# Labour Justice

This book argues that the imagination of the worker-citizen, inherent in citizens' constitutional duty to work, is the very foundation of constitutional citizenship and its social justice agenda in India. The design of social justice in the constitution takes labour as its core ideological and political commitment, seeking to treat workers fairly for their social contribution through work. Employing this constitutional design, this book evaluates the recently repealed labour law in India against the constitutional metric of social justice. Drawing on the components of social justice, the book evaluates the new labour law in its capacity to promote a market-based distribution that respects basic individual liberties, a complementary redistribution of public goods that upholds the principle of solidarity, and worker participation in decisions about the operation of the market and the state. In offering such evaluation, the book conceives of work in its wider social relationship in contrast to its narrower private exchange rationale.

**Supriya Routh** is an Associate Professor and Canada Research Chair in Labour Law and Social Justice at the Peter A. Allard School of Law, University of British Columbia, Vancouver. His research interests include theoretical conceptualisations of work and labour law, workers' organisation initiatives, international labour law, atypical and informal workers in the Global South, human rights, and human development and sustainability.

# Labour Justice

## A Constitutional Evaluation of Labour Law

Supriya Routh

Shaftesbury Road, Cambridge CB2 8EA, United Kingdom

One Liberty Plaza, 20th Floor, New York, NY 10006, USA

477 Williamstown Road, Port Melbourne, VIC 3207, Australia

314–321, 3rd Floor, Plot 3, Splendor Forum, Jasola District Centre, New Delhi – 110025, India

103 Penang Road, #05–06/07, Visioncrest Commercial, Singapore 238467

Cambridge University Press is part of Cambridge University Press & Assessment, a department of the University of Cambridge.

We share the University's mission to contribute to society through the pursuit of education, learning and research at the highest international levels of excellence.

www.cambridge.org
Information on this title: www.cambridge.org/9781009445337

© Supriya Routh 2024

This publication is in copyright. Subject to statutory exception and to the provisions of relevant collective licensing agreements, no reproduction of any part may take place without the written permission of Cambridge University Press & Assessment

First published 2024

*A catalogue record for this publication is available from the British Library*

ISBN 978-1-009-44533-7 Hardback

Cambridge University Press & Assessment has no responsibility for the persistence or accuracy of URLs for external or third-party internet websites referred to in this publication, and does not guarantee that any content on such websites is, or will remain, accurate or appropriate.

For Shuvali,
*the joy of my life!*

# Contents

| | |
|---|---|
| *Preface* | ix |
| *Acknowledgements* | xxiii |
| Introduction: The Law of Labour—Evaluating the Labour Law Reforms | 1 |
| **1** Labour's Constitution: Pursuing Economic, Social and Political Justice | 29 |
| **2** Individual Autonomy, Freedom of Contract and the Labour Market | 68 |
| **3** Solidarity and Social Welfare | 100 |
| **4** Industrial Democracy and Republican Citizenship: Collective Action in Resource Redistribution | 135 |
| Conclusion: Realising Labour Justice | 170 |
| *Bibliography* | 200 |
| *Index* | 221 |

# Preface

This book is premised on the understanding that work is a political idea of wide import and regulation of work is an exercise in public reasoning, whereby citizens accept the general idea of such regulation (labour law) because it is justified by an appeal to broadly accepted political ideals in contrast to justifications based primarily on private self-interested motives. The political notion of work and, relatedly, the just treatment of workers are articulated through the imagination of citizenship. The concept of duty-bearing citizenship is central to the articulation of the social justice agenda under the Constitution of India, 1950. Citizenship is understood as a basis for social cooperation, and the latter is essential to the formation and development of the independent constitutional state. At the same time, the conceptual and institutional project of social justice under the Indian Constitution unfolds with reference to social cooperation inherent in the idea of Indian citizenship. Indian citizenship cannot merely be defined on the basis of legal rights that citizens can validly demand against the state. The idea of citizenship carries with it substantial constitutional duties. These duties are central to the understanding of citizenship in India. The Constitution enumerates a number of citizenship duties, which every Indian citizen is expected to abide by and fulfil. One among these duties receives significant prominence under the Constitution, which is the duty to individually and collectively excel in their activities, including work or labour (as a core human activity), in a manner that contributes to the development of society (or the state). That this duty to work (and to excel in one's respective work) is fundamental to defining

Indian citizenship is evident from the constitutional structure that furthers the social justice project of the constitutional state. The social justice project of the Constitution unfolds primarily through Parts III and IV of the Constitution, dealing with fundamental rights of individual citizens and fundamental duties of the state, respectively. Although the social justice project under the Constitution develops with reference to citizens' duty to work and their social cooperation as workers, a duty-based conceptualisation of citizenship is yet to receive much prominence in political and legal scholarship. While citizenship obligations have been recognised in prominent accounts of citizenship, these obligations are conceived primarily as participatory and deliberative political duties, rather than an obligation to contribute by means of individual and collective labour.

The idea of liberal constitutional citizenship has conventionally been associated with rights-demanding citizens on the basis of their membership of a political community.[1] 'Citizenship is a status bestowed on those who are full members of a community.'[2] Thomas Marshall proposed three components of citizenship: *civil*, or the rights promoting individual freedom; *political*, or the right to participate in the political affairs of the state; and *social*, or the rights promoting economic security and necessities for a civilised existence. In addition to these core components of citizenship, Marshall also proposed the idea of industrial citizenship, a 'secondary system ... parallel with and supplementary to the system of political citizenship'.[3] The foundation of this industrial citizenship is the reciprocity between capital and organised labour, effectuated through collective bargaining, with the participation of trade unions. In this sense, industrial citizenship is in a league of its own, separate from the three principal components of political citizenship. Industrial citizenship is a secondary citizenship, a citizenship by analogy. While labour law scholars have sporadically engaged with the notion of industrial citizenship,[4] scholars of citizenship outside of this group have not seriously engaged with Marshall's idea of industrial citizenship, instead focusing on the three major components of political citizenship. Marshall's account of citizenship is so influential that later authors, either in agreement or in disagreement, responded to it rather than reinventing the very idea of citizenship.

The theme that permeates Marshall's classical account of citizenship is the notion of reciprocity. In relation to social rights, such reciprocity manifests, for example, in the state's obligation to educate children in return for (that is, with the expectation of) educated citizens' future participation – as part of their public duty to participate – in the political and economic affairs of society.[5] Charles Tilly more explicitly points out the reciprocity inherent in the idea of citizenship when he notes that citizenship rights are bargained exchanges between citizens and the state.[6] Citizenship is a 'special sort of contract ... as it entails enforceable rights and obligations based on persons' categorical membership and agents' relation to the state'.[7] In this view, citizens and the state are related in a reciprocal relationship wherein the citizens' duty to civic and political participation is reciprocated with their citizenship rights, including their social rights. However, social rights' position in a much more comprehensive and integral relationship with the principle of reciprocity (in relation to the state), outside purely political participation, has received scant attention apart from their explication on the basis of the principle of solidarity – that is, the 'responsibility towards the welfare of the community'.[8] While Marshall does designate the duty to work as paramount, he ends up dismissing this duty as vague and distant in relation to that of the state and social rights in particular.[9] The duty to work might be more meaningful when it relates to the local community constituting industrial citizenship – the secondary system of citizenship – but it is not the foundation of citizenship.[10] Such a position ends up distancing the duty to work from the principle of solidarity at the level of the state.

There seems to be some convergence between the Western ideas of citizenship, where the constitutional nation-state developed in a specific manner, and Indian ideas of citizenship, where the constitutional nation-state emerged under substantially different circumstances.[11] Both of these perspectives articulate the idea of citizenship through a combination of rights and obligations. Because of one's legal status as a citizen, one could make legitimate demands against the state, and the state is obligated to meet such demands from its citizens. Although citizenship per se qualifies one to claim – and receive – certain entitlements against the state, *good citizens* have obligations to the state. Broadly, citizens' participation in the affairs of the state is taken to be the mark of good citizens. As noted, conventionally, civic and political engagements are understood to be the core obligations of citizenship. Depending on the context, these obligations have specific requirements, including educated and contemplative citizenry, participation in local governance, deliberative law-making, and so on. While some deployed the idea of citizen's obligations in order to normatively formulate a docile and obedient citizenry, others used the concept to further an enlightened and disobedient citizenry.[12] While some accounts of citizenship explicitly note the reciprocity inherent in the right–duty interaction of citizenship, in others such reciprocity remains underspecified.

Non-Eurocentric ideas of citizenship have often attempted to distinguish themselves from Eurocentric ideas of citizenship on a number of grounds. Many of these bases of distinction are pertinent and acutely attend to the problems of the universalised idea of constitutional citizenship for a diverse world.[13] However, even when the idea of (formally equal and universalised) citizenship is problematised and nuanced, especially in the context of the Global South, the idea of citizenship generally seems to be articulated through the conventional notions of political engagement and legitimate entitlements.[14] Where these (Eurocentric and non-Eurocentric) accounts substantially differ is at the level of political engagement – that is, the actual unfolding of individual citizen's relationship to the state. Relatedly, critical accounts of citizenship also nuance the foundational ideas of the citizen and the state. Importantly, in non-Eurocentric accounts, the relationship between political engagement and legitimate entitlements is more explicitly reciprocal. And this reciprocity is felt at the different levels – formal and informal – of administration and politics where individuals interact with the state. Populations in the vast swaths of the Global South are accustomed to the politics of *establishing* their citizenship before demanding citizenship rights. Often, the very purpose of establishing their citizenship is to demand rights from the state rather than the intention of belonging to a shared identity as citizens.

Three interrelated dimensions of Indian citizenship – the legal status of citizenship, the rights-based citizenship and identity- and belonging-centred citizenship – have received emphasis from political theorists.[15] While these components of citizenship do not exhaust all there is to the idea of Indian citizenship, they go on to show the prominence of certain characteristics in defining the idea of citizenship in India. As much as their content is Indian, these dimensions of citizenship are universal. Collectively, the three dimensions of Indian citizenship articulate the idea of the political citizen. This idea of the political citizen is, of course, indispensable for the imagination of Indian democracy.[16] In centralising the role of the political citizen in Indian democracy, productive contributions of the citizens on the basis of a duty to contribute largely remain in the background, unworthy of theoretical attention. Yet it is this notion of productive, contributory citizens that the Constitution relies on in conceiving individual rights, social welfare and participatory deliberation. In this sense, the relationship of reciprocity noted earlier is explicitly articulated in the Constitution, but not in a manner theorised by political scientists and legal scholars. The (reciprocal) relationship between contributory productive citizenship and social rights is primary – not secondary and an afterthought (as in Marshall's industrial citizenship) – under the Constitution. Citizens' productive contribution to the development of the state places them in a direct relationship with the state. This version of citizenship and its relationship to the idea of social rights is, then, not an analogy of the idea of political citizenship – it is a fundamental part of the idea of citizenship. It is, therefore, important to revisit the idea of Indian citizenship in order to explicate this contributory idea of citizenship, which is central to the overall imagination of the constitutional framework in the country.

The process of establishing one's citizenship by means of one's contribution, and demanding citizenship rights in return, is largely framed by the idea of the worker-citizen under the Constitution. While the term 'worker-citizen' is not explicitly used in the Constitution, it is a logical interpretation of the idea of constitutional citizenship. It is a 'fundamental' duty of every citizen of India to contribute to the nation's development through their individual and collective activity so that the nation 'constantly rises to higher levels of endeavour and achievement'.[17] As important as it may be, only civil and political participation by the citizens cannot propel a nation to continued higher level of endeavour and achievement. Individual and collective *activity*, which surely includes work – labour – is centrally important to the development of the nation. To be sure, the imagination of the worker-citizen does not stand in isolation, completely separated from or contradictory to the idea of the political citizen. The worker-citizen and the political citizen are inseparable aspects of the overall imagination of the Indian citizen. This inseparability is also evident from the overarching constitutional agenda. When imagining citizens' contribution to the achievements of the nation, the Constitution does not understand national achievement only in economic terms; its focus is the overall development of the nation that also includes social and cultural development. This broad understanding of the national aspiration could be seen in the constitutional mandate on citizens' fundamental duties, the state's fundamental duties and the safeguard of (individual and communal) fundamental rights within the Indian territory.[18] Just as the political citizen serves this broader imagination, the worker-citizen too contributes to the sustenance of this idea.

As noted, although central to the imagination of citizenship, and consequently the institutional framework of social justice under the Constitution, the idea of the worker-citizen remains largely under-theorised, and its links to other components of the Constitution remain unexplored. Whereas political theorists have noted the significance of 'taxpayer' citizen, 'consumer' citizen and 'property-owner' citizen, they have yet to develop the idea of worker-citizen in any detail.[19] Prominently, the idea of the worker-citizen – citizens' duty to work – appears in Marshall's account only in dismissal. This general omission (and dismissal) is somewhat surprising, especially since the idea of the worker-citizen is not only a conceptual possibility, existing solely in the interpretive adventures of an author, but also a concrete idea frequently articulated in the practical politics of citizenship. Politics of the urban poor frequently invoke the idea of worker-citizenship by emphasising their 'contribution' to productive industries of the urban space as well as their social reproduction of the city.[20] Their relational and reciprocal claim to citizenship highlights their contribution as a justificatory basis of their citizenship – that is, the rights and entitlements associated with their citizenship.

That their contribution to the development of the state is a result of their personal undertaking – *work as a livelihood activity* – is more explicitly asserted by informal workers in India. Informal workers constitute the significant majority of the Indian workforce. According to most accounts, more than 90 per cent of the Indian workforce is informal. Informal workers are, of course, workers engaged in working arrangements that exist outside the legal form or the conventional industrial employment pattern on the basis of which law operates in (re)distributing rights and obligations between workers and employers. Since law often does not recognise specific working arrangements, including worksites, of informal workers (thereby denying them industrial citizenship), such workers invoke the idea of contributory worker-citizens in order to claim their right to livelihood through a range of informal economic activities in the city-spaces that are generally off-limits to such workers because of the operation of law (such as access to public land for street vendors and public receptacles for waste recycling workers).[21] Informal workers not only demand their mere right to livelihood against the state, they also claim livelihood security and rights at work against the state on the basis of the aforementioned justification.

Informal workers often do not relate to their work by means of an employer. In fact, in the majority of circumstances, informal workers do not have an employer; when they have one, their relationship with the employer is not unambiguously contractual. Thus, contractual bargaining, the process of negotiating rights against an employer, which the law safeguards, is of little use to them. Under these circumstances, informal workers' claim to a secure livelihood by means of social security provisioning is often based on their claims against the state rather than an employer.[22] These claims are laid on to the state firmly on the basis of their identity as worker-citizens. These workers demand that the state see them as citizens and treat them as contributory members of society. More practically, of course, informal workers' collective action against the state is often based on their capacity to influence local and regional electoral politics where they are seen as 'vote banks' to acquire and sustain.[23] Unsurprisingly, therefore, the response of the different state governments against the demands of informal workers is also varied on the basis of the necessities of regional politics (and local calculations of vote banks).[24] Irrespective of practical political considerations, informal workers' demands on to the state are morally framed as workers' claim to reciprocal treatment on the basis of their work – and continued commitment – to subsidise productive economic relations and offer conditions for the social reproduction of labour.[25] This relationship of reciprocity between the worker-citizen and the (beneficiary) state is, thus, most evident in the context of informal workers. Informal workers' collective action, then, gives practical expression to the relationship between citizens' constitutional duty to excel in their (socially contributory) activity and the state's corresponding duty to offer livelihood security and welfare in exchange for the performance of such duty.

In fact, the imagination and the institutional framework of social justice – fairness – in social cooperation[26] under the Constitution depend on the centrality of the concept of the worker-citizen. The point, then, is not that the duty to work, thereby contributing to society, is vague and distant from the point of view of the worker-citizens but that the duty grounds the constitutional framework of social justice. In this sense, the duty is real and imminent. It has conceptual and practical ramifications. In India, social cooperation, which 'makes possible a better life for all [citizens] than any would have if each were to live solely by [their] own efforts',[27] is conceived primarily as the process by which workers (individually and collectively) participate in productive and socially reproductive activities. If the terms of social cooperation are to be just, cooperative citizenry excelling at promoting the state to higher levels of achievement must be treated fairly.

It is this overarching principle of social justice that receives its institutional backing in the forms of Fundamental Rights (Part III) and Directive Principles of State Policy (Part IV) under the Constitution. In offering the institutional framework of social justice, the Constitution balances individual liberty with social solidarity and centralises participatory democracy to keep the former two as subjects of continued political deliberation and decision-making. In promoting the goals of social justice, the first creates conditions for market-based distribution, the second consolidates state-based redistribution and the third negotiates within and between the two. Since the entire structure of social justice under the Constitution is based on the imagination of the worker-citizen in their contributory relationship to society (the state), it is appropriate to evaluate the legislative agenda on worker welfare – labour law – on the basis of its ability to meet the constitutional demand of social justice. This book undertakes this evaluation by looking at the deeply impactful changes introduced in Indian labour law through the sweeping reforms of 2019–2020.

By means of the comprehensive reforms of 2019–2020, the Indian Parliament has charted a new path for labour regulation in the country. Before assessing this new direction of labour law, we should remember that labour law in India is not merely a statute regulating workplace relationships; it is a legal instrument implementing the constitutional social justice programme. It is a means to realise constitutional ends. From this perspective, the reforms are of momentous significance. Accordingly, an evaluation of labour law is not only important for understanding its capacity to regulate workplace relationships but also its ability to further the constitutional goal. Whereas the first relates to an examination of specific rights, entitlements, doctrines and principles of labour law, the latter pertains to the overall narrative – normative aim – of labour law. To be sure, these two are not mutually exclusive aspects of the subject matter but instead inseparably linked together. Their difference lies predominantly in the emphasis of the analysis. In this book, the emphasis lies on the latter – that is, the overall narrative of labour law in India. Even when specific interpretations of legal principles are offered, they are offered with the aim of evaluating this overall narrative.

Some of the prominent features of this overall narrative of labour law after the reforms are significant withdrawal of the state from labour relations, expansion of the scope of market-based distribution in labour relations, recognition of the misfit between heterogeneously organised informal economic activities and the conventional structure of labour law, articulating informal workers' social security programme, (yet) disproportionally exposing informal workers to the insecurities of the market, undermining the scope of collective action and participatory deliberation, and (ironically) entrenching the government (at the cost of workers' representative) in deliberative institutions geared towards decision-making on worker entitlements. These prominent features together offer an overall narrative of labour law that is alarming in its potential to deviate from the constitutional goal. This book evaluates labour law in its post-reform manifestation through the lens of the constitutional imagination of social justice, emphasising the changes introduced by the reforms in particular. Each chapter in the book takes up one broad component of the post-reform labour law and evaluates it from the perspective of its constitutional fit.

Chapter 1 develops the evaluative criteria for the examination of labour law by conceptually discussing the constitutional imagination of social justice and linking the different programmatic components of the Constitution to such imagination. In the process of developing the evaluative criteria, this chapter also engages in a brief conceptual discussion of some liberal theories of social justice. This discussion, occurring in the third section of the chapter, is abstract and may be skipped by the reader; skipping this section will not impact the overall understanding of the chapter. Chapter 2 examines the market-expanding role of the labour law reforms. For many commentators, this is the primary objective of the latest reforms. While the Constitution does contemplate a role for labour exchanges through the market, this chapter examines whether the market expansion promoted through the reforms simultaneously meets the limits imposed by the Constitution on such exchanges. This latter evaluation leads us to Chapter 3, which engages with the coverage and adequacy of social security offered by labour law. Neither the constitutional permissibility of market exchanges nor the limits imposed on such exchanges could be evaluated without a concurrent engagement with the scope of social security for the workforce. The permissible scope of market exchanges depends on the comprehensiveness of social security provisioning under the constitutional design. In this sense, workers' social security entitlements are an inseparable component of labour law. They are not two different silos existing side by side.

Chapter 4 picks up the rather contentious issue of workers' collective action and participatory deliberation. This component of the labour law is contentious, in particular, because all major trade unions in India alleged that Parliament reformed labour laws without adequate consultation with workers' organisations, including trade unions. In that backdrop, this chapter analyses whether the reforms promote or constrain workers' collective action and participatory deliberation. In evaluating the post-reform labour law, the book does not seek to adjudicate whether the labour codes are within the juridical authority of the Constitution (that is, intra vires the Constitution). It aims to understand whether the labour codes further fairness in labour relations (that is, social cooperation) in the sense intended by the Constitution. Here, furthering fairness would mean keeping the balance between the different components of the constitutional social justice agenda. The book does not attempt to offer a comprehensive statutory reading of the different provisions of the labour codes, but instead focuses on the major changes that effect radical and long-term impact on labour law jurisprudence in the country. Thus, some specific issues receive more attention while other minor changes remain relatively less analysed. It is expected that once the broader narrative of labour law is well understood, the minor issues will make sense in their fit with the broader issues.

While the book's aim is to examine labour law in light of the constitutional agenda, it is simultaneously a contribution towards a juridical (and policy) approach to labour justice. The book indicates how Indian labour laws should be analysed and interpreted by practitioners of labour law, including the judiciary. By offering a constitutional narrative of labour law, the book explicitly takes cognisance of the conceptual foundation of labour law to better understand – and potentially recalibrate – the grammar of labour law, referring to the set of rights, obligations and legal categories that are employed to determine specific legal issues and disputes in labour relations.[28] Explicit recognition of – and commitment to – this conceptual foundation expands the juridical toolkit to better respond to the sui generis challenges of the heterogeneous labour relations in the country. It is important to recognise this social justice approach to labour law because unlike in traditionally industrialised common law jurisdictions, the foundation of this branch of law is not purely contractual, but social relational in India. This explicit recognition stands in contrast to the more influential contractual model of labour relations that had been originally exported from Europe to India and had long been the dominant juridical model of labour relations in the country.

Indian labour force and labour law are radically different from the reality of the labour force and the imagination of labour law in industrialised Western jurisdictions. Yet there are similarities too, both in the organisation of the labour force and in the conceptualisation of labour law. At a general level, while the difference lies in the heterogeneous manner of 'informal' work organisations of the vast majority of the labour force in India, the similarities relate to the formal industrial workforce and the employment relationship-based idea of labour law. Beyond this general level, the ways workers obtain work, work relationships are constituted, worksites are conceived, negotiations are undertaken, workers participate in collective action, deliberative frameworks unfold, society (the state) is involved, social security is instituted and politics is employed are all different from the conventional Western model for the majority of the workforce. Legal tools developed to engage with the conventional model cannot per se be expected to resolve the complications of the sui generis scenario.

The conventional labour law model has been a colonial legacy for the country. While it generally works in the formally organised industries and factory floors, it becomes a burden outside the conventional industrial relations model. This realisation, although delayed, is now an identifying characteristic of the Indian labour law jurisprudence. Just as the similarities between the two (Western and Indian labour laws) could not be ignored, the differences should not be overlooked. It is by engaging with both the Western model and the Indian uniqueness that a more complete picture of the labour law jurisprudence in the country emerges. The Constitution too works on a similar philosophy. It combines Western notions with Indian characteristics. Ignoring one in favour of the other will present a skewed idea of the nation's foundational principles. This consciousness should be central to the work of scholars commenting on India, and the Global South more generally. Foundationally, Indian labour law is social relational and is tethered to the idea of citizenship. This social relational nature of labour law is constitutionally grounded. Constitutionally recognised citizenship duty to contribute to the betterment of the society by means of individual and collective activity is the basis of (reciprocal) labour welfare rights of the worker-citizens. Any interpretation of labour law that ignores this constitutional genesis of the subject matter is bound to fail the constitutional compass and the enormous labour force of the country that contributes to the development of the nation yet barely ekes out a decent living through their livelihood activities.

Vancouver, Canada<br>
17 December 2023

## Notes

1. T. H. Marshall and Tom Bottomore, *Citizenship and Social Class* (London: Pluto Press, 1992), 24–25; Charles Tilly, 'Where Do Rights Come From?' in *Collective Violence, Contentious Politics, and Social Change: A Charles Tilly Reader*, ed. Ernesto Castaneda and Cathy Lisa Schneider, 168–182 (New York and Abingdon: Routledge, 2017).
2. Marshall and Bottomore, *Citizenship and Social Class*, 18.
3. Marshall and Bottomore, *Citizenship and Social Class*, 26, 40.
4. Guy Mundlak, 'Industrial Citizenship, Social Citizenship, Corporate Citizenship: I Just Want My Wages', *Theoretical Inquiries in Law* 8, no. 2 (2007): 719–748.
5. Marshall and Bottomore, *Citizenship and Social Class*, 16–17.
6. Tilly, 'Where Do Rights Come From?' 169–170.
7. Charles Tilly, 'Citizenship, Identity and Social History', *International Review of Social History* 40, supp. 3 (1995): 1–17, 8.
8. Marshall and Bottomore, *Citizenship and Social Class*, 41.
9. Marshall and Bottomore, *Citizenship and Social Class*, 45–46.
10. Marshall and Bottomore, *Citizenship and Social Class*, 47.

11. See Niraja Gopal Jayal, *Citizenship and Its Discontents: An Indian History* (Cambridge [MA] and London: Harvard University Press, 2013), for a comparative discussion of ideas of citizenship as evolved in the West and in India. Also see Partha Chatterjee, *The Politics of the Governed: Reflections on Popular Politics in Most of the World* (New York: Columbia University Press, 2004), 36–37, for a discussion on how the constitutional nation-state developed differently in India as opposed to in Europe because of the former's long colonial experience.
12. Jayal, *Citizenship and Its Discontents*, 133–135.
13. For example, see Jayal, *Citizenship and Its Discontents*, 133–135; Chatterjee, *The Politics of the Governed*; Partha Chatterjee, *Lineages of Political Society: Studies in Postcolonial Democracy* (New York: Columbia University Press, 2011), 12–13; James Holston, *Insurgent Citizenship: Disjunctions of Democracy and Modernity in Brazil* (Princeton, NJ: Princeton University Press, 2008); Sanjeev Routray, *The Right to Be Counted: The Urban Poor and the Politics of Resettlement in Delhi* (Redwood City, CA: Stanford University Press, 2022).
14. Routray, *The Right to Be Counted*, 1–2, 264–265.
15. Jayal, *Citizenship and Its Discontents*, 2; Routray, *The Right to Be Counted*, 2.
16. Jayal, *Citizenship and Its Discontents*, 4–5.
17. Constitution of India, 1950, Article 51A (hereinafter, 'Constitution').
18. Constitution, Parts III, IV, IVA.
19. Holston, *Insurgent Citizenship*, 246–249, 260–263 (if not the idea of worker-citizen, some references to workers' rights as part of a citizenship claim could be found in Holston's work); Routray, *The Right to Be Counted*, 18, 265.
20. Routray, *The Right to Be Counted*, 265, 269–274.
21. Routray, *The Right to Be Counted*, 269; Supriya Routh, *Enhancing Capabilities through Labour Law: Informal Workers in India* (Abingdon and New York: Routledge, 2014) (noting that informal workers' access to city-spaces is often limited by legal actions – criminal and tortious – on trespassing).
22. See Rina Agarwala, *Informal Labor, Formal Politics, and Dignified Discontent in India* (New York: Cambridge University Press, 2013).
23. Agarwala, *Informal Labor, Formal Politics, and Dignified Discontent in India*, 192–196.
24. Agarwala, *Informal Labor, Formal Politics, and Dignified Discontent in India*, 192–196.
25. Agarwala, *Informal Labor, Formal Politics, and Dignified Discontent in India*, 198.

26. John Rawls, *A Theory of Justice* (Cambridge, MA: Harvard University Press, 1999 [1971]), xv, 3.
27. Rawls, *A Theory of Justice*, 4.
28. Brian Langille, 'The Narrative of Global Justice and the Grammar of Law', in *Global Justice and International Labour Rights*, ed. Yossi Dahan, Hanna Lerner and Faina Milman-Sivan, 186–208 (Cambridge, UK: Cambridge University Press, 2016).

# Acknowledgements

Although the inspiration for this book comes from the comprehensive labour law reforms in India, the book emerged out of several years of thinking and discussing the idea of work and its regulation. I have accumulated intellectual debts from many remarkable friends and colleagues, too many to individually mention them here in a couple of pages. I will, therefore, limit myself to noting assistance and encouragement that I received in thinking about and writing the different chapters of the book. I have been interested in exploring the role of labour law in realistically promoting social justice for workers, particularly those who have traditionally been left out of the protection afforded by the conventional labour law because of the conceptual and structural limitations of the legal framework. My discussions with Brian Langille, Alain Supiot, Diamond Ashiagbor, Alan L. Bogg, Guy Davidov, Adelle Blackett, Ruth E. Dukes, Tonia A. Novitz, Martin Dumas, Ania Zbyszewska, Victor V. Ramraj, Arun K. Thiruvengadam and Jeremy Webber have been foundational in my own thinking on the relationship between labour law, constitutional law and social justice. I thank all of them for engaging me in fruitful and passionate deliberations on the interlinkages among the different agendas over the years. I continue to learn immensely from them.

The more immediate impetus for the writing of this book came from Barbara Palli and Frédéric Géa, when they invited me to write on the recent labour law reforms in India, which effectively changes the character of labour law in the country. In beginning to write about the recent reforms, I felt the need to engage in a more comprehensive analysis of labour law in India, resulting in this book.

I thank both of them for inviting me to write on the theme and commenting on the introduction to this book. Alan Bogg's invitation to think about the superior role of legislation (as opposed to adjudication) in realising social justice has been particularly helpful in articulating some of the arguments in the book. I have tremendously benefitted from the discussions at the Workshop on Courts and Legislators in the Constitution of Freedom of Association at the University of Bristol, which I attended at Alan's invitation. Similarly, thanks are due to Isabelle Daugareilh for the useful discussions on the exclusion of informal workers, including post-industrial versions of informal workers such as gig- and platform-based workers, from the scope of labour law. My discussions with colleagues at Duke University's Revaluing Care in the Global Economy network have been helpful in understanding the regulation of work as a broader political project.

My discussions with Tvisha Shroff and Colin Fenwick have been helpful in writing parts of Chapter 2, and my exchanges with Saurabh Bhattacharjee have been helpful in writing Chapters 2 and 3. Ewan McGaughey and Shae McCrystal have commented on parts of Chapter 4 of the book. In particular, I have benefitted from my exchanges with Ewan while writing Chapter 4. I thank all of them for being generous with their time, suggestions and resources. I thank my colleagues Kathy Chan and Patricia Cochran for offering their thoughtful reflections on some of the chapters of the book. My friend Michael Large has read the entire first draft of the book and, true to his nature, offered unreserved critique where it warranted. I offer my heartfelt thanks to the two anonymous reviewers of the book, who offered sympathetic yet critical reviews of the manuscript. The reviewers helpfully identified some loopholes in the manuscript that I had originally missed. Their constructive comments helped me strengthen some parts of the book. However, they should not be held liable for the weaker parts and mistakes, if any; those remain my sole responsibility.

Parts of some of the chapters of the book were previously published elsewhere. A former version of the introduction has appeared as 'Labour's Justice? Evaluating Labour Law Reforms in India' in *L'avenir du droit du travail: Perspectives international et compare*, edited by Frédéric Géa and Barbara Palli and published by Éditions Bruylant (2023). Parts of Chapter 4 originally appeared in 'Workers and Competition Law in India: Workers' Associations Are Mostly Not Cartels' in *The Cambridge Handbook of Labor in Competition Law*, edited by Sanjukta Paul, Shae McCrystal and Ewan McGaughey and published by Cambridge University Press (2022). However, I have reworked those parts specifically for the purpose of this book.

I also thank the Peter A. Allard School of Law, particularly Dean Ngai Pindell, for offering me a writing term during the autumn of 2022 to help me conclude the manuscript. In writing the book, I have received remarkable research assistance from Alex Alstad, Himaloya Saha, Brendan Ready, Liam Byrne and Erica Johnston. I thank them for their assistance. I thank Anwesha Rana, senior commissioning editor, and Anandadeep Roy, associate commissioning editor, at Cambridge University Press for their help and persistence with the project. I also thank Priyanka Das at the Press for her excellent editorial assistance with the book.

Last but not least – an important acknowledgement of the care work that Bidisa and Shuvali perform on a regular basis for me. I acknowledge, without compensating, the socially reproductive work performed by these two amazing women that goes behind reproducing my everyday labour. Finally, my parents' – Sandhya and Sumangal – unflinching conviction in what I do inspires me every moment.

# Introduction

## The Law of Labour

*Evaluating the Labour Law Reforms\**

### Introduction

This book argues that the 2020 labour law reforms in India, where Parliament consolidated twenty-nine federal statutes into four labour codes, fail to meet the Indian Constitution's labour mandate. In so failing to meet the constitutional mandate, the reforms have far-reaching consequences for labour rights in the country. Labour, understood broadly as an individual's personal undertaking contributing to broader socio-economic pursuits, occupies a prominent position in the constitutional framework in India. As a category, labour is pivotal to the social justice agenda envisaged under the Constitution. The Preamble to the Constitution of India, 1950, aspires to social, economic and political justice. The other values fundamental to the foundation of the republic are freedom, equality and solidarity. While the latter values are inherently important for the constitutional framework of the nation, they are also the conceptual and programmatic components of the constitutional social justice agenda.

---

\* An earlier version of this chapter was published as Supriya Routh, 'Labour's Justice? Evaluating Labour Law Reforms in India', in *L'avenir du droit du travail: Perspectives international et compare*, ed. Frédéric Géa and Barbara Palli, 235–252 (Bruxelles: Éditions Bruylant, 2023). All rights reserved. Reproduced by permission of Éditions Bruylant.

On the basis of its social justice agenda, India's Constitution could be positioned somewhere between classical liberalism and social democracy.[1] In classical liberalism, on the one hand, the constitution stipulates basic rules of contract, property and tort to regulate market exchanges, which are the primary means of distributing goods and services.[2] In social democracy, on the other hand, the constitution catalogues extensive rules of redistribution that secure citizens' legal entitlements, such as education, nutrition, work, healthcare, social security, unionisation, maternity benefit, legal aid, and so on.[3] Mark Tushnet notes that in classical liberalism, the distribution of goods and the principles of such distribution are primarily the concern of private law, whereas in social democracy, they are primarily a public law issue.[4] The Indian Constitution uses – balances – both of these approaches by simultaneously allocating a role for the market (structured through private law) and guaranteeing welfare rights (secured through public law).

## The Constitutional Social Justice Agenda

The Indian Constitution's social justice agenda is furthered through a combination of individual freedom, social solidarity and participatory democracy. It is the balance among these three aspects of the social justice agenda that captures the uniqueness of the agenda for Indian society. The Constitution guarantees every citizen of India the individual freedom to practise their chosen occupation and engage in a trade or business of their choice without undue interference.[5] Alongside the right to formal equality – non-discrimination on the grounds of religion, race, caste, sex, place of birth – the right to individual freedom safeguards workers' autonomy to participate in the labour market. By means of justiciable constitutional rights to equality and freedom, the Constitution prioritises workers' choice and autonomy without limiting the extent of worker engagement in the market or dictating the economic goals of such engagement. These safeguards are how the Constitution removes impediments to worker participation in the market without being paternalistic in the process. At the same time, the state could restrict freedom of trade – market freedom – in the public interest, including in the interest of safeguarding individual freedoms and social justice.[6] This restriction recognises that inviolable market freedom may be inimical to the cause of social justice.

In any case, worker participation in the market, while important, is only one component of the multidimensional social justice framework envisaged under the Constitution. The market-focused distribution of economic resources is supplemented by the solidarity-based social welfare provisioning mandated under the Constitution, drawing its strength from the socialist ambition of the Constitution. The constitutional aspiration to promote 'fraternity' in ensuring a dignified life for the citizens is detailed in the constitutionally mandated duties of the state.[7] Since the Indian Constitution is based on the ideals of individual freedom and social solidarity, workers who are unable to meaningfully participate in market exchanges or are systematically disadvantaged from market participation are supported by the 'social state', which has a responsibility – a constitutional one – towards such workers.[8] A just social order secured by the state should minimise inequalities of income, social status and opportunities among individuals and groups, including workers engaged in different occupations. The state's 'fundamental' duty includes resource redistribution and securing work for the citizenry.[9] Just social outcomes are, then, a combination of market-based distribution and state-based redistribution of rights, resources and opportunities.

While the fundamental duties of the state are to be furthered through legislative action rather than constitutional litigation, the Constitution does not advance justice merely through substantive legislative entitlements; the very access to the legal system on an equal basis is also part of the just constitutional order.[10] Equal opportunity to participate in formulating and accessing the legal framework of entitlements is, then, part of the just economic democracy[11] that the Constitution seeks to further. Accordingly, the third component of the multidimensional agenda of justice, one that permeates all the other components of the constitutional ideal of social justice, is participatory citizenship. In particular, the labour-focused social justice agenda of the Constitution recognises the prominent role of workers' participation in the management of their workplace and collective action in a dynamic social justice framework. The Constitution safeguards workers' rights to form associations, unions and cooperative societies.[12] Although the Supreme Court decrees – incorrectly, as we will argue in Chapter 4 – that the right to unionise does not include collective bargaining or work cessation in furthering the bargaining agenda, the state is duty-bound to ensure worker participation in management as a legal right.[13] The state is also mandated to promote participatory control and autonomous functioning of cooperative societies, including workers' cooperatives.[14]

The ideal of social justice facilitated through participatory democracy is an unalterable part of the Constitution's basic structure.[15] Depending on the nature of political demands, Parliament may amend specific constitutional entitlements, but it cannot abandon the ideal of social justice. Although the welfare state plays a leading role in promoting social justice, social welfare cannot come at the cost of curbing individual freedom. '[T]he whole scheme underlying the Constitution is to bring about economic and social changes without taking away the dignity of the individual.'[16] Individual freedom to engage in activities and pursuits that one values, including the desire to participate in collective action, occupies a place of eminence in the country's constitutional framework.[17] That individual agency – the freedom and initiative of conceiving and executing one's life plan – occupies a prominent position in the constitutional social justice agenda is evident from the fact that the agenda is premised on socio-economic redistribution by means of *labour*, which requires an active commitment to participate in the social justice project. In other words, since the constitutional social justice narrative, in the regular course (that is, not considering individuals who are incapable of agency for a range of reasons), unfolds primarily through labour relations, it demands citizens' active participation – agency – in labour exchanges. To emphasise, the overarching components of social justice in India are threefold: individual freedom, social welfare and democratic participation. In the context of workers, it is their voice and (collective) participation that connect the other two components of social justice, allowing them to transform the constitutional ideal into concrete and detailed legal entitlements. They do so by means of the participatory law-making process envisaged under the Constitution.[18]

Evidently, then, the constitutional social justice agenda unfolds through two simultaneous realms – private markets and public social welfare – corresponding with the two dimensions of social justice: individual freedom and social solidarity. While the private market operates through the logic of self-interested autonomous individuals making decisions on their own behalf, social welfare operates on the ideal of solidarity – fraternity – in 'assuring the dignity'[19] of fellow citizens. The Constitution, thus, seeks to strike a harmonious balance between market-based individual freedom and solidarity-based social welfare.[20] Since the constitutional scheme entrusts the state to realise constitutional ideals through law, we should evaluate legislated entitlements using these constitutional ideals. Note that evaluating enacted legislation is not the same thing as adjudicating the 'authority' of such legislation. The aim of constitutionally evaluating legislation is to understand whether the legislation properly realises constitutional goals rather than whether such legislation is beyond the constitutional authority of the body that enacts it (that is, ultra vires the Constitution).

## The Role of Legislation

The ideal of social justice as a common political framework for a plural community, of necessity, is articulated at a higher level of abstractness. The authority of law rests on its ability to act as an instrument for coordinating citizens' behaviour in furthering the mandates of the common political framework.[21] In this instrumental sense, law captures the essence of the abstract ideal and converts it into concrete formulations to be carried out in quotidian practice, including negotiating the deliberative space for the citizenry. To be sure, even when law should fit and further the ideal of social justice, it must also negotiate the disagreements citizens have about the ideal itself in actual communities.[22] Jeremy Waldron notes that since legislation – as collective political action – is the principal tool for guaranteeing entitlements for the citizenry, its task is to find practicable ways (under conditions of disagreements) to realise the ideal of social justice in actual contexts.[23] Legislation, thus, should be accountable on two fronts: its commitment to the ideal of justice and its sensitivity to actual contexts. As will be elaborated in Chapter 1, these two components are not separate concerns; they converge in (some) conceptual imaginations of social justice. Although politics may require periodic legislative enactments, amendments and repeals, in all its iterations legislation should always adhere to the constitutive principles of society.[24] In principle, then, the role of legislation is to realise social justice in all its political complexities.

Grégoire Webber, Paul Yowell, Richard Ekins, Maris Köpcke, Bradley W Miller and Francisco J. Urbina demonstrate the advantage of enacted legislation over constitutional adjudication in actually realising constitutional human rights safeguards.[25] According to them, legislation specifies and clarifies the contours of a bill of rights with a precision absent in the judicial review process.[26] In well-functioning democracies, legislation signifies responsiveness to social evolution.[27] It is the legislature in its representative capacity that is entrusted with understanding the details of effective legal intervention, devising a reasoned justification for such an intervention, widely circulating the reasoning, scrutinising their reasoning and intervention through criticism and debate, and approving the legislation through representative bodies.[28] Webber, Yowell, Ekins, Köpcke, Miller and Urbina note that '[r]ights can only be realised if they are specified' through enacted legislation.[29] Even without an absolute conviction in the efficacy of legislation, it is uncontroversial that legislation creates a network of entitlements and specific duties – actions and abstentions – involving individuals and institutions that are generally acceptable to society at large.[30] The role of legislation, therefore, is to create a dynamic and coherent scheme of 'just relations' within a distinct area of social interaction.[31]

In particular, it is the role of the legislature to make sure that everyone, not only a selected few, can access certain common goods, including 'life, liberty, security, equality, privacy, family life, property, religion, expression, association, and assembly', so that every individual and group can fulfil their aspirations.[32] Legislative intervention in realising the bill of rights operates through a broad range of social interactions shaped inter alia by the law of contract, tort law, property law and criminal law.[33] Because of its core concern with the distribution of economic power and resources, labour relations are an area of continued political conflict and compromises.[34] Labour relations, therefore, are an area of social interaction that requires the responsiveness of the legislative process.[35] Since labour as a category occupies a central position in the redistribution of the common good in the Indian context, labour law as a legislative domain holds – ought to hold – a disproportionately large influence over the Indian population. This influence will be assessed in this book, not by examining every specific aspect of the 2020 labour law reforms (for example, the Industrial Relations Code [hereinafter, 'IR Code'], 2020) in their capacity to realise specific constitutional rights (for example, the right to occupation or trade), but by examining the reforms collectively in their ability to further the justiciable and non-justiciable constitutional rights that comprise the constitutional framework of social justice. In this holistic way of analysing the latest labour law reforms, our gaze is not merely fixated on the different labour codes; we also pay specific attention to the trade-offs between the different legal entitlements specified in these codes. It is these trade offs – say, between freedom of (employment) contract and social protection – that will help ascertain whether Indian labour law meets its constitutional mandate.

The bill of rights in Part III and the directive principles of governance in Part IV of the Indian Constitution aim to further social justice for the country's citizens. The approach adopted in this book is that it is through a subtle, contextually (and historically) determined 'balance' between the bill of rights and the policy directives that the Constitution seeks to advance an egalitarian society. This balance is not formulaic and, thus, not conditional on an absolute priority of certain rights (including justiciable rights) over others. Instead, the right measure of balance is dependent on the de facto realisation of social justice in actual contexts, and actual contexts in the Indian workforce are remarkably diverse. Since the Constitution mandates that the social justice mission be realised through legislative initiatives, we should evaluate the labour law reforms of 2020 using the constitutional metric. Accordingly, the book's central question is whether the 2020 labour law reforms in India, insofar as actually realising workers' rights, securing their socio-economic well-being and structuring social institutions wherein workers are able to satisfy their aspirations, strike a balance between individual freedom (Part III) and social solidarity (Part IV) in furthering the normative goal of social justice.

This context-sensitive evaluation of labour law should also take into account workers' participation, including through collective action, in evaluating the strength of the reforms. Participation plays a multifaceted role in the legislative realisation of constitutional principles. As we will discuss in Chapter 4, workers' participation in the labour law discourse supplies legitimacy to legal entitlements, validates the congruity of reforms to actual needs, ensures the effectiveness of enforcement and encourages wider compliance with the legislative agenda. Worker participation is also important for inclusivity, an underlying promise of the redistributive goal of the Constitution. Since the inclusive social justice mission of the Constitution seeks to recognise the dignity of every individual, it is to be expected that a legislative initiative realising the mission should not exclude certain groups and communities from its legislative purview. In a democratic society, dignity demands that people have a say over decisions meant to affect them, or else the decisions suffer from a legitimacy deficit (this issue will be explored in Chapters 1 and 4).

At the same time, we must be cognisant that the orthodox (post-independence) labour law framework has largely excluded informal workers – workers who do not belong to the traditional formal contractual employment structure – from its coverage, even though they constitute the overwhelming majority of the Indian workforce. Informal workers' working arrangements and relationships to patrons, clients and institutions are variously constituted. This diversity is difficult to capture in any a priori legal formulation. Therefore, direct participation of informal workers is essential in order for the law to facilitate distributive justice for informal workers. Unless the labour law discourse integrates continued worker participation, including by informal workers, there is a risk that a significant percentage of the workforce will remain excluded from the labour-centric social justice mission. And since the labour law reforms ought to be evaluated on a holistic basis, not only from the point of view of industrial employees, inclusive participation itself remains a factor in assessing the legislative balance – that is, in weighing the multidimensional legal entitlements advanced to promote labour justice through the latest reforms.

## A Contextual Evaluation of Labour Law

As noted, this book adopts a holistic approach to evaluate labour law in India as shaped by the latest reforms. The holistic approach signifies that instead of focusing on specific aspects of the labour law reforms or pursuing particular interpretations, a contextual assessment of the overall character of labour law in the country is the need of the day, which this book seeks to accomplish. This book primarily offers a conceptual and doctrinal account of labour law. While the book does provide statutory interpretation, it is not merely an exercise in statutory analysis, offering commentary on specific statutes after their consolidation through reforms. Its engagement with statutes furthers the overall analysis of labour law as a coherent regulatory approach in the aforementioned constitutional context. By evaluating the potential influence of the different components of post-reform labour law on divergent worker groups, this book unearths the capacity of Indian labour law to become an instrument furthering the constitutional social justice agenda.[36] In offering a conceptual account of labour law, the book engages in interdisciplinary analysis that is tethered to its constitutional context. The book not only engages in a doctrinal evaluation of legal principles but also examines how law works and ought to work – in society. It draws on political theory, anthropological narratives and quantitative and qualitative data to comment on the essential qualities and impact of the recent labour law reforms. That said, some chapters offer a more intensive doctrinal scrutiny of labour law, focusing on whether the law is normatively thorough and internally coherent.

Legislative power on the subject matter of labour is constitutionally distributed between Parliament and the state legislatures.[37] The general subject matter of labour welfare is listed in the 'Concurrent List' of the constitutional scheme of law-making power, on which Parliament and state legislatures concurrently legislate.[38] While Parliament is empowered to enact legislation for the territory of India, state legislatures exercise the power within their respective territories.[39] Thus, within the territory of a state, federal and state legislation (or state amendments) can exist on subject matters of '[t]rade unions, industrial and labour disputes', '[s]ocial security and social insurance; employment and unemployment' and '[w]elfare of labour including conditions of work, provident funds, employers' liability, workmen's compensation, invalidity and old age pensions and maternity benefits'.[40] It should be noted, however, that Parliament enjoys a certain degree of prominence in this constitutional division of legislative power. For example, if statutory provisions enacted by Parliament and the state legislatures are found to be incompatible, it is the parliamentary law that will prevail over state legislation in general.[41] Additionally, Parliament has exclusive power to legislate on any subject matter that is not listed in the 'Concurrent List' or the 'State List'.[42] It also enjoys exclusive law-making power in order to implement the country's international obligations.[43] And under exceptional circumstances ('national interest' or 'emergency'), Parliament can legislate on subject matters in the 'State List'.[44]

Employing its superior constitutional power to legislate on labour welfare, the Indian Parliament thoroughly amended labour law for the country during 2019–2020; the majority of amendments were introduced in 2020 (hereinafter, '2020 reforms'). As the book will show, the 2020 labour law reforms introduced numerous changes to the country's labour law scheme, thereby forcing a permanent and far-reaching revision of the nature of labour law and workers' rights. The changes range from diminishing the government's role in industrial 'employment' relations to extending social protection for informal workers and others in between. This book analyses the different legislative amendments from three broad perspectives: market-based employment relations, solidarity-based worker welfare and participatory industrial democracy. These three facets of the reforms are then weighed together in their combined ability to further social justice for Indian workers. Accordingly, this book undertakes a critical constitutional and legislative analysis, including that of judicial interpretations of the different components of the labour law regime. Documentary research of the social science literature to situate the legal regime in its actual social context complements this analysis. The combined methods – of doctrinal analysis and contextual evaluation – are employed simultaneously throughout the book.

The Indian Parliament instituted the labour law reforms of 2020 through four codes: the IR Code, 2020;[45] the Code on Wages, 2019;[46] the Occupational Safety, Health and Working Conditions Code, 2020;[47] and the Code on Social Security, 2020.[48] One of the remarkable features of the labour law reforms has been organised labour's sustained and widespread opposition to them. Trade unions across the country, including the trade union wing of the Bharatiya Janata Party (BJP) (the political party in power), the Bharatiya Mazdoor Sangh, have called for multiple general (that is, political) strikes and protests against the labour law reforms. The intensity of protests against the reforms, yet the eventual adoption of them, would easily qualify the reforms as 'hard reforms' wherein labour and capital are unrelenting in their respective positions on the core values of labour regulation.[49] Worker organisations protested the lack of consultation and meaningful participation in enacting the reforms. Insofar as participation in the law-making process and wider community engagement are concerned, the reforms are alleged to be deficient.[50] It is also alleged that Parliament bypassed broad consultation and democratic participation during the reform process in order to force the 'ease of doing business' at the cost of promoting labour welfare in the country.[51] Indeed, some prominent features of the reforms prima facie lend themselves to such criticism.[52]

Traditionally, industrial relations in India have largely involved a tripartite relationship between employers, employees and the government. While the relationship was – is – based on a formal employment contract between the employer and the employee, the government acted as an interested party monitoring these contractual relationships. The law substantially limited the contracting parties' (that is, the employer and the employee) freedom in employment contracts through the requirements to report to the governmental authority and obtain prior approval for contractual (managerial) decision-making, particularly in decisions about laying off and terminating employees.[53] Pre-reform labour law in India looked past both the narratives of formal 'freedom of contract' in the labour market and the 'permissible inequality' of the employment relationship inherent in the employer's legal (common law) right to control her business and employees. The legal regime recognised with Max Weber that the 'formal right of a worker to enter into any contract whatsoever with any employer whatsoever does not in practice represent for the employment seeker even the slightest freedom in the determination of his own conditions of work, and it does not guarantee him any influence on this process'.[54] On the other hand, because of proprietary rights, the employer is free to impose her will on the employee.[55] Indian labour law tackled this disparity of contractual freedom, including the lopsided ownership-backed freedom of the employer, by imposing reasonable limits on the employer's freedom. In imposing limits on the employer's decision-making prerogative about her business, labour law traditionally understood the employment relationship as a de facto unequal contract wherein the inequality between the contracting parties exists for the duration of the relationship. Since employees, because of both their constrained choice in market participation and the absence of proprietary interest in the (employer's) business, are decidedly the weaker party in the relationship, the government is duty-bound to safeguard their interests.[56]

This governmental mandate to minimise the inequality in employment relationships was incorporated prominently in chapter VB of the Industrial Disputes Act, 1947.[57] Chapter VB instructed an employer to seek and receive governmental approval before laying off and terminating her employees, and before closing down her establishment, if she employed 100 or more employees.[58] Upon receiving an application from an employer, the government was to investigate and decide whether to grant permission for the lay-offs, terminations or the establishment's closure. The government's decision was theoretically final and binding on the employer, and refusal to comply with the governmental order would expose the employer to a penalty.[59] The tripartite relationship – as evident in the employer's legal obligation to secure prior governmental approval for major decisions affecting the employment relationship – being the historical characteristic of industrial relations, one of the most contentious parts of the reforms has been the amendment that minimises the role of the government in employer decisions to lay off, terminate or cease operations. Whereas before the reforms, an employer employing 100 or more employees needed prior governmental approval for laying off and terminating employees, the reforms mandated the approval requirement only for employers employing 300 or more employees.[60]

This is not to say the new industrial relations scheme conceptually abandons the 'unequal contracting parties' narrative. The law still requires employers to obtain prior approval from the government before laying off and terminating employees and before closing down an establishment, albeit only for larger employers.[61] By introducing this change, the legislature expands the operation of the 'formal contractual freedom' in labour market relationships and simultaneously narrows the scope of the constitutional 'governmental duty' in addressing labour market inequalities. The increased prominence of the market-based contractual freedom narrative could also be traced elsewhere in the reforms. For example, the law permits the expanded use of sub-contracted and fixed-term workers and allows the government to exempt employers, including labour contractors, from meeting the minimum statutory standards in employment contracts in the interests of the employer, the industry and the public.[62] As will be elaborated more fully in Chapter 2, by means of the 2020 labour law reforms, the legislature concedes the moral and regulatory authority of the erstwhile social space to the market space, thereby seeking to transform a predominantly 'tripartite' social relationship into a primarily 'bipartite' relationship of market exchange.

This legislative approach also permeates through how the new social security regime applies to the workforce. The raison d'etre of the Code on Social Security is to 'extend social security to *all employees and workers* either in the organized or unorganized or any other sectors'.[63] Since the very justification of the code rests on its ability to devise the legal right to social security for the entire workforce, the most appropriate place to begin evaluating the impact of the legislation on the workforce is to assess its coverage. As is extensively noted, the significant majority of the Indian workforce – that is, about 90 per cent of the workforce – is engaged in the so-called unorganised sector, which is also known as the informal sector.[64] The overarching distinguishing character of this sector is that working arrangements in the sector differ from the traditional industrial relations model, which is based on a modified formal contractual framework – contractual freedom as modified by the vestiges of the master–servant relationship – between an employer and an employee. While the terms 'unorganised' and 'informal' signify distance from the 'formal' (that is, orthodox) industrial relations, informal working arrangements are heterogeneous and numerous. Informal working arrangements can be found in productive activities such as home-based work, small-scale 'street' vending, transportation work, domestic work, waste recycling and a range of other types of manual work, to note only a few. It is *how* a productive activity is organised, much less than the actual occupation or trade, that determines whether it is informal or not. Work-on-demand, or 'gig' work, and online platform-based work too are broadly informal, insofar as they do not fit the traditional notions of industrial relations.[65]

Since labour law traditionally emerged within the 'formal' contractual industrial relations model, one of the unmet challenges of this branch of law has been to address the concerns of informal workers engaged in unorthodox working arrangements. It is this mischief that the Code on Social Security seeks to address. However, the code's claim to universal social security coverage, inclusive of informal workers, is overstated. To informal workers, the social security law primarily secures the *legal right* – legitimate claim to substantive resources obligating a party (the state) to make it available or face legal consequences – to national and state social security boards.[66] It is these boards that shall be duty-bound to devise social security 'schemes' for informal workers.[67] On the advice of the (national and state) boards, the government is obligated to devise executive schemes on social security for informal, gig and platform-based workers covering issues such as life and disability coverage, health and maternity benefits, old-age benefits, accident insurance, provident fund, employment injury benefit, housing provisioning, educational provisioning, skill upgradation, childcare facility, funeral assistance, and so on.[68] Thus, while informal workers possess rights to executive schemes against the government, they do not possess the legal right to substantive entitlements (for example, life and disability coverage or health and maternity benefits) under the schemes. When the law does enumerate a specific claim, such as the employees' health insurance, it leaves it to the government's discretion to replicate the legal right of formal workers as an executive entitlement for informal workers.[69] While there may be some valid reasons for relying on executive schemes instead of legal rights in securing informal workers' social security, as will be analysed in Chapter 3, such a strategy may end up exposing social security entitlements to political (executive) interferences without affording enough power to workers to counter this interference.

Insofar as the coverage of the remaining approximately 10 per cent of the workforce – that is, formal industrial employees – is concerned, the social security regime secures entitlements to employees' provident fund, pension, deposit-linked life insurance, medical insurance (for employees and their families), maternity benefits, compensation for injury during employment, construction workers' welfare fund and gratuity at termination.[70] The law also contemplates social security benefits for self-employed workers, which is to be instituted by the central government.[71] While the entitlements of formal workers are wide-ranging, exclusions from legislative coverage should be central in the evaluation of the social security framework, as should be the role of the government-led substantive social security privileges. For instance, the law only makes employers who employ at least twenty employees contribute to the employees' provident fund.[72] Furthermore, the reforms also exempt cooperatives operating without electricity and employing less than fifty persons from provident fund obligations. Additionally, the central government is empowered to exempt establishments from the purview of the provident fund obligations if the government is convinced that it is not financially viable for those establishments.[73] Likewise, workers employed in establishments employing at least ten workers are only entitled to medical insurance through the Employees State Insurance Corporation. While the law safeguards gratuity for all employees working in factories, mines, oilfields, plantations, ports and railways, in other establishments, including shops, workers can only demand gratuity if there are at least ten employees. Similarly, while all employees in a factory, mine or plantation are entitled to maternity benefits, it is available to workers in other establishments (that is, not being a factory, mine or plantation) only when such establishments employ ten workers or more.[74] To contextualise the reach of the social security entitlements in the larger context of India's total workforce, according to one estimate, during 2013–2014 only about 1.37 per cent of the commercial establishments in India employed ten or more workers.[75]

Even for formal workers, entitlements to provident funds, pensions and medical insurance still depend on governmental discretion and executive programming, albeit to a lesser extent. On the other hand, formal workers' access to gratuity on termination, maternity-related benefits and compensation for workplace accidents rest on the more secure foundation of legal rights.[76] Given the heterogeneity of the Indian workforce, while executive programmes may offer some flexibility in formulating the substantive content of workers' social security entitlements, such a legislative blueprint consolidating governmental discretion will only succeed when it simultaneously empowers collective worker engagement in the formulation of such programmes. It is only when workers can engage in the law-making process through collective action that executive entitlement schemes may be responsive to workers' contextual aspirations. Unfortunately, however, the labour law reforms turned out to be seriously deficient in promoting workers' collective action and participatory industrial democracy.

Trade union opposition to the reforms makes it evident that they largely fall short of the aspirations of India's workforce. Ten major central trade unions went on a nationwide general strike to protest the labour codes' enactment.[77] While the labour and employment minister asserted that wide-ranging consultations had taken place, trade unions allege that there was insufficient consultation leading to the reforms.[78] Some commentators note that the government took advantage of a fragmented political opposition and the COVID-19 pandemic-induced restrictions on gatherings and agitations to fast-track the legal reforms.[79] This deficit in consultation in the law-making process seems to be motivated by the government's commitment to improving the country's ranking in the World Bank's Ease of Doing Business (EoDB) index rather than any desire to promote inclusive industrial democracy.[80] Accordingly, major trade unions have demanded that the government withdraw the new labour laws.[81] The main union objections to the reforms have been the introduction of the hire-and-fire regime and the general withdrawal of the government from the industrial relations structure. In fact, as Chapter 4 shows, the expansion of the market logic and the contraction of the social space accompany the simultaneous weakening of collective worker power through the recent reforms.

Through the reforms, the law mandates the recognition of a trade union as a bargaining agent by the employer. While mandatory recognition of a trade union as a bargaining agent has been part of some states' labour law framework, the IR Code, for the first time, mandated it at the national level.[82] Although organised labour has demanded this for a long time, the recognition of trade unions as bargaining agents is, in fact, consistent with the pro-market legislative alignment of the rest of the reforms. If the industrial relations regime is increasingly marketised, wherein the contracting parties (that is, the employer and the employee) are to determine the details of their contractual obligations under conditions of minimal external (that is, governmental) interference, then it follows that employers must recognise trade unions as 'formally equal' bargaining agents. It is logically inconsistent to endorse the market space without recognising the formal equality of the employer and the trade union as workers' representatives. Any hint of non-recognition of the workers' representative organisation would be an affront to the legitimacy of the market space. Additionally, the recognition of a single bargaining unit for an establishment improves the 'market efficiency' of the bargaining process by reducing the administrative costs associated with an employer having to bargain with multiple trade unions as opposed to bargaining with only one representative agent.

Although the IR Code – as a legal necessity – formally recognises workers' representative organisations as bargaining agents, it goes on to substantively weaken worker power in industrial relations. One of the primary bargaining tools of the workers is the cessation of work – industrial strike – to exert economic pressure on the employer. Before enacting the IR Code, only employees in public utility services needed to serve prior notice to the employer of their intention to strike.[83] Serving of such notice, at least fourteen days (notice period of maximum sixty days) before the strike, is now compulsory in *all* industries.[84] Once the strike notice is served, it triggers a report to the conciliation officer and the government (or an authority prescribed by the government), who are expected to intervene in the employer–employee deadlock that led to the notice.[85] This means that Parliament has not only impeded industrial employees' bargaining power by constraining the right to strike, it also thrusts industrial relations further into the domain of juridical expertise rather than industrial democracy. The reforms make immediate conciliatory and tribunal intervention in bargaining disagreements more likely, thereby making legal experts rather than worker voice more important in industrial negotiations.[86]

Additionally, as argued in Chapters 3 and 4, while there is some recognition of worker participation in the various social security boards, by generally weakening labour's actual collective power – not only by constraining strike action and juridifying employment relations, but also by potentially limiting the number of trade unions in industrial bargaining – Parliament may have created a recipe for weakening India's independent labour movement in the long term. Limiting the number of bargaining unions in each industry may not lead to the waning of the independent labour movement in the short and medium terms. However, over time, some major trade unions – likely with the support of a friendly government – will consolidate their power by marginalising other collective organisations. This consolidation of worker power in only a few politically connected trade unions could result in the further marginalisation of most informal workers from the industrial democratic process, broadly conceived. It is worth noting here that unlike formal industrial employees, who bargain with their employer in determining their working conditions, informal workers' working conditions are mainly negotiated with the government (at various levels) rather than the employer. In view of the overwhelming heterogeneity of informal workers and the character of their negotiation, there is merit in permitting divergence in the nature and form of collective worker organisation. It is not only trade unions but also cooperatives, societies, trusts and worker-promoted companies that serve as representatives of the country's heterogeneous informal workers.[87]

These different organisations adopt a range of strategies to promote worker well-being. The normative aim of the labour law regime in the country should be to engage these different organisations in the law-making process as an acknowledgement of the fragmented nature of the country's labour relations and workers' contextual aspirations. The following discussion outlines how the arguments of the book unfold through the different chapters that follow this introduction.

## An Outline of Arguments

This book argues that by failing to recognise the inherent diversity of labour relations in the country, making the social space subservient to the market space and downgrading industrial democracy, the labour law reforms of 2020 fail to meet the social justice agenda of the Constitution. In particular, the reforms fail to strike a proper balance between individual liberty, social solidarity and industrial democracy in the context of the country's unique industrial relations scenario. The book does not argue that the new labour codes are ultra vires the Constitution, but that they collectively fail to further the constitutional agenda of social justice both in its legislative configuration and in its normative aspiration. This theme of the book is carried out through the following chapters.

Chapter 1 analyses the centrality of labour as a dynamic idea in advancing the constitutional goal of social justice. In India's Constitution, labour is conceived as one of the principal formative components of the nation wherein citizens' – workers' – agency results in social (or national) contribution. Society – the nation – reciprocates by ensuring a dignified life for workers. Labour is, thus, what the Constitution envisions as the basis for the just distribution of the country's resources, rights and opportunities. The Constitution does not define social justice but articulates the idea primarily through the Preamble, Part III (bill of rights) and Part IV (policy obligations of the state) of the document. As expressed through these parts of the Constitution, the idea of social justice could generally be understood as a commitment to distributional fairness that promotes a dignified life for every citizen, allowing them to participate fully and equally in their community as responsible citizens. Since labour constitutes the core of the constitutional social justice project and since social justice is an unalterable basic structure of the Constitution, the book argues that we should examine the latest comprehensive labour law reforms employing the constitutional benchmark of social justice. In furthering that commitment, this chapter elaborates on the tenets of the constitutional social justice project.

Individual liberty, contractual freedom and market participation are justiciable fundamental rights under the Constitution. The Constitution safeguards every citizen's freedom to engage in any trade, business, occupation and profession. Chapter 2 examines the role of the IR Code in facilitating worker autonomy and their ability to meaningful market participation. This chapter shows that although the code recognises the inequality of contractual freedom between the employer and the employee, it substantially expands the operation of formal contractual freedom by making the government largely withdraw from industrial (that is, employment) relations. Workers' substantive entitlements are seen primarily as negotiated contractual claims. Although the IR Code furthers the narrative of individual autonomy-powered labour market exchanges, one should not analyse the code in isolation. Even when recognising the freedom of contract between the employer and the employee, the labour law reforms, in principle, limit such market freedom through minimum wage regulation and workplace safety, health and working conditions mandates.[88] The chapter also evaluates the extent to which these latter entitlements balance the risks of labour market uncertainties that the IR Code exposes industrial employees to.

As noted, Chapter 2 argues that the labour law reforms in India expand the significance of contractual freedom in industrial relations at the cost of political (that is, governmental) intervention. This contractual freedom is grounded in the bill of rights – fundamental rights – of the Constitution. While this market freedom is (constitutionally) crucial for promoting an individual worker's agency-centred advancement, a just society must supplement it with social provisioning. Social provisioning is necessary not only to remove barriers to market entry and rectify market distortions but also to promote workers' dignity by directly promoting their well-being. The latter is articulated through the constitutional ideals of solidarity and socialism. Chapter 3 will assess the reforms insofar as their capacity to meet the constitutional mandate of social provisioning is concerned. Given the expanded operation of the market in industrial relations, social security entitlements should offer an elevated level of protection to the workforce to meet the constitutional balance between individual liberty and social solidarity. Chapter 3 argues that the social security reforms fail on this count. In examining the (workforce) coverage and comprehensiveness of substantive entitlements, this chapter notes that the social security framework fails to offer a reliable network of protection commensurate with the heightened risks associated with expanded market-based industrial relations. The specific context of the country's informal workers, including gig and online platform-based workers, exacerbates the failure of the social security framework.

Whereas individual liberty provides the foundation for the market-centric justiciable right to work (that is, trade, business, occupation and profession), the constitutional redistributive agenda is a political – governmental – programme executed through collective participation and industrial democracy. The constitutional redistributive programme, articulated through the directive principles of state policy (Part IV) of the Constitution, is declared to be 'fundamental in the governance of the country'.[89] India's 'governance' is premised on the participatory democratic process, including at the level of local administration and industrial management.[90] What follows is that collective action and democratic participation are constitutive elements of the Constitution's social justice mission. In this formulation, redistribution is a political agenda rather than a strictly legal one. The political governance process determines both the substantive contours of entitlements and the legal mechanism for their enforcement in specific contexts. Accordingly, Chapter 4 evaluates the recent reforms on the basis of their ability to facilitate worker collective action and participation in the law-making process. In particular, this chapter examines how legislative safeguards realise the justiciable constitutional rights to form trade unions and worker cooperatives in India. This analysis is important not only from the point of view of industrial management in formal firms but also for the purpose of understanding workers' participation in the broader production processes involving informal economic activities. In addition to evaluating the role of the reforms in informal workers' collective action, this chapter also analyses whether informal workers' – particularly self-employed ones – collective action is constrained through the operation of the competition law regime. Since many informal workers (for example, street vendors, transportation workers, freelancers and gig workers) could be seen to be undertaking their own businesses, their collective action may prima facie appear to be in restraint of trade.

The concluding chapter of the book is forward-looking. While it reviews the central arguments offered in the book and considers whether the balance among the different components of the constitutional social justice project is maintained and the normative aim of the project is furthered through the amended labour law in the country, its principal aim is to indicate research approaches and juridical attitudes that should be pursued on the basis of the core thesis of this book. In broadly evaluating the ability of labour law to further social justice, this chapter situates the theme in current and emerging debates in labour law and industrial relations, including those precipitated by the increasing prominence of on-demand work (or gig work), the use of artificial intelligence (AI) as a management (and production) strategy and the relationship between work and environment. In so situating the agenda, the chapter employs the constitutional foundation of labour law in India in order to recommend theorising labour law on the basis of the principle of social justice as opposed to the logic of the labour market exchange. Unfortunately, however, the conceptual misunderstanding of labour law as the law of the labour market has led some of the state governments in India to either attempt the suspension of labour law or exempt industries from some of the key provisions of the law to ease the burden on businesses during a market turbulence. In addition to appraising the accurate conceptual basis of labour law, the chapter emphasises the need to adopt a contextual sui generis interpretation of the law in practice that is independent of the inherited (colonial) rationale of the subject. Simultaneously, the chapter identifies some substantive future research agendas.

## Notes

1. Iris Marion Young, 'Between Liberalism and Social Democracy: A Comment on Tushnet', *Chicago Journal of International Law* 3, no. 2 (2002): 471–476; Mark Tushnet, 'State Action, Social Welfare Rights, and the Judicial Role: Some Comparative Observations', *Chicago Journal of International Law* 3, no. 2 (2002): 435–453.
2. Young, 'Between Liberalism and Social Democracy', 471–472; Tushnet, 'State Action, Social Welfare Rights, and the Judicial Role', 435–436.
3. Young, 'Between Liberalism and Social Democracy', 471–472; Tushnet, 'State Action, Social Welfare Rights, and the Judicial Role', 435–436.
4. Tushnet, 'State Action, Social Welfare Rights, and the Judicial Role', 438, 440.
5. Constitution of India, 1950, Article 19(g) (hereinafter, 'Constitution').
6. Constitution, Articles 19(6), 31A, 38, 39, 46.

7. Constitution, Preamble, Part IV.
8. Alain Supiot, 'Grandeur and Misery of the Social State', *New Left Review* 82 (2013): 99–113; Constitution, Article 38.
9. Constitution, Articles 37, 39, 41.
10. Constitution, Articles 31C, 37, 39A.
11. Constituent Assembly of India Debates (Proceedings), vol. 7, 19 November 1948 (opinion of B. R. Ambedkar), https://www.constitutionofindia.net/constitution_assembly_debates/volume/7/1948-11-19 (accessed on 16 August 2023).
12. Constitution, Article 19(1)(c).
13. *All India Bank Employees' Association v. National Industrial Tribunal & Others*, [1962] 3 SCR 269 (SC); *T. K. Rangarajan v. Government of Tamil Nadu & Others*, [2003] Appeal (Civil) 5556 of 2003 (SC); Constitution, Article 43A.
14. Constitution, Article 43B.
15. *His Holiness Kesavananda Bharati Sripadagalvaru v. State of Kerala*, (1973) MANU 0445 (SC), paras. 306–307 (per S. M. Sikri, chief justice), para. 564 (per J. M. Shelat and A. N. Grover).
16. *His Holiness Kesavananda Bharati Sripadagalvaru v. State of Kerala*, para. 619 (per J. M. Shelat and A. N. Grover).
17. See, generally, *His Holiness Kesavananda Bharati Sripadagalvaru v. State of Kerala*. Also see Amartya Sen, *Development as Freedom* (New York: Alfred A. Knoph, 1999), 18; Peter Evans, 'Collective Capabilities, Culture, and Amartya Sen's Development as Freedom', *Studies in Comparative International Development* 37, no. 2 (2002): 54–60.
18. Constitution, Articles 19(1)(a), 19(1)(c), 38, 40, 43A, 51A(j); *His Holiness Kesavananda Bharati Sripadagalvaru v. State of Kerala*, para. 749 (per K. S. Hegde and A. K. Mukherjea).
19. Constitution, Preamble.
20. *His Holiness Kesavananda Bharati Sripadagalvaru v. State of Kerala*, para. 564 (per J. M. Shelat and A. N. Grover), paras. 705, 755, 758 (per K. S. Hegde and A. K. Mukherjea), para. 1531 (per H. R./ Khanna), paras. 1762, 1748 (per K. K. Mathew's dissent), paras. 1860, 1861, 1862 (per M. H. Beg's dissent).
21. Jeremy Waldron, *Law and Disagreement* (New York: Oxford University Press, 1999), 7.
22. Waldron, *Law and Disagreement*, 4, 6.
23. Jeremy Waldron, *The Dignity of Legislation* (New York: Cambridge University Press, 1999), 2–3, 5, 156–162.

24. Waldron, *Law and Disagreement*, 5.
25. Grégoire Webber, Paul Yowell, Richard Ekins, Maris Köpcke, Bradley W. Miller and Francisco J. Urbina, *Legislated Rights: Securing Human Rights through Legislation* (New York: Cambridge University Press, 2018).
26. Webber, Yowell, Ekins, Köpcke, Miller and Urbina, *Legislated Rights*, 1.
27. Webber, Yowell, Ekins, Köpcke, Miller and Urbina, *Legislated Rights*, 3.
28. Webber, Yowell, Ekins, Köpcke, Miller and Urbina, *Legislated Rights*.
29. Webber, Yowell, Ekins, Köpcke, Miller and Urbina, *Legislated Rights*, 55, 69–70.
30. Webber, Yowell, Ekins, Köpcke, Miller and Urbina, *Legislated Rights*, 56–57, 60, 65–66.
31. Webber, Yowell, Ekins, Köpcke, Miller and Urbina, *Legislated Rights*, 56, 58–60.
32. Webber, Yowell, Ekins, Köpcke, Miller and Urbina, *Legislated Rights*, 6.
33. Webber, Yowell, Ekins, Köpcke, Miller and Urbina, *Legislated Rights*, 20–21, 28, 53.
34. Alan Bogg, 'Common Law and Statute in the Law of Employment', *Current Legal Problems* 69, no. 1 (2016): 67–113, 75.
35. Bogg, 'Common Law and Statute in the Law of Employment'; Webber, Yowell, Ekins, Köpcke, Miller and Urbina, *Legislated Rights*, 3.
36. Carrie Menkel-Meadow, 'Uses and Abuses of Socio-Legal Studies', in *Routledge Handbook of Socio-Legal Theory and Methods*, ed. Naomi Creutzfeldt, Marc Mason and Kirsten McConnachie, 35–57 (Abingdon and New York: Routledge, 2020), 43, 46. For a similar approach to the analysis of labour jurisprudence, albeit from the perspective of one Supreme Court justice, see Sharath Babu and Rashmi Shetty, *Social Justice and Labour Jurisprudence: Justice V.R. Krishna Iyer's Contributions* (New Delhi: SAGE Publications, 2007). Also see Debi S. Saini, 'Labour Legislation and Social Justice: Rhetoric and Reality', *Economic and Political Weekly* 34, no. 39 (1999): L-32–L-40.
37. Constitution, Article 246, Seventh Schedule.
38. Constitution, Seventh Schedule, List III: Concurrent List.
39. Constitution, Article 245.
40. Constitution, Seventh Schedule, List III: Concurrent List, Entries 22, 23 and 24.
41. Constitution, Article 254.
42. Constitution, Article 248. Also see Seventh Schedule, List II: State List (state legislatures have exclusive authority to enact legislation on subject matters in the State List).

43. Constitution, Article 253.
44. See Constitution, Articles 249, 250, 251.
45. Act no. 35 of 2020.
46. Act no. 29 of 2019.
47. Act no. 37 of 2020.
48. Act no. 36 of 2020.
49. Rahul Suresh Sapkal and K. R. Shyam Sundar distinguish between 'soft' and 'hard' reforms on the basis of the ability of such reforms to cause serious negative disruptions in jobs and wages and the inflexible position of trade unions and employers with respect to such reforms. See Rahul Suresh Sapkal and K. R. Shyam Sundar, 'Determinants of Precarious Employment in India: An Empirical Analysis', in *Precarious Work*, ed. Arne L. Kalleberg and Steven P. Vallas, 335–361 (Bingley: Emerald Publishing Limited, 2018), 335, 341–342.
50. For example, see K. R. Shyam Sundar, 'No Dialogue with Trade Unions, India's Labour Laws Are Now a Product of Unilateralism', *The Wire*, 7 July 2020. Also see Damini Nath, 'Can't Keep Deferring Labour Reforms in the Name of Consultation, Says Labour Minister Gangwar', *The Hindu*, 2 October 2020.
51. Anamitra Roychowdhury, *Labour Law Reforms in India: All in the Name of Jobs* (Abingdon and New York: Routledge, 2018), 282–283; Aishwarya Bhuta, 'Imbalancing Act: India's Industrial Relations Code, 2020', *Indian Journal of Labour Economics* 65, no. 3 (2022): 821–830; T. K. Rajalakshmi, 'The New Labour Codes: Labour's Loss'. *Frontline*, 23 October 2020. For an analysis that Parliament – policymakers generally – may have been influenced by a range of (methodologically and conceptually) erroneous studies on the rigidities of Indian labour law during the process of reforms, see Aditya Bhattacharjea, 'Labour Market Flexibility in Indian Manufacturing: A Critical Survey of the Literature', *International Labour Review* 160, no. 2 (2021): 197–218. Also see Vidu Badigannavar and John Kelly, 'Do Labour Laws Protect Labour in India? Union Experiences of Workplace Employment Regulations in Maharashtra, India', *Industrial Law Journal* 41, no. 4 (2012): 439–470, for an analysis developed on the basis of the disjuncture between law in books and law in practice in order to challenge the narrative of inflexibility of pro-worker labour regulation in the country; Gopal Krishna Roy, Amaresh Dubey and Suresh Ramaiah, 'Labour Market Flexibility and Changes in Employment: Spatial and Temporal Evidence from Indian Manufacturing', *Indian Journal of Labour Economics* 63, no.

1 (2020): 81–98, for a state-level analysis refuting the inflexibility of labour law thesis; Anamitra Roychowdhury, 'Application of Job Security Laws, Workers' Bargaining Power and Employment Outcomes in India', *Economic and Labour Relations Review* 30, no. 1 (2019): 120–141, for an analysis of de facto labour flexibility practised by the Indian industry. It is important to note that Indian labour law has historically allowed some labour flexibility to industrial establishments in the performance of their non-perennial activities. Employers could engage contract labour, through an intermediate (contractor), to adjust their workforce to meet their seasonal or unforeseen needs. While an employer – principal employer – takes full advantage of a contract worker, she is not primarily responsible for the welfare of such a worker under the Contract Labour (Regulation and Abolition) Act, 1970 (Act no. 37 of 1970). It is the contractor who bears the primary obligation for the welfare of such workers. Thus, when the Indian industry advocated and lobbied for labour flexibility, their demand has to be understood as a demand for labour flexibility in core industrial activities (in distinction to non-perennial activities). In Pankaj Kumar and Jaivir Singh, *Issues in Law and Public Policy on Contract Labour in India: Comparative Insights from China* (Singapore: Springer, 2018), the authors discuss the role of contract labour in facilitating a flexible labour market in India that is attractive for global capital and compares India's contract labour regime with the labour flexibility of China.

52. It should be noted that the 2020 labour law reforms are a culmination of more than two decades of governmental initiative in this respect. The reform initiative began in the aftermath of the liberalisation of the Indian economy in 1991. In 1999, the government of India constituted the Second National Commission on Labour through a resolution. The terms of reference to the commission were 'to suggest rationalisation of existing laws relating to labour in the organised sector' and 'to suggest an "umbrella" legislation for ensuring a minimum level of protection to the workers in the un-organised sector'. The commission submitted its report to the government in 2002. The commission recommended a range of so-called rationalising proposals to modernise labour laws in India. The purpose of such modernisation was to update the country's industrial relations framework to meet the needs of globalisation. In this respect, the commission broadly recommended increased labour flexibility and a general withdrawal of the state from labour relations, essentially proposing to transform the tripartite labour relations framework in the country to a predominantly bilateral contractual

relationship in order to keep up with the demands of globalisation. It is this general approach that defines the characteristics of the latest reforms. See Ministry of Labour, *Report of the National Commission on Labour*, vols. 1–2 (New Delhi: Ministry of Labour, Government of India, 2002). Also see K. R. Shyam Sundar, 'Labour Flexibility Debate in India: A Comprehensive Review and Some Suggestions', *Economic and Political Weekly* 40, nos. 22–23 (2005): 2274–2285; K. R. Shyam Sundar, 'Second National Commission on Labour (SNCL) and Reform of Industrial Relations System: Some Comments', *Indian Journal of Industrial Relations* 42, no. 2 (2006): 252–270.

53. See the Industrial Disputes Act, 1947 (hereinafter, 'ID Act'), chs. VA and VB, which is now repealed by the Industrial Relations Code, 2020 (hereinafter, 'IR Code').
54. Max Weber, 'Freedom and Coercion', in *Max Weber on Law in Economy and Society*, ed. Max Rheinstein, 188–191(Cambridge, MA: Harvard University Press, 1954).
55. Weber, 'Freedom and Coercion'.
56. See Constitution, Article 38. Article 38(2) reads:

> The State shall, in particular, strive to minimize the inequalities in income, and endeavour to *eliminate inequalities in status, facilities and opportunities*, not only amongst individuals but also amongst groups of people residing in different areas or engaged in different vocations. (Emphasis mine)

57. Act no. 14 of 1947.
58. ID Act, sections 25K, 25M, 25N, 25O. Chapter VB was introduced in the ID Act in 1976. At the time of the introduction, Chapter VB was to apply to establishments employing 300 or more employees. This number was reduced to 100 in 1982 in order to expand the application of the chapter (the amendment actually came into force in 1984). Through the 2020 labour reforms, the minimum employee threshold for requiring prior governmental approval was increased back to 300.
59. ID Act, sections 25Q, 25R.
60. Also see note 58.
61. See IR Code, ch. X.
62. See IR Code, sections 39, 40, 41, 96 and the Third Schedule.
63. Code on Social Security, 2020 (Act no. 36 of 2020) (hereinafter, 'Code on Social Security'), Preamble (emphasis mine).

64. See Government of India, *Economic Survey 2018–19*, vol. 2 (New Delhi: Government of India, 2019), 266 (noting 93 per cent of the Indian workforce is informal); International Labour Organization, *India Labour Market Update*, ILO Country Office for India, July 2017 (New Delhi: International Labour Organization), 3 (putting the informal workers' percentage at 92).

65. However, the Code on Social Security conceives gig workers and online platform-based workers as different categories from that of 'unorganised' workers. See the definitions of 'gig worker', 'platform work' and 'platform worker' in the Code on Social Security, section 2(35)(60)(61). Online platform-based work-on-demand (or gig work) is generally not seen as informal work because policymakers (and law and industrial relations scholars) often associate informality with traditional and pre-capitalist forms of work that failed to evolve into the industrial relations model. This orthodox understanding is analytically flawed. If we understand informality by its distance from the industrial relations 'form' emerging out of the industrial revolution period in Europe, there is no logical basis to exclude newer innovations in business models that bypass the 'form' as innovations in informality, with the ultimate motive of profit maximisation. For a better characterisation of platform-based work as informal work and (platform-based) gig workers' core concerns in India, see Premilla D'Cruz and Ernesto Noronha, 'Indian Freelancers in the Platform Economy: Prospects and Problems', in *Globalization, Labour Market Institutions, Processes and Policies in India: Essays in Honour of Lalit K. Deshpande*, ed. K. R. Shyam Sundar, 257–276 (Singapore: Palgrave Macmillan, 2019).

66. See Code on Social Security, section 6. The Code on Social Security mandates that the central government and the state governments 'shall' constitute social security boards respectively for the national and the state jurisdictions.

67. Code on Social Security, section 6(7)(15).

68. Code on Social Security, sections 109, 114.

69. Code on Social Security, section 45, First Schedule. Although employees' health insurance is not legally guaranteed for establishments employing less than ten workers, the central government 'may' in their discretion frame such an executive scheme for informal workers, including gig and platform-based workers.

70. Code on Social Security, sections 15–16, 21, 26, 28, 32, 34, 36, 38–40, 53, 59–61, 64–67, 74–75, 100.

71. Code on Social Security, section 15(1)(d).
72. Code on Social Security, First Schedule.
73. Code on Social Security, section 20(2).
74. Code on Social Security, chs. IV, VI, First Schedule.
75. See Government of India, *All India Report of Sixth Economic Census, 2016*, ch. 2, 26–27, http://mospi.nic.in/all-india-report-sixth-economic-census (accessed on 10 November 2021). The report further notes that 95.5 per cent of commercial establishments employed less than six workers, whereas 3.13 per cent employed six to nine workers.
76. Code on Social Security, sections 53, 59, 60, 74, 75, 85, 87, 133.
77. Anamitra Roychowdhury and Kingshuk Sarkar, 'Labour Law Reforms in a Neo-Liberal Setting: Lessons from India', *Global Labour Journal* 12, no. 1 (2021): 58–64.
78. Nath, 'Can't Keep Deferring Labour Reforms in the Name of Consultation'.
79. Roychowdhury and Sarkar, 'Labour Law Reforms in a Neo-Liberal Setting', 59.
80. Roychowdhury and Sarkar, 'Labour Law Reforms in a Neo-Liberal Setting', 59.
81. *The Hindu*, 'Trade Unions to Strike on November 26 against Labour Laws', 2 October 2020; Yogima Seth Sharma, 'Central Trade Unions Want Ministry to Put on Hold Four Labour Codes & Re-Start Discussions', *Economic Times*, 20 January 2021.
82. IR Code, sections 14, 27. States such as Kerala, West Bengal and Maharashtra already had provisions for the recognition of trade unions as bargaining agents. See the Kerala Recognition of Trade Unions Act, 2010 (Act no. 16 of 2010). Also see West Bengal Trade Unions Rules, 1998 (issued under Trade Unions Act, 1926 [Act no. 16 of 1926], as amended by the Trade Unions [West Bengal Amendment] Act, 1983 [West Bengal Act no. 48 of 1983]); Maharashtra Recognition of Trade Unions and Prevention of Unfair Labour Practices Act, 1971 (Act no. 1 of 1972).
83. See ID Act, section 22.
84. IR Code, section 62.
85. IR Code, section 62(6).
86. IR Code, sections 44(7)(c), 60.
87. See Supriya Routh, 'Informal Workers' Aggregation and Law', *Theoretical Inquiries in Law* 17, no. 1 (2016): 283–320.
88. See, generally, Code on Wages, 2019 (Act no. 29 of 2019); Occupational Safety, Health and Working Conditions Code, 2020 (Act no. 37 of 2020).

89. Constitution, Article 37.
90. See Constitution, Article 40, on self-governing village-level administration, or *panchayat*. Also see Constitution, Article 43A, on workers' participation in management of industries; Article 43B, on democratic control of cooperative societies.

# 1

# Labour's Constitution

## Pursuing Economic, Social and Political Justice

### Introduction

One of the core normative aims of the Indian Constitution is the creation of an active citizenry. An Indian citizen is duty-bound to respect the constitutional principles, follow the ideals that guided the Indian independence movement, protect the sovereignty and unity of the country, defend the country, promote harmony and brotherhood, preserve the nation's heritage and culture, protect and improve the natural environment, develop scientific temper and inquisitiveness, safeguard public property, provide opportunities for their children's education and strive towards excellence in all spheres of individual and collective activities.[1] It is by imagining Indian citizens as agents of historical continuation and progressive change through their individual and collective activities that the slave mentality[2] of the Indian subjects under the British rule could be overcome. While it is true that the Constitution aimed to create independent political agents capable of self-determination,[3] the ideal of enterprising citizens, or worker-citizens, is also required to overcome the slave mentality and simultaneously pursue a nation-building agenda. In fact, the Constitution's three major trajectories – that of securing political freedoms, planning economic development and undertaking social reform[4] – all take the idea of worker-citizens as the core of their agenda. Although different dimensions of Indian citizenship may be contested,[5] the secular Indian identity is so intimately connected to the idea of the worker-citizen that it is around this ideal that the Constitution develops its social justice narrative. Yet this aspect of the Constitution has rarely received a sustained analysis from constitutional law scholars, including by those offering a tour d'horizon of the Constitution.[6]

Since the Constitution signifies a break from the past,[7] Indian citizens are conceived as agents of change. Work, or labour, is the primary process through which this agency finds – ought to find – a concrete personal expression in accordance with the Constitutional plan. The de facto reach of the concept of work, and consequently of the worker identity, is much more pervasive than that of the fundamental duty-bearing *political* citizen. Work is a fundamental condition of life for the overwhelming majority of Indian citizens. If we take into account an expansive definition of work as also including unpaid and care work, the magnitude of the worker identity becomes staggering. In view of this enormous reach of work – as a process that affects the majority of the citizenry in a way that no other process does – it occupies a central position in the Constitutional framework. Individual and collective agencies constitute the foundation of the idea of the worker identity. It is by means of their willingness, initiative, creativity, talent, skill and ambition that Indian workers are expected to strive towards excellence in their respective activities. True, this is an ideal-type imagination of workers. And that is precisely the point. In order to construct a constitutional ideal of social justice, it is necessary to conceive of an ideal-type citizen. The worker-citizen is the ideal-type citizen since work is conceived not only as an idea that is instrumentally significant as a means of personal income and socio-economic contribution[8] but also as intrinsically important[9] for the citizen. Work is where the citizen's and the state's ambitions genuinely converge.

Unsurprisingly, therefore, work is the basis of social cooperation and, thus, the foundation of the constitutional social justice project. In expanding this idea, the first section examines the attributes of the worker-citizen and worker-citizens' inherent relationship to the social justice project in the country. The second section elaborates the idea of social justice under the Constitution on the basis of judicial articulations of the idea. Drawing on political philosophy, the third section identifies the principal components of a liberal theory of justice. Instead of a comprehensive treatment of conceptual ideas of social justice, the aim of this section is to note a broad general structure of a theory of justice, which could serve as background knowledge for charting the major components of social justice under the Constitution. The fourth section elaborates the different components of the social justice framework under the Constitution. It is this framework that is employed as a standard to evaluate the post-reform labour law in India. The chapter ends with a brief conclusion, leading to the next one.

## Worker-Citizens as Subjects of Justice

Since the worker-citizen is not an exclusively individualistic idea of citizenship and since individual fulfilment and social responsibility both are part of the worker-citizen narrative, the idea of active citizenship through work is not entirely captured by the juridical idea of individual dignity. The idea of the worker-citizen extends beyond the concept of dignity of the individual worker. Individual dignity is a necessary but not sufficient condition for the imagination of active citizenship. It is by combining worker agency with the conditions of dignified existence that we arrive at the idea of the worker-citizen. As Upendra Baxi notes, even though it is difficult to harmonise the judicial articulations of dignity, the predominant narrative of human dignity under the Constitution could be understood as a concept of empowerment.[10] Empowerment, in this sense, means the capacity for autonomous action. The juridical idea of dignity, then, respects every individual's capacity for autonomous action, and from this respect flows the judicial attempt to create conditions wherein each individual is able to exercise her autonomy in planning and pursuing her life.

The Indian Constitution understands dignity in close relationship to that of solidarity ('fraternity'), which means that social support – social solidarity – in the form of public services are considered to be dignity-affirming rights.[11] By employing the idea of dignity, constitutional jurisprudence aims to channel state policies in a manner that helps develop the capacity of – that is, *empowers* – citizens for autonomous action. In *Bandhua Mukti Morcha v. Union of India*, the Supreme Court had to deal with forced labour under precarious conditions in stone quarries.[12] The workers in the stone quarries were forced to work under a debt bond system, whereby workers were paying a supposed debt through their manual labour, which either they or their parents had received from the employer. There were severe restrictions on the mobility of these workers; many of them were injured and diseased but did not receive medical attention; their workplaces flouted required safety norms; their wages were less than the stipulated minimum; they had access to only polluted drinking water; they barely had any residential accommodation and appropriate clothing; and murder and sexual harassment were common incidents.[13]

In the judgment, Justice P. N. Bhagwati noted that the right to live with human dignity includes protection of the health and strength of workers, protection of children against abuse, all-round development of children, educational facilities, just and humane conditions of work and maternity relief.[14] According to the court, these requirements are minimum necessities for a life with human dignity.[15] These necessities are, then, constitutive elements of an autonomous citizen capable of independent decision-making and considerate agency. The court also noted that while it was not possible for the court to direct the state to undertake legislative or executive action to promote these 'basic essentials' constituting human dignity, the court could direct the state to comply with such requirements when a legislative or executive scheme already existed.[16] As important as this reflection is for our understanding of the different components of dignity, it also emphasises the role of politics – participatory and deliberative policymaking – in creating conditions for a dignified life for workers. Dignity is not dependent on judicial dictates; it is an outcome of the political process. The civil society (broadly speaking) and the legislature promote dignity through the processes of collective action and participatory deliberation. The judiciary affirms the political process and the outcome.

In *Francis Coralie v. Union Territory of Delhi*,[17] the Supreme Court iterated that the right to life is not about mere animal existence; it means the right to live with human dignity.[18] The court observed that human dignity means the availability of provision for adequate nutrition, clothing, shelter; facilities for reading, writing, expressing oneself in any form; freedom of movement; and socialising with fellow human beings. According to Justice Bhagwati, speaking for the court, the concept of human dignity, thus, includes the right to 'basic necessities of life' and 'bare minimum expression of the human-self'.[19] However, the caveat the court added was that human dignity, in the sense the court expressed it, is always subject to economic development of the country.[20] Here is, then, another affirmation by the court of the significance of the political process, which should determine the priorities of the state within the scope of its economic capacities. In decisions such as *Consumer Education and Research Centre v. Union of India* and *Kirloskar Brothers Limited v. Employees' State Insurance Corporation*, the Supreme Court held that the right to health and medical assistance promotes the dignified life of workers.[21] Additionally, the court included tradition and cultural heritage as part of the concept of dignity.[22] The court also noted that it is the state's responsibility to secure facilities and opportunities so that workers could attain a minimum standard of health, economic security and decent living.[23] By consistently emphasising state responsibility, the court articulated the integral nature of the idea of dignity and politics within the constitutional framework.

Thus, it is evident that the Supreme Court envisages *provision for* certain entitlements, *facilities for* certain guarantees, *relief* of certain sorts and all-round development of individuals as constitutive of the idea of fundamental human dignity.[24] What follows from such an understanding of human dignity is that the state (and, also perhaps, non-state entities) needs to make certain provisions, certain facilities and some relief available to its citizens in order to respect and further their human dignity. In this sense, respecting dignity signifies that human beings are treated 'as persons capable of planning and plotting their future' and thereby having the capacity to 'control their future'.[25] According to Joseph Raz, if this control over the future is taken away by interfering with an individual's overall circumstances so that she is effectively stripped of all options that help shape her future, it amounts to enslavement of the individual and violation of her dignity.[26] Overcoming such enslavement by expanding individual choices, we may recall, is a core ambition of the Indian Constitution, according to Jawaharlal Nehru. And in this normative aim, dignity is the precondition to individual agency. Additionally, a more expansive understanding of dignity also requires a vibrant political process, as indicated by the court.

Ronald Dworkin captures the relationship between basic respect for human life and individual agency in terms of self-respect and authenticity, both as constituent parts of an expansive idea of human dignity.[27] While self-respect means respecting one's mere human life instead of one's accomplishments, authenticity refers to an individual's responsibility to contemplate what would be a successful and satisfactory life for her and live that life through her own agency.[28] In this view, authenticity depends on self-respect. It is only when people respect themselves that they are able to act in furtherance of their life's agenda.[29] Under the Indian constitutional framework, public services cater to self-respect, which is the basis of an individual's capacity for agency. However, in the Indian context, what is unique is the public nature of individual agency in contrast to the inward-looking individual agency that Dworkin formulates. While in the Dworkinian perspective authenticity relates to the goals of an individual, under the Indian Constitution it should also be seen as pursuing the ambition of the nation.

The worker-citizen is, therefore, simultaneously a private and public agent and a central theme of constitutional preoccupation. It is also important to note that, unlike the Dworkinian formulation, individual responsibility and agency are not captured as part of the (fraternity-engendered) constitutional idea of dignity as empowerment; instead, fundamental dignity remains the precondition to such responsibility and agency.

In view of labour's intrinsic significance (for example, satisfaction for workers) and instrumental importance (for example, contribution to material well-being and nation-building), it is by means of the labour process – exchange of labour – that redistribution of the common good, including material resources, is conceived under the Constitution. The social justice programme in the Constitution takes labour as its core ideological and political commitment and conceives of institutions (that is, rules and values) and procedures (that is, frameworks of engagement) of social justice with reference to labour processes – that is, ideals and processes surrounding exchanges and contributions of labour. The overarching aim of the Constitution of India is to promote fairness in working arrangements (or labour relations) so that every worker-citizen possesses the maximum available choice to live an autonomously decided satisfactory life. And because of the constitutional commitment to the ideals of solidarity and socialism, it is primarily the state's responsibility to recognise workers' social contribution in their varied undertakings and to promote fairness in their working relationships. The social justice principle of the Constitution, therefore, entails that social–economic–political–cultural processes should secure the dignity of every worker and create opportunities for the realisation of their agency.

The social justice formulation of the Indian Constitution operates through three overarching domains: the market, the state and the civil society. The market is the domain characterised by freedom of exchange between self-interested individuals (for example, employer–employee relationship). The state intervenes through mandating social support pursuant to the principle of solidarity (for example, provident fund and maternity benefits). And the civil society offers the space for deliberations on and evaluations of the other two domains of social justice. To be sure, this three-dimensional structure is a straightforward and formal representation of the social justice formulation. There are overlaps and blind spots in this structure of social justice. However, the structure offers a useful evaluative framework to analyse legislative initiatives and, crucially for our purposes, the 2020 labour law reforms in India. Later in this chapter, and prior to engaging in that evaluative exercise, we will identify some of the linkages and blind spots in this constitutional social justice formulation. Before assessing the components of the uniquely worker-centric social justice construct of the Constitution, it is worthwhile to briefly note the basic structure of this idea of social justice.

## Social Justice as a Basic Structure of the Indian Constitution

Social justice was a rallying cry and a unifying force during India's independence movement, and accordingly, it is prominently articulated in the Constitution.[30] In introducing the 'Resolution Re: Aims and Objects' in the Constituent Assembly, Nehru stated that social justice, including support for backward and depressed classes, should guide the policies of independent India.[31] As Arun Thiruvengadam notes, this aim may have been broadly shared by the judiciary, which explains the judiciary's initial deference to a range of progressive executive actions all over the independent nation.[32] Although this deferential attitude towards the executive changed rapidly, the judiciary consolidated social justice as a fundamental principle of the Constitution by limiting the scope of constitutional amendments.

The Supreme Court emphasised that the social justice principle is part of the 'basic structure' of the Constitution and, therefore, a permanent and unamendable component of the Constitution.[33] The court developed the basic structure doctrine through four judgments on the scope of constitutional amendments.[34] The basic structure constitutes 'the identity' of the Constitution.[35] Sudhir Krishnaswamy clarifies that the basic structure limitation on law-making power is in addition to the other limitations – including the limitation on the basis of fundamental rights – imposed by the Constitution.[36] Even though the basic structure doctrine is a distinct form of limitation and a fundamental feature of the Constitution, Krishnaswamy suggests that the constitutive feature of the doctrine is to be ascertained from the different provisions of the Constitution.[37] At the same time, the doctrine is not a mere collection of different articles of the Constitution.[38] The thematic ideas constituting the basic structure, such as supremacy of the Constitution, republican and democratic forms of government, secularism, separation of powers and the federal character of the Constitution, emanate from the 'basic foundation [of] dignity and freedom of the individual', as indicated by Justice

S. M. Sikri in *His Holiness Kesavananda Bharati Sripadagalvaru v. State of Kerala*.[39]

Dignity as empowerment and the agency aspect of individual freedom, as noted earlier, are constitutive features of the worker-citizen ideal in the Constitution. This ideal is furthered through the 'noble and grand vision' of the Constitution that simultaneously safeguards individual liberty and promotes economic, social and political justice.[40] The following is how the court preferred to articulate the idea of social justice as a fundamental feature of the Constitution:

> It is true that on a concept such as social and economic justice there may be different schools of thought but the Constitution makers knew what they meant by those concepts and it was with a view to implement them that they enacted Part III (Fundamental Rights) and Part IV (Directive Principles of State Policy) – both fundamental in character[.] [Social justice warrants] on the one hand, basic freedoms to the individual and on the other social security, justice and freedom from exploitation by laying down *guiding principles for future governments*.[41]

Accordingly, Parts III and IV – as elaborations of the idea of social justice – are basic structures of the Constitution.[42] And since social justice is an unalterable foundational feature of the Constitution and a guiding principle for governments, state action (including by the executive and the legislature) aimed at regulating socio-economic exchanges (such as the regulation of labour), in turn, should be evaluated on the basis of such foundational characteristics. Before we undertake such an evaluation of Indian labour law after the labour law reforms of 2020, we should clarify the essential features of social justice under the Constitution and, in particular, the delicate balance between individual liberty and redistributive policies.

The idea of social justice in the Constitution is broadly a liberal idea of justice. Although in *Kesavananda Bharati*, the court noted that distributive justice is a fundamental feature of the Constitution, the judges were quick to add that redistribution cannot come at the cost of violating individual liberty.[43] Granted that there are non-liberal features in the Constitution; however, the Indian Constitution is primarily a liberal constitution in both respecting individual liberty and restricting governmental power.[44] Although the role of liberalism in Indian political thought is contested, liberal ideas could be historically traced in the country's social–political debates.[45] The constitutional institutionalisation of liberal characteristics such as individual liberty, equal citizenship and state secularism are not only formal governing principles, they are generally internalised by the Indian citizenry.[46] It is argued that the Indian Constitution offers a thick concept of liberalism, which articulates the idea of autonomous individual citizens while also acknowledging the social embeddedness of the citizens.[47] This thick concept of liberalism, it may be noted, helps reconcile individual liberty with social solidarity.

Unsurprisingly, this reconciliation has resulted in the precedence being given to individual liberty over social solidarity in constitutional adjudication. More specifically, the judicial interpretation of the social justice mandate has accorded precedence to liberty in the sense that constitutional socio-economic rights are justified using instrumental reasoning that they promote individual liberty. For example, in *People's Union for Democratic Rights v. Union of India*,[48] the Supreme Court explained that economic, social and cultural rights secured as directive principles are the prerequisites for the meaningful realisation of civil and political rights safeguarded as fundamental rights.[49] The case concerned the violation of several labour laws in the construction work initiated by the government in preparation for the Asian Games. These construction works were performed by contract workers employed by the government through a contractor, wherein the contractor owned principal responsibility for the enforcement of mandatory regulations.[50] When rampant violations of several labour laws – including subversion of minimum wage regulation and gender-based wage discrimination – were brought to the notice of the court, the government denied any responsibility and instead shifted the onus on to the contractors.[51] In this situation, although socio-economic rights are essential for the marginalised workers, the court acknowledged that the judiciary could only play a limited role in furthering the realisation of such rights, which is primarily the function of the legislature and the executive.[52] However, by treating such rights as instrumental in promoting workers' freedom, the court could legitimately nudge the government to promote these socio-economic entitlements.[53]

In *M. C. Mehta v. State of Tamil Nadu*,[54] taking suo moto cognisance of employment of child labour in hazardous industries, the Supreme Court invoked the justiciable fundamental right against child labour and directive principles such as the right to education (which is now a fundamental right under Article 21A), right to health of children, right against exploitation of children, right to work and social protection and right to adequate standard of living in furtherance of abolishing child labour from hazardous industries in the country.[55] The court articulated that it is not only the executive who is required to implement directive principles; the judiciary too is duty-bound to apply directive principles in matters of public interest, such as the abolition of child labour.[56] In furtherance of its duty to promote freedom from exploitation (in this case, of child labour), the court instructed the government to enforce the Child Labour (Prohibition and Regulation) Act, 1986.[57] The court also directed the government to facilitate the employment of adult members of a family so that child labour could be avoided.[58] However, since these directions require resources to be spent by the government, the court noted that it is not asking the government to undertake these responsibilities immediately but '[i]nstead, ... leave[ing] the matter to be sorted out by the appropriate [g]overnment'.[59] Ultimately, then, the court leaves it to the existing legislative safeguards, democratic institutions and processes of the polity, which includes the government, to solve the problem of child labour.

In *Consumer Education and Research v. Union of India*,[60] dealing with occupational health hazards of employees resulting from asbestos exposure in the asbestos industry, the Supreme Court interpreted a range of directive principles related to health, safety and social protection as constituent parts of the fundamental right to life under Article 21 of the Constitution. The court noted that in order to live a dignified life, workers are entitled to the rights to livelihood, social security, humane conditions of work and opportunities for leisure and that the state is duty-bound to promote these basic claims of workers that are enumerated as directive principles.[61] Having noted the instrumental value of these entitlements for workers' dignified life and liberty, the court issued several directions to the government and the asbestos industry.[62] The court advised that the concerned workers, on whose behalf the court was petitioned, need to be examined for diseases and compensated by the industry.[63] Other directions pertained to compulsory insurance coverage for all employees in the industry, extension of safety regulations to small-scale industries and compulsory maintenance of medical records even after the workers retire.[64]

*Bandhua Mukti Morcha v. Union of India*[65] concerned the precarious conditions of bonded workers – that is, workers rendering labour without remuneration as repayment of an earlier debt incurred either by them or their ancestors – along with other workers in stone quarries in the district of Faridabad in the Indian state of Haryana. Although these workers were illegally engaged, their situation comes closer to the conditions of marginalised informal workers (many of whom often work unmonitored) in the sense that these workers were undocumented, outside the state's monitoring and regulatory purview, and mostly landless agricultural workers.[66] In its judgment, the Supreme Court noted that employment of workers without remuneration and against their free will amounts to forced labour, which stands prohibited by Article 23 of the Constitution – a fundamental right.[67] The court further stated that it is a basic human right of every individual in the country to live with dignity and be free from exploitation.[68] The right to live with human dignity, the court reasoned, entails the right to health of workers, right against abuse of children, right to educational opportunities, right to humane conditions of work and right to maternity relief – all specified directive principles.[69]

While one of the primary reasons why the Indian judiciary adopted the strategy of reading the non-justiciable directive principles as inseparable parts of the justiciable fundamental rights is that the strategy helps in judicially enforcing the directive principles, the court in this instance found that in spite of such a strategy, the judiciary cannot compel the state to act on promoting socio-economic rights in the absence of specific statutory enactments in that respect.[70] The court concluded that directive principles could be judicially realised only when statutory safeguards exist.[71] It follows that the social justice mandate of the Constitution needs legislative enactment for its proper realisation and that it is the duty of the state to implement the social justice mandate through legislative enactments. On the particular reasoning outlined here, mere constitutional adjudication – even if supported by an activist judiciary – is not enough to realise social justice. The proper juridical form of social justice is legislation, backed by participatory deliberation.

In *Bandhua Mukti Morcha*, the court directed the government(s) to appropriately implement existing laws for vulnerable workers. Approvingly citing a letter circulated by the Ministry of Labour, Government of India, to the various state governments on the strategies for rehabilitation of precarious and marginalised workers, the court identified the following aspects for the amelioration of the living conditions of such workers:[72]

(i) devising a comprehensive strategy for their physical, economic and psychological rehabilitation;
(ii) safeguarding civil rights of the workers;
(iii) provision for agricultural land, low-cost housing, easy credit, skills training, wage employment, healthcare, sanitation, essential commodities and education of children;

(iv) encouragement of traditional activities, such as traditional arts and crafts, and collection and processing of forest produce;
(v) purposive integration of a range of social protection schemes in devising more efficient social security for workers; and
(vi) mainstreaming the choice of workers for policymaking and focusing on their individual and family aspirations.

These guidelines are, indeed, statements of the different components of the social justice framework under the Constitution, which is discussed in the fourth section. Before discussing the different components of the social justice agenda, the major characteristics of a liberal idea of social justice are briefly identified. This exercise is done by surveying some of the prominent ideas of social justice in political philosophy. The purpose of the following section is not to engage with any one theory of social justice or to use any theory as an evaluative framework to examine labour law. Instead, the aim is to briefly document the essential features of social justice and notice (in the next section) how the constitutional idea of social justice fits with such a conceptual narrative.

## Components of a (Liberal) Theory of Social Justice

There is some consensus that fairness is the basis for theoretical approaches to social justice.[73] Fairness guides the rules and institutions of social justice. At a general level, theories of distributive justice aim to fairly distribute individual liberty and allocate resources for individuals to promote their material well-being.[74] Liberal theorists of social justice also seem to agree that individual liberty should have some priority over other distributive principles in theories of justice.[75] While these are the general characteristics of a theory of justice, structurally such a theory should have two components:[76] first, a measuring standard or subject matter of justice, which adequately compares unjust and just or less-just and more-just social situations, and, second, a rule of distribution, which states how the subject matter of justice is to be distributed. Examples of the former (that is, the subject matter) are happiness, income, wealth, social primary goods and capabilities. Examples of the latter (that is, the rule) are procedural rules specifying threshold-level material distribution (that is, income distribution by means of freedom of contract and social insurance, as per John Rawls) and distributive patterns apportioning individual liberty (that is, equal distribution of fundamental liberties, in Rawls' theory).[77]

Different theories of social justice offer varied responses to the two components of justice. Two of the most influential concepts of justice for liberal constitutional democracies are Rawls' theory of justice and the capability-sensitive idea of justice.[78] Both of these conceptual articulations of justice emerged as critiques of utilitarianism's subjective focus on happiness or desire satisfaction as the measuring standard of social justice. In response to the subjective bias of utilitarianism – an individual's subjective understanding of their happiness – Rawls offers an objective resource-focused approach to justice, whereas Amartya Sen and Martha Nussbaum articulate a consequentialist idea of justice that assesses the actual role – consequences – of resources in people's heterogeneous lives. While Rawls offers a comprehensive – self-contained – ideal theory of justice for ('perfectly just') liberal constitutional democracies, capability theorists, particularly Sen, propose a 'comparative' – that is, non-ideal – concept of justice.[79] The difference between the ideal-theorising and the comparative perspective is that while in the ideal theory decisions about institutions facilitating justice could be conclusively settled by applying the principles of justice, in the comparative approach arrangements of just institutions are never fully settled and are subject to continued evaluation and democratic deliberation. The aim of the comparative perspective is to move from less-just to more-just situations rather than settle, once and for all, the ideal conditions of justice. However, with respect to their overall structure, both of these approaches share broad similarities.

Rawls offers a basic structure for the political constitution with just economic and social arrangements, including legally protected individual liberty, private property and competitive markets.[80] The basic constitutional structure promotes people's freedom and choice, enabling them to be what they want to be by means of their agency.[81] According to him, social justice demands that '[a]ll social values – liberty and opportunity, income and wealth, and the social bases of self-respect – are to be distributed equally' unless their unequal distribution benefits everyone.[82] For Rawls, the measure of individual advantages and disadvantages and, accordingly, the subject matter of justice are the social primary goods.[83] Primary goods are those goods that a rational individual wants regardless of whatever else she wants.[84] The primary social goods are rights, liberties, opportunities, income, wealth, self-respect and confidence in one's worth. In comparing individual advantages or disadvantages in a society, possession of such primary goods by citizens should be compared 'without looking closely at what individuals, possessed of heterogeneous abilities and preferences, can do with them'.[85]

Insofar as the distribution of the subject matter is concerned, the first lexicographic[86] rule – distributive pattern – proposes that basic individual liberties should be equally distributed.[87] Thus, individual liberties have priority over the rule of resource distribution. The rule of distribution – the second rule – specifies that social and economic inequalities should work for the benefit of the least advantaged people and are attached to offices and positions to which everyone has access under conditions of fair equality of opportunity.[88] This rule, then, stipulates that an equal distribution of resources is to be preferred, unless by means of unequal distribution the position of the least advantaged is improved without, at the same time, lowering the position of others (that is, the difference principle).[89] These rules of social justice form the foundation of the 'basic structure of society and govern the assignment of rights and duties and regulate the distribution of social and economic advantages'.[90]

Rawls' second principle of distribution works under the assumption of a free market system, which means that just distributions of material resources take place *efficiently* when individuals, under conditions of equality of liberties and equal market opportunities (that is, 'positions'), strive to access material resources.[91] The free market, here, is the site of 'social cooperation' that leads to everyone's mutual advantage; it is the site of cooperative production of 'greater benefits' for the citizenry.[92] The free market, however, should function under institutional constraints that 'preserve the social conditions necessary for fair equality of opportunity' such as opportunities for education, skills, cultural knowledge and limits on accumulation of wealth.[93] Although freedom of contract (that is, market exchange) is central to the distribution of income and wealth, it is not a basic liberty, which means that such freedom could be limited if necessary for the purpose of just distribution of income and wealth.[94] The difference principle – the rule of distribution – also grounds the ideal of fraternity or social solidarity. Since, under the rule, unequal distribution is just only when it benefits the least advantaged without disadvantaging the more fortunate citizens, it could be interpreted as citizens (in the original decision-making stage at the Constituent Assembly) 'not wanting to have greater advantages unless this is to the benefit of others who are less well off'.[95]

While for Rawls, the basic structure – fundamental institutions of liberal constitutional democracies – is the primary subject of justice,[96] for capability theorists, expanding real freedom and choice for individuals so that they can achieve what they value in their lives are the aims of justice.[97] The capability approach to social justice (irrespective of internal variations among the different capability theorists) is, thus, interested in '[w]hat really happens to people'.[98] In contrast to the central characteristic of the Rawlsian theory, Sen notes that getting institutions right – once and for all – is not the same thing as accomplishing a just society. A theory of social justice cannot merely focus on institutions; it should also analyse actual behaviour of individuals in their interactions with those institutions to arrive at a judgement on justice. Actual 'realizations and accomplishments' are, then, the concerns of the capability-sensitive approaches to justice.[99] Institutions do matter, but institutions must be modified, abandoned and replaced, depending on whether they are really able to facilitate people's ability to live their lives. Ongoing critical examination of social institutions, in their ability to promote social justice, is also a prominent component of the capability approach to justice. This instrumental focus on institutions as a means of promoting an individual's 'functionings' – doing what she wants to do – needs an analysis of individual freedom – capability – in their heterogeneous circumstances.[100] While Rawls is concerned with an ideal society (with assumed individual and institutional behaviours) where institutions of justice will succeed, the capability approach to justice centralises (individual and communal) diversity in real societies as its analytical preoccupation.[101]

Like the Rawlsian theory, capability-sensitive social justice perspectives emphasise that the measuring standard for the evaluation of justice should be 'objective' (in contrast to the subjective criteria favoured by utilitarianism, such as happiness, desire satisfaction or preference).[102] However, the subject matter of social justice in the latter is 'capabilities' (individual freedoms to do the things that one values in their lives) in certain core areas of human lives, and the procedural rule of just distribution is 'sufficientarian' – that is, the distribution of core capabilities should be such that it secures individual citizens 'a certain *basic level* of capability'.[103] The procedural rule, in this narrative too attaches some prominence to individual liberties (as intrinsically important), particularly the political liberties.[104] Just as Rawls delineates a list of primary goods, Nussbaum offers a list of capabilities (or freedoms) for some central functionings (or actual achievements) as a moral basis of constitutional principles, the absence of which excludes individuals from the minimally acceptable threshold level of human worth.[105] Sen too agrees with the significance of some of these basic capabilities even when reluctant to offer a list of his own. He notes that fundamental political principles should aim to roughly equalise basic capabilities of individuals so that they can do certain basic things.[106] In Sen's work, basic capabilities appear as examples, not as a complete list.[107] He endorses basic education, health, clean environment and gender equality as some of the basic capabilities that everyone should possess.[108]

Capability theorists underline the need for continued reflection and public deliberation on the components of justice, both the central capabilities and the threshold rule of distribution of functionings.[109] While it is true that democratic participation and deliberation are important in both the Rawlsian and the capability perspectives, in the capability approach to justice citizens' deliberation features in a more pertinent manner. Public deliberation is a permanent and continuous characteristic in the capability approach, one that permeates the subject matter of justice (capabilities) and the rule of distribution (for example, sufficientarian). Since, in this view, the quest for justice is an ongoing and inconclusive process (always moving from less-just to more-just situations), mere theoretical formulation does not settle questions about social justice.[110] A vibrant civil society is essential in operationalising and scrutinising social justice in actual societies. It is by means of deliberations in the civil society that important values (basic capabilities), institutions, behaviours and relationships between citizens and institutions must be examined and (provisionally) settled in the context of specific communities and societies.

The civil society – the space for democratic deliberations – is not only the legitimate space for prioritising the capabilities to basic functionings, it is also the space to decide *how* to advance such capabilities. In fact, the market and the state are two of the prominent spaces through which the subject matter of justice is distributed under both the aforementioned conceptualisations of social justice. The complementary role of the market and the state in distribution is a point of agreement between the Rawlsian and the capability perspectives. Rawls observes that the (competitive) market is naturally advantageous for distributive concerns because it is consistent with – and gives scope for the expressions and practices of – equal liberties and fair equality of opportunity.[111] The market is where the instrumental force of individual liberties receives its productive expression in the free choice of occupations and profitable exchanges. For Sen, the market characterises an even deeper site for individual freedom. It is the site of freedom of exchange and interaction, such as the 'interchange of *words, goods and gifts*'.[112] Secondarily, the market is also the producer of wealth. In view of the broader role of the market, Sen notes that any concept of social justice should have some scope for the market space.[113]

While the market may occupy a prominent position in liberal theories of justice, both Rawls and Sen are, however, against market fundamentalism. Rawls notes:[114]

> There is a divergence between private and social accounting that the market fails to register. One essential task of law and government is to institute the necessary corrections.

Thus, free markets may be efficient in the distribution of consumption goods on the basis of demand and supply, but 'the market fails altogether in the case of public goods'.[115] Social provisioning of public goods, through the institutions of the state, must supplement the market-based distribution of material resources.[116] Although the state is considerably responsible for the redistribution of material resources, it should not be seen as a generous public good provider.[117] Just as the civil society must question the scope of the market, it should also scrutinise the role of state institutions in promoting social justice.[118] 'To ask how things are going and whether they can be improved is a constant and inescapable part of the pursuit of justice'.[119]

From the previous discussion, it is clear that the idea of civil society is not confined to the formal procedures of the electoral representative system. The civil society, in this perspective, is the site of the practice of deliberative democracy.[120] This practice signifies the discursive content of democracy – that is, the actual engagement of citizens in publicly deliberating values, policies and choices.[121] This substantive notion of democracy prioritises freedom of speech, access to information and freedom of dissent, rather than the mere opportunity to elect a representative.[122] This perspective on democracy, then, is a dynamic idea of civil society that needs extensive participation and collective decision-making by the citizenry. This imagination of the civil society is not only important in conceiving the social justice framework generally; from a capability perspective, it also has an ongoing and permanent function. To be sure, the idea of civil society, particularly in the Indian context, should not be understood only in terms of traditionally recognised institutions of dialogue, such as the media, political parties, trade unions and non-governmental organisations (NGOs). Formal and informal associations, groups and interest representations – whatever form they take and even if they remain amorphous – should also be understood as part of a broader and complex idea of civil society.[123]

As noted, there are differences between the Rawlsian perspective and the capability-sensitive social justice formulations. In spite of the differences, the comparability of the two is also acknowledged by the theorists. Sen concedes that Rawls' ideal (transcendental) theory may be able to address comparative concerns of justice, which is the focus of his approach to justice.[124] He also notes that distributional equity with reference to individual capabilities is compatible with a conceptual framework prioritising individual liberties.[125] Rawls, on the other hand, notes that the capability approach helps in showing the 'propriety of the use of primary goods'.[126] He reasons that by specifying primary goods and applying the just rules of distribution, 'we may come as close as we can *in practice* to a just distribution of [... capabilities]'.[127] Although Rawls acknowledges the importance of focusing on individual capabilities, he characterises the capability approach as an unworkable idea because of the difficulty in computing comprehensive information (on various political, social, economic, environmental, cultural, physiological, psychological and other factors) necessary for the promotion of capabilities to specific functionings.[128]

While there is some truth to this difficulty of open observability, especially when analysing the constitutional specification of rights and entitlements, the capability approach can still guide an observable (even if not comprehensive) entitlement framework in plural societies by focusing on ends rather than means.[129] Capabilities offer a more direct way to acknowledge how resources work under specific circumstances. Of course, focusing on some basic capabilities would suggest some overlap between primary goods and factors necessary for the expansion of such capabilities. The capability approach is context-sensitive by allowing the civil society and the democratic process a larger role in realising social justice. This context sensitivity is helpful in offering a social justice evaluation in deeply diverse societies. Bearing in mind the broad similarities between the two approaches and the constraint of accounting only for the 'observable' factors, I aim to draw a schematic framework of social justice within liberal societies in general and observable in the Indian constitutional structure in particular. In turn, my schematic framework of social justice will eventually guide the evaluation of the recent changes in labour law in India.

Even when individual capabilities offer a more direct way of comparing just and unjust, or less-just and more-just, for the purpose of identifying a constitutional concept of social justice, the focus is necessarily on rights and entitlements specified under the Constitution. Thus, the major components of a liberal constitutional social justice framework are (*a*) individual liberties, which are compatible with and find expression in the distributive conditions of the market space; (*b*) social solidarity, promoting equitable material (that is, public goods) (re)distribution, through the state; and (*c*) effective ongoing participation of the civil society,[130] actively deliberating and modelling the nature of the two aforementioned distributive perspectives in specific social contexts.[131] In the following section, I argue that the social justice agenda of the Indian Constitution roughly fits the aforementioned structure with a strong emphasis on state-based redistributive guarantees and ongoing participatory input from the civil society while also maintaining the role of the market as the site of individual exchanges. It is this structure, I argue, that should guide the evaluation of legislative programmes, including the amended labour law in India.

Admittedly, this conceptual survey of the components of a social justice framework is inadequate. It is also slightly adjusted to capture the social justice framework of the Indian Constitution as an evaluative benchmark. The conceptual accounts of social justice discussed here (and those not discussed) are significantly more nuanced and detailed than their portrayal in the preceding discussion. Moreover, there are differences between the aforementioned approaches to justice and the other theories of justice not discussed. However, the purpose of this section is not to detail comprehensive accounts of prominent ideas of justice. Instead, the primary objective has been to identify the principal characteristics of these two broad conceptual accounts of justice. In other words, we have worked to capture the broad agreements and complementarities of the two prominent theoretical accounts. This discussion of the conceptual accounts of justice will not be pursued any further than what has been done in this section. The discussion in this section has a limited overarching aim: to serve as a prelude to the following section, where the components of the constitutional social justice agenda are identified as a basis of legislative evaluation. Thus, this section is an attempt to fit the constitutional narrative into a conceptual framework that can serve as an evaluative standard for recent changes in labour law.

## The Architecture of Accountability for Legislative Standards

As noted earlier, the Indian Constitution is structured around the ideal of social justice. The principle of fairness (as the essence of justice), then, sets the parameters of legislative entitlements and executive actions. Accordingly, when we engage in an evaluation of a legislative agenda governing socio-economic interactions involving a fundamental aspect of human life (that is, labour),[132] the standard of such evaluation needs to conform to the principle of fairness. However, since the principle of fairness is highly abstract, the evaluative standard must be specified in terms of observable components flowing from the abstract idea of fairness. Drawing on the discussion in the previous section, it is suggested here that when we evaluate – even if roughly – the post-reform labour law, the components of the evaluative standard should be the following: (*a*) the scope and protection of market-based distribution, respecting basic individual liberties; (*b*) the complementary redistribution of public goods through state action, upholding the principle of solidarity; and (*c*) the institutionalisation and promotion of public participation in decisions about the operation of the market and the state in advancing social justice. It is argued that all three of these components flow from the Constitution.

As we have seen, the social justice narrative and practice under the Indian Constitution primarily unfolds through relationships involving the labour process – the exchange and contribution of labour. The market occupies a central position for such exchanges and contributions. Although both the exchange and the contribution of labour are not limited solely to the market (for example, care work, socio-ecological work, unpaid work, charitable and voluntary work), a fact acknowledged in the constitutional duties, the market surely is an important site for the exchange of labour. The market is the primary site for the distribution of material goods, and market exchanges – contracts – are the basis of such distribution. Market exchanges of labour for income and other consumer exchanges that have the labour exchange as their basis (that is, income from labour exchange goes towards further exchange of commodities) form the core of the market. Market-based private contracts are, therefore, the foundational basis of distribution that is compatible with citizens' freedom of choice and agency-driven accomplishment. Labour markets are, then, (ideally) the sites of 'social cooperation' under conditions of individual freedom.

The underpinnings of private contractual exchange, individual liberty, substantive equality and freedom of trade[133] are protected under the

Constitution. As Justices K. S. Hegde and A. K. Mukherjea concluded in *Kesavananda Bharati*, the '[c]onstitutional plan is to eradicate poverty without destruction of individual freedoms'.[134] While individual liberty is intrinsically important, it is also instrumentally a prerequisite to eradicating poverty through market participation. Individual liberty has the broadest possible scope under the Constitution, seen in light of the range of functionings that individual liberties facilitate.[135] Individual liberties, however, have to meet the equality standard of the Constitution – that is, they should be compatible with the liberties of all other citizens. Prominently, the freedom of contract (exchange and contribution) in occupations, businesses, trades and vocations – as a pilot, an exporter, an evangelist, a musician, a dancer, a professor, a lawyer, a doctor or a journalist, for example – is a core instance of individual liberty, even when it is not explicitly enumerated as a justiciable right under the Constitution.[136] It is by means of freedom of contract – freedom of market exchange – that equally free individuals get to further their life's plan on the strength of their agency.

Even when the constitutional narrative reserves an important place for market-based (income and wealth) distribution, the market is not an unrestricted domain. By limiting contractual freedom through reasonable restrictions on the grounds of public interest, the Constitution imposes indirect public policy limits on the freedom of market exchanges.[137] Contractual exchanges are also restricted more directly if they violate the fundamental rights (basic freedoms) of individual citizens. For example, the judiciary has repeatedly nullified contracts (with the government) when such contractual relationships failed to treat individual citizens equitably.[138] Thus, as important as market-based distributions may be, the freedom of the market may be restricted when it undermines the fundamental rights of citizens and injures public interest. In any case, in the constitutional scheme, the market and individual liberties underlying market exchanges constitute only one of the two distributive trajectories of the practice of social justice. State action in the redistribution of material resources for the promotion of overall public goods complements market-based distribution.[139]

In *Kesavananda Bharati*, several judicial opinions converge on the point that no understanding of dignity could be sustained if socio-economic rights were not a constitutive part of that formulation alongside the civil-political rights.[140] What is required for the promotion of human dignity is a proper balance between individual rights and social needs.[141] The mandate of social needs is met not only through the imposition of reasonable limits on the market but also through the redistribution of material resources through the institutions of the state. The directive principles of the Constitution guarantee material redistribution to the citizenry.[142] However, the directive principles, offering the foundational principles of governance by the state, do not have the same priority as individual liberties insofar as they are not justiciable. Thus, constitutional entitlements based on the solidarity principle, such as the general social welfare, distribution of material resources, minimising inequalities of income and status and promoting equal opportunities, or, more specifically, securing diverse means of work (livelihoods), equal pay for equal work, protection of health and strength of workers, opportunities for children, access to justice, decentralised self-government, social protection against unemployment, and so on,[143] even if they are fundamental in the governance of the country, cannot per se be the grounds of judicial claims against the state. Although these directives, and several others mentioned in Part IV of the Constitution, are the foundations of the state-led redistributive programme, they are the demands of democratic politics rather than purely juridical claims.

However, in keeping with its view that dignity needs both the promotion of individual freedoms and state action, the judiciary has extensively read the constitutional directives as constituent parts of the justiciable fundamental rights. As is extensively noted, this strategy of expanding the content of the idea of dignified life as including resource redistribution has, to a large extent, attenuated the distinction between justiciable and non-justiciable rights.[144] Politically, too, the Indian state has assertively embraced its role as the welfare state responsible for the redistribution of public goods. In fact, the constitutional balance between the market-promoting individual liberties[145] and state-based social rights is struck in favour of a larger role for state-based redistributions. The removal of the right 'to acquire, hold and dispose of property'[146] could be seen as a *constitutional moment* consolidating the prominence of state-based redistributions at the expense of market-centred distributions. Although the removal of the fundamental right to property was not an instantaneous moment, instead evolving through a lengthy politico-juridical process, it does signify a break from the past and a deep constitutional commitment towards state-led redistribution, particularly the redistribution of land resources.[147] In independent India, the right to property moved from being a justiciable fundamental right to a constitutional right for the purpose of promoting public welfare.[148] In fact, the recent advocacy around reinstituting the right to property as a fundamental right is also based on the concern for securing the gains of public welfare that have been achieved on the basis of land reforms and redistribution and to prevent the state's acquisition of property for private parties (that is, private businesses).

In any case, what follows from this discussion is this: the balance between the role of the market and the state in the constitutional social justice architecture is tilted in favour of state-based redistribution while leaving substantial scope for the operation of the market. The constitutional social justice 'benchmark', then, should be premised on this understanding of the balance between the market and the state. However, as scholars of comparative constitutional law indicate, 'the constitutional system ... of India ... grapple[s] with the right balance between state and market, public intervention and private freedom – and this balance is shifting over time'.[149] More recently, they note, there is a general executive (that is, governmental) recalibration of this balance, favouring liberalisation of the economy and market-based development, sacrificing the state-based welfare entitlements of the citizenry.[150] It is argued that such a reorientation shifts the balance of the Constitution in a way not permitted by the basic structure of the Constitution.[151] It is true, as argued earlier, that in the constitutional scheme, a state-based redistributive agenda is preferred over the market-based distribution. However, a reorientation of the institutions of social justice, even if controversial, is not unimaginable if such reorientation remains within the permissible range of the Constitution.[152]

No analysis of such a *permissible range* could be undertaken merely by looking at the aforementioned balance, without simultaneously taking into account the third component of the constitutional social justice narrative, which is the ongoing participation of the civil society. It is, in fact, a testimony to the significance of civil society participation that the balance between the state and the market has shifted over time. The role of the civil society, understood here broadly as the political discursive space not identical with the market or the state, is not limited only to the original installation of the institutions of social justice. Its constitutional role is that of an ongoing evaluator and adjuster, evaluating the continued appropriateness of the institutions of social justice in view of social evolution and making necessary changes to such institutions in view of actual social needs and sensibilities. What the civil society cannot do (that is, limits to civil society action), however, is invalidate the social justice orientation of the Constitution, potentially leading to a different constitutional arrangement. Thus, merely because the market-state balance has shifted cannot per se be a ground to adjudicate such shift as illegitimate unless such shift is greater than the permissible range under the Constitution and brought about without active participation from the civil society.

Active and ongoing participation of the civil society in the social justice narrative is constitutionally safeguarded. Considering the relative ease with which amendments to the Constitution could be made,[153] it would appear that the Constitution furthers a continuous pursuit of social justice through the engagement of the civil society rather than adhering to a rigid idea of institutions and procedures of justice. The Constitution permits an expansive role for the political process by making it easy to amend the Constitution, underscored by the more-than-hundred amendments to the document. Although the scope of the amending power has been narrowed – and the main tenets of social justice settled – by the judiciary over the years, the political process is still possessed of significant power to change the Constitution.[154] Depending on the significance of the constitutional provision, the Constitution could be amended through three formal manners.[155] While less significant provisions could be amended only through a simple majority in Parliament, more significant provisions require a supermajority (two-thirds of members present and voting in both houses of Parliament).[156] In addition to these two, subject matters of special importance to the constitutional framework require the supermajority of Parliament and ratification by at least half of the states for their amendment.[157] The formal ease to constitutional amendments means that changes enjoying 'political support' are likely to be introduced to the constitutional structure.[158]

The Indian Constitution simultaneously characterises stability and change.[159] While the *stability* pertains to the foundational spaces of justice – the market and the state – the *change* relates to the balance between the two. Within the limits of the constitutionally settled prominence of the social justice ideal, between the two interpretations in which one would lead to an understanding of the institutions of the polity as largely fixed and the other where such institutions are understood always to be in transition and open to democratic evaluation, the latter interpretation should be preferable in view of the constitutional deference to the political process through amendments. This interpretation should be preferred irrespective of the basic structure doctrine developed by the judiciary because although the judiciary made certain constitutional features unamendable, it has not altered the rationale of amendments, which is the adaptability of the Constitution to emerging social needs. In this interpretation, then, an active civil society becomes the third component of the constitutional social justice framework.

We must be careful, however, not to imagine any specific ideal of civil society in the aforementioned characterisation. As Partha Chatterjee cautions, the characteristics of the deliberative public space in India may not always coalesce around the familiar narrative of state–civil society relationships.[160] In addition to the formal state–citizen (that is, state–civil society) relationship, populations interact with the institutions of the state – primarily the government – as welfare recipients (in contrast to equal rights-bearing citizens).[161] In the latter situation, the civil society (Chatterjee calls this space 'political society') may often be amorphous, and the currency of its interaction with the state is welfare entitlements rather than civil-political rights.[162] Accordingly, in imagining the third component of the social justice framework, the civil society should be imagined broadly as the participatory deliberative space irrespective of the institutional forms (for example, trade unions, lobbying groups or NGOs) that such space ends up accommodating.

In any case, the observable components of the constitutional social justice narrative are market-based distribution, state-led redistribution and civil society participation. Constitutional scholars have lately warned us of the crisis of constitutionalism in India, including along the lines of these three components of the social justice framework.[163] Scholars are particularly concerned about recent governmental policies – from the amendment of the citizenship law to the reforms of labour law – which, they argue, challenge the fundamental constitutional values.[164] In the next three chapters, we will evaluate whether this alarm is justified, particularly with reference to the changes introduced in labour law. It will be argued that while there exist sufficient reasons to be concerned about the labour law reforms, in their entirety they largely 'lie within the allowed range'[165] of the constitutional social justice agenda. However, the labour law reforms fall short of the social justice benchmark due to their democratic deficit, in terms of insufficient civil society participation. Tarunabh Khaitan has already noted this deficit in the current model (at the time of writing) of the Bharatiya Janata Party (BJP)-led government of India, the one that accomplished the labour law reforms.[166] Alongside undermining a range of democratic accountability mechanisms, the current government of India has significantly undermined the civil society, including trade unions, by sidelining the discursive component of the social justice mandate of the Constitution.[167] In the backdrop of such sidelining, I assess the potential of collective action under the current labour law in Chapter 4.

As Jeremy Waldron observes, law executes the idea of social justice in actual contexts by focusing on specific tasks.[168] Moving forward, we will examine whether the specific tasks executed through the labour law reforms meet the three tenets of social justice outlined earlier. In Chapter 2, we will analyse the labour law reforms on the basis of their capacity to fairly promote market distribution. In Chapter 3, we will consider how well the labour law reforms complement market distribution with state-led redistribution. In Chapter 4, we will discuss the degree to which the labour law reforms facilitate continued civil society participation in decision-making processes affecting the other components of the social justice mission, specifically through the participation of workers' organisations.

As Rawls notes, the justice of legislation or social policies has two parts: a just procedure leading to a just outcome.[169] While the formal procedure of statutory enactment is constitutionally articulated (for example, simple majority in Parliament), an outcome is just when it meets the demands of social justice, including people's continued participation in decision-making processes. The latter tenet is not adequately captured by the (mere) procedural formalities of statutory enactment.[170] Although in evaluating the labour law reforms my primary focus is on the unjust outcome, a democratic deficit also taints the procedure and undermines its legitimacy. Of course, analysing the reforms on the basis of the three constitutional social justice parameters is not a mathematical validation process. The idea is to ascertain, even if roughly, whether the legislative scheme meets the overarching constitutional promise of fairness.

## Conclusion

This chapter discussed the conceptual and practical components of the social justice architecture of the Constitution. The purpose of this discussion is to designate an evaluative criterion for the analysis of India's labour law after the 2020 reforms. This evaluative criterion is particularly suitable for the examination of labour law at two levels: conceptual and political (or practical). Conceptually, it is through the legislative enterprise that the ideal of social justice finds concrete, workable directions in specific contexts. Politically, the constitutional ideal of social justice is articulated mainly in its significance to labour relations. Therefore, in addition to its general fit with the imagination of social justice, it is a specific responsibility of labour law to discharge its constitutional burden in the contextual circumstances of work-based relationships. Indian citizens are conceived as contributing worker-citizens, who not only value work for its inherent significance and material importance, but also contribute to social development through their work. This social relational foundation of work lies at the core of the ideal of justice as fairness.

Of course, this understanding of citizenship and the corresponding analysis of social justice at work is not a truism about the Indian Constitution. It is an interpretation of Indian citizenship and the constitutional idea of social justice. Although this interpretation does not make an assumption that the constitutional vision is clear and unproblematic, the idea of worker-focused social justice agenda and the institutions through which such an idea transpires is a reasonably plausible interpretation of the Constitution. Social justice is a foundational idea of the Constitution. And if one assesses the specified principles of social justice in the different articles of the Constitution, it is also not difficult to see the significant emphasis placed on fairness in labour relations – broadly conceived as relationships at work (without limiting it to merely industrial market-based exchanges) – in constitutional articulation of rights to resources and opportunities. To be sure, while the constitutional development of the idea of social justice with reference to the worker-citizen is a plausible reading of the Constitution, it is not immune to criticism. And such criticism should be appreciated for its contribution to the debate on labour justice. In any case, irrespective of the issue of whether the Indian Constitution unfolds around the idea of worker-citizens, the three components of the constitutional social justice framework rest on a firmer ground, through judicial pronouncements and institutional consolidation.

That workers should be treated fairly, thus, is a concern that should permeate market-based relationships, state-led assistance and the scope of worker participation. Along the way, we will examine the reforms in terms of their ability to meet these constitutional mandates. It will be argued that, seen in isolation, the reforms may appear to remain within the permissible range prescribed by the Constitution with respect to each of the aforementioned trajectories. However, if we adopt a broader lens, the combined effect of the reforms on labour law is unsatisfactory. The latest reforms upset the current balance between the market space and the state-led space by allowing a greater scope for market-based distribution without simultaneously creating a complementary state-based redistributive framework. However, where the reforms mostly fail is in their incapacity to meet the participatory benchmark of the social justice agenda. This participatory or discursive deficit occurs not only at the consultation stage leading to the enactment but also in the legislative standards relating to workers' collective action. The deficit in permitting effective participation of the civil society in modelling the other components of social justice differs from the formal institutional legitimacy – the procedural requirements associated with enacting a valid piece of legislation – mandated by the Constitution. Quite apart from representative (electoral) legislative processes, the participatory deficit presents a disturbing deficiency in discussion-oriented policymaking. The next chapter will evaluate the labour law reforms in their capacity to promote market freedom of workers.

## Notes

1. Constitution of India, 1950, Article 51A (hereinafter, 'Constitution').
2. Jawaharlal Nehru, 'The Psychology of Indian Nationalism', in *Selected Works of Jawaharlal Nehru*, vol. 2, ed. Sarvepalli Gopal, 259–270 (New Delhi: Orient Longman, 1972–1982), 266.
3. Madhav Khosla, *India's Founding Moment: The Constitution of a Most Surprising Democracy* (Cambridge [MA] and London: Harvard University Press, 2020), 3–4, 22; Niraja Gopal Jayal, *Citizenship and Its Discontents: An Indian History* (Cambridge [MA] and London: Harvard University Press, 2013), 12.
4. Arun Thiruvengadam, *The Constitution of India: A Contextual Analysis* (Oxford and Portland [OR]: Hart Publishing, 2017), 1–2.
5. Jayal, *Citizenship and Its Discontents*, 2.
6. Sujit Choudhry, Madhav Khosla and Pratap Bhanu Mehta, 'Locating Indian Constitutionalism', in *The Oxford Handbook of the Indian Constitution*, ed. Sujit Choudhry, Madhav Khosla and Pratap Bhanu Mehta, 1–14 (Oxford: Oxford University Press, 2016).
7. Khosla, *India's Founding Moment*, 4–5, 16; Thiruvengadam, *The Constitution of India*, 3. Historian Granville Austin denotes this break as 'social revolution'. See Granville Austin, *The Indian Constitution: Cornerstone of a Nation* (Bombay: Oxford University Press, 1966), xiii, 26–27, 308–309.

8. Work is important for workers as a *means* to their livelihood and for the state as a *contribution* to the national development. See Constitution, Articles 39(a), 51A(j).
9. Because of its inherent personal (as distinguished from public) importance, citizens have a justiciable fundamental right to practise a profession, occupation, trade or business. See Constitution, Article 19(1)(g).
10. Upendra Baxi, 'The Place of Dignity in the Indian Constitution', in *The Cambridge Handbook of Human Dignity: Interdisciplinary Perspectives*, ed. Marcus Düwell, Jens Braarvig, Roger Brownsword and Dietmar Mieth, 429–436 (Cambridge, UK: Cambridge University Press, 2014). In a departure from this traditional understanding of dignity as empowerment, the Supreme Court has recently employed the idea of dignity as a constraint on autonomous action by conceptualising human dignity as a community value which could not be infringed through an individual's autonomous action. See *Justice K. S. Puttaswami (Retd.) v. Union of India*, Writ Petition (Civil) No. 494 of 2012 (SCC, 2018), paras. 113–116. Also see Deryck Beyleveld and Roger Brownsword, *Human Dignity in Bioethics and Biolaw* (Oxford: Oxford University Press, 2001), 11, 33–38, for a discussion of dignity as a constraint on autonomous action.
11. Baxi, 'The Place of Dignity in the Indian Constitution', 430–431.
12. *Bandhua Mukti Morcha v. Union of India*, (1984) 2 SCR 67.
13. *Bandhua Mukti Morcha v. Union of India*, (1984) 2 SCR 67, 96–98.
14. *Bandhua Mukti Morcha v. Union of India*, (1984) 2 SCR 67, 103.
15. *Bandhua Mukti Morcha v. Union of India*, (1984) 2 SCR 67, 103.
16. *Bandhua Mukti Morcha v. Union of India*, (1984) 2 SCR 67, 103.
17. *Francis Coralie v. Union Territory of Delhi*, (1981) 2 SCR 516.
18. *Francis Coralie v. Union Territory of Delhi*, (1981) 2 SCR 516, 528–529.
19. *Francis Coralie v. Union Territory of Delhi*, (1981) 2 SCR 516, 529.
20. *Francis Coralie v. Union Territory of Delhi*, (1981) 2 SCR 516.
21. See *Consumer Education and Research Centre v. Union of India*, (1995) 3 SCC 42; *Kirloskar Brothers Limited v. Employees' State Insurance Corporation*, (1996) 2 SCALE 1.
22. *Consumer Education and Research Centre v. Union of India*, (1995) 3 SCC 42; *Kirloskar Brothers Limited v. Employees' State Insurance Corporation*, (1996) 2 SCALE 1.
23. *Consumer Education and Research Centre v. Union of India*, (1995) 3 SCC 42; *Kirloskar Brothers Limited v. Employees' State Insurance Corporation*, (1996) 2 SCALE 1.

24. India is not the only jurisdiction to attribute such a meaning to human dignity. Other jurisdictions such as Hungary and South Africa also adopt such an interpretation of dignity. Such an orientation also increasingly permeates specific human right provisions. See Christopher McCrudden, 'Human Dignity and Judicial Interpretation of Human Rights', *European Journal of International Law* 19, no. 4 (2008): 655–724, 670–672, 674–675, 693–694.
25. Joseph Raz, *The Authority of Law: Essays on Law and Morality* (New York: Oxford University Press, 1979), 221.
26. Raz, *The Authority of Law*, 221–222.
27. Ronald Dworkin, *Justice for Hedgehogs* (Cambridge [MA] and London: Belknap Press of Harvard University Press, 2011), 203–204.
28. Dworkin, *Justice for Hedgehogs*, 204.
29. Dworkin, *Justice for Hedgehogs*, 209–212.
30. Thiruvengadam, *The Constitution of India*, 223; Tarunabh Khaitan, 'Directive Principles and the Expressive Accommodation of Ideological Dissenters', *International Journal of Constitutional Law* 16, no. 2 (2018): 389–420, 406–407.
31. See 'Constituent Assembly of India Debates (Proceedings)' vol. 1, Friday, 13 December 1946, https://eparlib.nic.in/bitstream/123456789/760449/3/CA_Debate_Eng_Vol_01_edited_page_217-218.pdf (accessed on 14 December 2023).
32. Thiruvengadam, *The Constitution of India*.
33. See *His Holiness Kesavananda Bharati Sripadagalvaru v. State of Kerala*, (1973) MANU 0445 (SC).
34. See Thiruvengadam, *The Constitution of India*, 222–229, for a succinct discussion of the conflict between the judiciary and the executive in the evolution of the basic structure doctrine.
35. Sudhir Krishnaswamy, *Democracy and Constitutionalism in India: A Study of the Basic Structure Doctrine* (New Delhi: Oxford University Press, 2009), 137, 145.
36. Krishnaswamy, *Democracy and Constitutionalism in India*, xviii–xix, 11–15.
37. Krishnaswamy, *Democracy and Constitutionalism in India*, 3.
38. Krishnaswamy, *Democracy and Constitutionalism in India*, 132–133, 139, 142.
39. Krishnaswamy, *Democracy and Constitutionalism in India*, 135–136, 148, 159. Some judges also hold socialism and equality to be basic features of the Constitution of India. See Krishnaswamy, *Democracy and Constitutionalism in India*, 161.

40. *His Holiness Kesavananda Bharati Sripadagalvaru v. State of Kerala*, paras. 15, 305–306, 310–311, 421, 424 (judgment by S. M. Sikri).
41. *His Holiness Kesavananda Bharati Sripadagalvaru v. State of Kerala*, para. 547 (judgment by J. M. Shelat and A. N. Grover) (emphasis mine).
42. *His Holiness Kesavananda Bharati Sripadagalvaru v. State of Kerala*, paras. 564, 619–620, 633–634 (judgment by J. M. Shelat and A. N. Grover), paras. 685, 705, 755 (judgment by K. S. Hegde and A. K. Mukherjea).
43. *His Holiness Kesavananda Bharati Sripadagalvaru v. State of Kerala*, paras. 705, 758 (judgment by K. S. Hegde and A. K. Mukherjea), para. 1531 (judgment by H. R. Khanna).
44. Chakravarthi Ram-Prasad, 'Pluralism and Liberalism: Reading the Indian Constitution as a Philosophical Document for Constitutional Patriotism', *Critical Review of International Social and Political Philosophy* 16, no. 5 (2013): 676–697, 682–690; Jürgen Bast and Arun K. Thiruvengadam, 'Origins and Pathways of Constitutionalism', in *Democratic Constitutionalism in India and the European Union: Comparing the Law of Democracy in Continental Polities*, ed. Philipp Dann and Arun K Thiruvengadam, 75–103 (Cheltenham, UK: Edward Elgar, 2021), 84–88 ; Mathew John, 'Social Institutions in the Shadow of Liberal Constitutionalism: An Indian Perspective', in *Constitutionalism beyond Liberalism*, ed. Michael W. Dowdle and Michael A. Wilkinson, 129–148 (Cambridge, UK: Cambridge University Press, 2017), 130.
45. C. A. Bayly, *Recovering Liberties: Indian Thought in the Age of Liberalism and Empire* (New York: Cambridge University Press, 2012), 343–357; Rajeev Bhargava, 'Liberal, Secular Democracy and Explanations of Hindu Nationalism', *Commonwealth and Comparative Politics* 40, no. 3 (2002): 72–96, 76–82.
46. John, 'Social Institutions in the Shadow of Liberal Constitutionalism', 147; Bast and Thiruvengadam, 'Origins and Pathways of Constitutionalism', 84–85; Bhargava, 'Liberal, Secular Democracy and Explanations of Hindu Nationalism', 82–84; Khaitan, 'Directive Principles and the Expressive Accommodation of Ideological Dissenters', 400.
47. See, generally, Ram-Prasad, 'Pluralism and Liberalism'.
48. *People's Union for Democratic Rights v. Union of India*, (1982) 3 SCC 235.
49. *People's Union for Democratic Rights v. Union of India*, (1982) 3 SCC 235 (opinion of P. N. Bhagwati, delivering the judgment).
50. *People's Union for Democratic Rights v. Union of India*, (1982) 3 SCC 235 (opinion of P. N. Bhagwati, delivering the judgment).

51. *People's Union for Democratic Rights v. Union of India*, (1982) 3 SCC 235 (opinion of P. N. Bhagwati, delivering the judgment).
52. *People's Union for Democratic Rights v. Union of India*, (1982) 3 SCC 235 (opinion of P. N. Bhagwati, delivering the judgment).
53. *People's Union for Democratic Rights v. Union of India*, (1982) 3 SCC 235 (opinion of P. N. Bhagwati, delivering the judgment).
54. *M. C. Mehta v. State of Tamil Nadu*, AIR 1997 SC 699.
55. *M. C. Mehta v. State of Tamil Nadu*, AIR 1997 SC 699 (judgment delivered by B. L. Hansaria).
56. *M. C. Mehta v. State of Tamil Nadu*, AIR 1997 SC 699 (judgment delivered by B. L. Hansaria).
57. *M. C. Mehta v. State of Tamil Nadu*, AIR 1997 SC 699 (judgment delivered by B. L. Hansaria).
58. *M. C. Mehta v. State of Tamil Nadu*, AIR 1997 SC 699 (judgment delivered by B. L. Hansaria).
59. *M. C. Mehta v. State of Tamil Nadu*, AIR 1997 SC 699 (judgment delivered by B. L. Hansaria).
60. *Consumer Education and Research v. Union of India*, (1995) 3 SCC 42.
61. *Consumer Education and Research v. Union of India*, (1995) 3 SCC 42.
62. *Consumer Education and Research v. Union of India*, (1995) 3 SCC 42.
63. *Consumer Education and Research v. Union of India*, (1995) 3 SCC 42.
64. *Consumer Education and Research v. Union of India*, (1995) 3 SCC 42.
65. *Bandhua Mukti Morcha v. Union of India*, AIR 1984 SC 802.
66. *Bandhua Mukti Morcha v. Union of India*, AIR 1984 SC 802. These workers were illegally employed because the bonded labour system stands abolished through the Bonded Labour System (Abolition) Act, 1976 (Act no. 19 of 1976) in accordance with Article 23 of the Constitution prohibiting forced labour.
67. *Bandhua Mukti Morcha v. Union of India*, AIR 1984 SC 802. See judgment delivered by P. N. Bhagwati.
68. *Bandhua Mukti Morcha v. Union of India*, AIR 1984 SC 802.
69. *Bandhua Mukti Morcha v. Union of India*, AIR 1984 SC 802. Also see Constitution, Article 21.
70. *Bandhua Mukti Morcha v. Union of India*, AIR 1984 SC 802. See judgment delivered by P. N. Bhagwati.
71. *Bandhua Mukti Morcha v. Union of India*, AIR 1984 SC 802.
72. *Bandhua Mukti Morcha v. Union of India*, AIR 1984 SC 802. See judgment delivered by P. N. Bhagwati.

73. Amartya Sen, 'The Place of Capability in a Theory of Justice', in *Measuring Justice: Primary Goods and Capabilities*, ed. Harry Brighouse and Ingrid Robeyns, 239–253 (New York: Cambridge University Press, 2010), 241.
74. Sen, 'The Place of Capability in a Theory of Justice', 248.
75. Sen, 'The Place of Capability in a Theory of Justice', 242.
76. Elizabeth Anderson, 'Justifying the Capabilities Approach to Justice', in *Measuring Justice: Primary Goods and Capabilities*, ed. Harry Brighouse and Ingrid Robeyns, 81–100 (New York: Cambridge University Press, 2010), 81–82.
77. Anderson, 'Justifying the Capabilities Approach to Justice'.
78. Ingrid Robeyns and Harry Brighouse, 'Introduction: Social Primary Goods and Capabilities as Metrics of Justice', in *Measuring Justice: Primary Goods and Capabilities*, ed. Harry Brighouse and Ingrid Robeyns, 1–14 (New York: Cambridge University Press, 2010), 6.
79. John Rawls, *A Theory of Justice* (Cambridge, MA: Belknap Press of Harvard University Press, 1999 [1971]), 8; Amartya Sen, *The Idea of Justice* (Cambridge, MA: Harvard University Press, 2009), xi, 5–8, 400–401.
80. Rawls, *A Theory of Justice*, 6.
81. Rawls, *A Theory of Justice*, 6–7.
82. Rawls, *A Theory of Justice*, 54.
83. Rawls, *A Theory of Justice*. The other kind of primary goods are the natural goods, such as health, vigour, intelligence, imagination, and so on, which are influenced by the social primary goods and their distribution but are not directly regulated by the rules of distribution.
84. Rawls, *A Theory of Justice*, 79, 348.
85. Robeyns and Brighouse, 'Introduction', 1.
86. 'Lexicographic' means that subsequent conditions could only be met after the previous ones have been met.
87. Rawls, *A Theory of Justice*, 53, 220, 266–267.
88. Rawls, *A Theory of Justice*, 53, 72. Rawls elaborates:

> The second principle applies ... to the distribution of income and wealth and to the design of organizations that make use of differences in authority and responsibility. While the distribution of wealth and income need not be equal, it must be to everyone's advantage, and at the same time, positions of authority and responsibility must be accessible to all. One applies the second principle by holding positions open, and then, subject to this constraint, arranges social and economic inequalities so that everyone benefits. (Rawls, *A Theory of Justice*, 53)

89. Rawls, *A Theory of Justice*, 65–66, 107.
90. Rawls, *A Theory of Justice*, 53.
91. Rawls, *A Theory of Justice*, 57, 62.
92. Rawls, *A Theory of Justice*, 109.
93. Rawls, *A Theory of Justice*, 63.
94. Rawls, *A Theory of Justice*, 54.
95. Rawls, *A Theory of Justice*, 90–91.
96. Rawls, *A Theory of Justice*, 73–74, 76.
97. Amartya Sen, *Development as Freedom* (New York: Alfred A. Knoph, 1999); Martha C. Nussbaum, *Creating Capabilities: The Human Development Approach* (Cambridge [MA] and London: Belknap Press of Harvard University Press, 2011).
98. Sen, *The Idea of Justice*, 68, 82–84, 354.
99. Sen, *The Idea of Justice*, 10, 413.
100. Sen, *Development as Freedom*, 18, 74–75. Sen defines 'capability' as the freedom to do and to be the things that one values doing and being. Actual achievements are 'functionings'. The relationship between capability and functionings could be better explained through an example. If an individual values doing *X*, *Y* and *Z*, but not *A*, *B* and *C*, then *X*, *Y* and *Z* functionings are the proper space to assess her capability. If she is only free to pursue *X* and *Y*, but *Z* remains out of her bounds, her overall capability is constitutive of functioning sets of *X* and *Y*. What matters, then, is her choice and her opportunities to choose.
101. Sen, *The Idea of Justice*, xvi, 7–8, 79–81, 410–412; Nussbaum, *Creating Capabilities*, x, 18, 35–36.
102. Anderson, 'Justifying the Capabilities Approach to Justice', 82–83.
103. Anderson, 'Justifying the Capabilities Approach to Justice'; Martha Nussbaum, *Women and Human Development: The Capabilities Approach* (Cambridge, UK: Cambridge University Press, 2000), 71–72 (emphasis mine). Note here the distinction between capabilities and functionings in capability-sensitive ideas of social justice. Whereas capabilities are *freedoms* to do things that one values, functionings are *actual achievements* that one attains by employing their capabilities. Thus, in a just society, the freedom to do (capability) leads to the actual doing (functionings) in any specific area of human endeavour.
104. Anderson, 'Justifying the Capabilities Approach to Justice'; Sen, *Development as Freedom*, 31–32, 36–40, 51–53, 123, 147–148, 152–155 (Sen

noting the significance of political liberties in Rawls' formulation). Also see Nussbaum, *Women and Human Development*, 12.
105. Nussbaum, *Women and Human Development*, 73–75, 77–80.
106. Amartya Sen, '"Equality of What?" The Tanner Lecture on Human Values, delivered at Stanford University, May 22, 1979', in *The Tanner Lectures on Human Values*, vol. 1, 195–220 (Salt Lake City, UT: University of Utah Press; Cambridge [UK], London, Melbourne and Sydney: Cambridge University Press, 1980), 217–218.
107. Amartya Sen, 'Human Rights and Capabilities', *Journal of Human Development* 6, no. 2 (2005): 151–166, 158.
108. Jean Drèze and Amartya Sen, *India Development and Participation* (New Delhi: Oxford University Press, 2002), 143–274.
109. Nussbaum, *Women and Human Development*, 77; Sen, *The Idea of Justice*, 106–111, 410–412.
110. Nussbaum, *Women and Human Development*; Sen, *The Idea of Justice*.
111. Rawls, *A Theory of Justice*, 240–241.
112. Sen, *Development as Freedom*, 6–7, 112–119 (emphasis mine).
113. Sen, *Development as Freedom*, 7, 25.
114. Rawls, *A Theory of Justice*, 237.
115. Rawls, *A Theory of Justice*, 239–240.
116. Rawls, *A Theory of Justice*, 236–237; Sen, *Development as Freedom*, 127–129.
117. Rawls, *A Theory of Justice*, 246; Drèze and Sen, *India Development and Participation*, 45.
118. Rawls, *A Theory of Justice*, 249; Sen, *The Idea of Justice*, 85; Drèze and Sen, *India Development and Participation*, 21, 45–46.
119. Sen, *The Idea of Justice*, 86.
120. Sen, *The Idea of Justice*, 345–354.
121. Sen, *The Idea of Justice*, 324.
122. Sen, *The Idea of Justice*, 327, 335–337.
123. See Partha Chatterjee, *The Politics of the Governed: Reflections on Popular Politics in Most of the World* (New York: Columbia University Press, 2004), 36–38, on the distinction between civil society and political society (his categorisation) and their role in the complicated practice of democracy in India.
124. Sen, *The Idea of Justice*, 16–17, 97–108, 144–145.
125. Sen, *The Idea of Justice*, 250.
126. Sen, *The Idea of Justice*, 250.

127. John Rawls, *The Law of Peoples* (Cambridge [MA] and London: Harvard University Press, 1999), 13 (emphasis mine).
128. Rawls, *The Law of Peoples*, 13–14.
129. Anderson, 'Justifying the Capabilities Approach to Justice'; Erin Kelly, 'Equal Opportunity, Unequal Capability', in *Measuring Justice: Primary Goods and Capabilities*, ed. Harry Brighouse and Ingrid Robeyns, 61–80 (New York: Cambridge University Press, 2010), 61. Also see, generally, Thomas Pogge, 'A Critique of the Capability Approach', in *Measuring Justice: Primary Goods and Capabilities*, ed. Harry Brighouse and Ingrid Robeyns, 17–60 (New York: Cambridge University Press, 2010).
130. Although the 'freedom' of the civil society to deliberate and participate is captured by political liberties (the first principle), its ongoing participation in shaping the other components of justice needs separate treatment. This characteristic is a major contribution of the capability perspective of justice that also finds a reference in the Rawlsian version.
131. Rawls summarises the main principles of a 'family of reasonable liberal conceptions of justice' thus:

   (a) 'basic rights and liberties of the kind familiar from a constitutional regime';
   (b) assignment of 'these rights, liberties, and opportunities a special priority, especially with respect to the claims of the general good and perfectionism values'; and
   (c) securing 'all citizens the requisite primary goods to enable them to make intelligent and effective use of their freedoms'.

   See Rawls, *The Law of Peoples*, 14.
132. See Hannah Arendt, *The Human Condition* (Chicago, IL: University of Chicago Press, 1969), where she notes work, labour, and action as the three conditions of human existence. Although the three aspects of human existence are not exclusive and their boundaries are contested, these three human conditions do offer a vision of core human existence.
133. Constitution, Articles 14, 19, 21.
134. *His Holiness Kesavananda Bharati Sripadagalvaru v. State of Kerala*, para. 705 (judgment by K. S. Hegde and A. K. Mukherjea).
135. See Constitution, Articles 14, 19, 21. Also see *Maneka Gandhi v. Union of India*, 1978 (1) SCC 248. However, see Anup Surendranath, 'Life and Personal Liberty', in *The Oxford Handbook of the Indian Constitution*, ed. Sujit Choudhry, Madhav Khosla and Pratap Bhanu Mehta, 756–776 (Oxford:

Oxford University Press, 2016), 757–758, arguing that such an expansive reading of liberty by the Indian Supreme Court lacks normative coherence.
136. *Maneka Gandhi v. Union of India* (judgments by P. N. Bhagwati and V. R. Krishna Iyer). Also see Rawls, *A Theory of Justice*, 54.
137. See Constitution, Article 19(6).
138. See Mahendra Pal Singh (ed.), *VN Shukla's Constitution of India* (12th edition) (New Delhi: Eastern Book Company, 2013 [1982]), 82–85, 89, 110, 113.
139. It might be useful to remember that although at independence (1947) the private sector dominated the market, from the late 1960s to the early 1990s public sector firms were the major players in the market. See Thiruvengadam, *The Constitution of India*, 159.
140. *His Holiness Kesavananda Bharati Sripadagalvaru v. State of Kerala*, (1973) MANU 0445 (SC).
141. *His Holiness Kesavananda Bharati Sripadagalvaru v. State of Kerala*, para. 758 (judgment by K. S. Hegde and A. K. Mukherjea), para 1531 (judgment by H. R. Khanna).
142. See Constitution, Part IV.
143. Constitution, Articles 38, 39, 39A, 40, 41.
144. Singh, *VN Shukla's Constitution of India*, 24, 207–211, 367–378; Thiruvengadam, *The Constitution of India*, 114–115, 127–129.
145. The market-promoting individual liberties should be seen as distinct from the intrinsic value of individual liberties. While individual liberties are intrinsically important – per se important because they promote freedom – they are also necessary as a means for promoting market transactions. It is this latter role of individual liberty that is emphasised here. To be sure, this distinction is ontological not practical – no such practical distinction can be made to sensitise a policy promoting one aspect of the freedom or the other.
146. The right to property was removed as a fundamental right (under Article 19) through section 2 of the Constitution (44th Amendment) Act, 1978.
147. See Namita Wahi, 'Property', in *The Oxford Handbook of the Indian Constitution*, ed. Sujit Choudhry, Madhav Khosla and Pratap Bhanu Mehta, 943–964 (Oxford: Oxford University Press, 2016), for a useful discussion of the political and juridical issues involved in the gradual evolution of property rights under the Constitution and the eventual abrogation of the fundamental right to property.
148. Wahi, 'Property'.
149. Philipp Dann and Arun K. Thiruvengadam, 'Comparing Constitutional Democracy in the European Union and India: An Introduction', in

*Democratic Constitutionalism in India and the European Union: Comparing the Law of Democracy in Continental Polities*, ed. Philipp Dann and Arun K Thiruvengadam, 1–41 (Cheltenham, UK: Edward Elgar, 2021), 29.
150. Dann and Thiruvengadam, 'Comparing Constitutional Democracy', 13.
151. Dann and Thiruvengadam, 'Comparing Constitutional Democracy', 29–30.
152. Rawls, *A Theory of Justice*, 176.
153. Mark Tushnet, 'The Indian Constitution Seen from Outside', in *The Oxford Handbook of the Indian Constitution*, ed. Sujit Choudhry, Madhav Khosla and Pratap Bhanu Mehta, 1019–1032 (Oxford: Oxford University Press, 2016), 1021.
154. Thiruvengadam, *The Constitution of India*, 208.
155. Thiruvengadam, *The Constitution of India*, 209. Also see Singh, *VN Shukla's Constitution of India*, 1070–1072.
156. Thiruvengadam, *The Constitution of India*, 209–210.
157. Thiruvengadam, *The Constitution of India*, 210.
158. Tushnet, 'The Indian Constitution Seen from Outside', 1021–1022.
159. Tushnet, 'The Indian Constitution Seen from Outside', 1021–1023; Madhav Khosla, 'Constitutional Amendment', in *The Oxford Handbook of the Indian Constitution*, ed. Sujit Choudhry, Madhav Khosla and Pratap Bhanu Mehta, 232–250 (Oxford: Oxford University Press, 2016), 235–236; Singh, *VN Shukla's Constitution of India*, 1090–1091; Thiruvengadam, *The Constitution of India*, 215–220.
160. Chatterjee, *The Politics of the Governed*, 3–4, 23.
161. Partha Chatterjee, *Lineages of Political Society: Studies in Postcolonial Democracy* (New York: Columbia University Press, 2011), 13–15.
162. Chatterjee, *The Politics of the Governed*, 37–38.
163. Bast and Thiruvengadam, *The Constitution of India*, 100; Tarunabh Khaitan, 'Killing a Constitution with a Thousand Cuts: Executive Aggrandizement and Party–State Fusion in India', *Law and Ethics of Human Rights* 14, no. 1 (2020): 49–95.
164. Dann and Thiruvengadam, 'Comparing Constitutional Democracy', 10–11, 14.
165. Rawls, *A Theory of Justice*.
166. See, generally, Khaitan, 'Killing a Constitution with a Thousand Cuts'.
167. Khaitan, 'Killing a Constitution with a Thousand Cuts', 85–95. See K. R. Shyam Sundar, 'No Dialogue with Trade Unions, India's Labour Laws Are Now a Product of Unilateralism', *The Wire*, 7 July 2020. Also see Damini

Nath, 'Can't Keep Deferring Labour Reforms in the Name of Consultation, Says Labour Minister Gangwar', *The Hindu*, 2 October 2020.
168. Jeremy Waldron, *Law and Disagreement* (New York: Oxford University Press, 1999), 4–6.
169. Rawls, *A Theory of Justice*, 171–175.
170. While the formal enactment procedure grants citizens a degree of representation through the electoral process, the continued discursive participation component of social justice lends significance to the ongoing, decentralised participation of groups and communities affected by a legislative enactment, in light of their lived experiences. Representative and directly participatory forms of democracy may often overlap, but the latter offers a more authentic content to enacted statutes. See, generally, Supriya Routh, 'Examining the Legal Legitimacy of Informal Economic Activities', *Social and Legal Studies* 31, no. 2 (2022): 282–308. Also see Supriya Routh, 'Do Human Rights Work for Informal Workers?' in *Re-Imagining Labour Law for Development: Informal Work in the Global North and Global South*, ed. Diamond Ashiagbor, 101–122 (London: Hart Publishing, 2019).

# 2

# Individual Autonomy, Freedom of Contract and the Labour Market

## Introduction

Individual liberty, contractual freedom and market participation are justiciable fundamental rights under the Indian Constitution. Individual rights to freedom of trade, business, profession and occupation are the bases of contractual freedom under the Constitution. However, freedom of contract is not identical to freedom of trade or profession. The scope of the latter is much broader than the former. An individual's profession, occupation, trade or business is also an expression of individual choices and aspirations – things that individuals value in their lives – when such choices are not substantially constrained.[1] Contractual freedom is of a narrower import compared to the freedom of trade or profession, but an important one that also facilitates the aforementioned individual aspirations under market conditions. An exclusive focus on contractual freedom as an indicator to evaluate the scope (and realisation) of freedom of trade sidelines other motivations of workers to engage in a specific profession, occupation or business. An exclusive focus on the freedom of market exchange (that is, contract) also comes at the cost of ignoring the prerequisites and corequisites of such exchange. Such focus does not capture the role of education, training, skills, resources, social circumstances, cultural sensitivities and other factors that help expand the *real freedom* of the parties to such an exchange.

To elaborate, there is a valid basis to argue, as John Gardner does, that an isolated focus on the freedom of contract is restrictive of overall individual freedom.[2] In the context of the employment relationship, if the primary legal emphasis lies on preserving or promoting the contractual feature of the relationship, the employee identity narrows down to that of an instrument of exchange (of labour), or contractor.[3] As instruments of exchange employees remain merely as means of performing the (employer's) contract. This instrumental understanding of employees articulates a narrow view of an employee's freedom, including her right to freedom of trade, by denying the capacity of choice and aspiration of such employee.[4] Work or employment is broader than mere contractual exchange since it also signifies a worker's aspiration and self-fulfilment. This (or *any*) human aspiration is bound to be broader than an instrumental – means to something – understanding of one's freedom of contract. Accordingly, a mere contractual understanding of employment, without also referring to other social commitments (including other individual freedoms), is restrictive of the very freedom (that is, freedom of trade) that it purports to promote.[5]

Even when labour market participation is narrowly assessed in terms of contractual freedom, such assessment must also take into account the prerequisites to such freedom, as noted earlier. De facto contractual freedom signifies that parties to a contract – market exchange – should be at a roughly equal position to exchange their respective promises (work and wages) reasonably free from extraneous (that is, extraneous to the contract) circumstances. Contractual freedom is important and compatible with other individual freedoms only when such freedom is a *real freedom* in the sense of being exercised with minimal constraints. When the freedom of contract is merely a *formal* entitlement that is blind to the conditions under which such freedom is conceived and exercised, such freedom is somewhat illusory and fails to meet the real purpose of the constitutional principle of freedom of trade. If social and legal factors end up constraining choices for some individuals (that is, workers) in contractual exchanges, thereby expanding the inequality of the contractual exchange, they are unable to promote the contractual freedom that is conceived under the Constitution and compatible with other freedoms of individuals. A mere emphasis on the freedom of contract, or market exchange, values only the *exchange* and the resultant outcome (that is, efficient distribution), but not the scope of the freedom underlying the exchange.

Thus, although contractual freedom is an important constitutional freedom, there are limits to conceptualising such freedom as satisfying the constitutional requirement of freedom of trade or profession. Additionally, achieving such contractual freedom – if it must be a real (realisable) freedom – is dependent on other background conditions that seek to equalise the market positions between the parties so that they are actually able to exchange under free market conditions without external circumstances constraining their exchanges. Since the core aims of the labour law reforms in India have been to promote individual autonomy and contractual freedom in order to facilitate primarily the market-based distribution of resources, the reforms should, first, be analysed in their capacity to expand workers' *real freedom* of trade under free market conditions. In this chapter, the role of the Industrial Relations Code, 2020[6] (hereinafter, 'IR Code') in facilitating workers' market participation under the condition of individual autonomy will be examined. It will be shown that although the IR Code is mindful of the inherent inequality in contractual exchange between the employer and the employee, it substantially constrains workers' freedom of contract by failing to consolidate the background conditions for the de facto realisation of such freedom.

In fact, the IR Code weakens the background conditions conducive to contractual freedom by making the government largely withdraw from employment relations. Although the reforms envisage workers' substantive entitlements primarily as negotiated contractual claims, additional limits are imposed on their freedom of contract. While the IR Code formally expands the contractual freedom of the parties – in the sense of facilitating the operation of the free market by limiting governmental intervention – the code, in fact, ends up limiting workers' freedom of trade, business, occupation and profession. In this context, the chapter will also comment on the extent to which regulation of minimum wage, workplace safety, health and working conditions promote the freedom of contract and counterbalance the risks of the labour market uncertainties that industrial employees are exposed to through the current IR Code.

The following section discusses the evolution of the contractual foundation of the employment relationship and the conceptual nature of such contract under the common law. The second section analyses the historical imagination of the employment relationship in India, which largely draws on – but is not identical to – the English common law conceptual framework of employment contract. This section discusses that historically the government had a more direct and determinate role in the employment contract in India. The third section shows how the conventional regulatory imagination of the employment contract in India fails in its goal of offering a level playing field in market relations involving informal workers. The fourth section assesses the IR Code and evaluates the role (and orientation) of the latest reforms in their ability to facilitate the constitutionally guaranteed freedom of trade.

## The Common Law of (Individual and Collective) Employment Relationship

The law of master and servant determined the conditions of labour exchange – employment relationship – in the United Kingdom and its colonies for more than 500 years.[7] Two prominent characteristics of this legal imagination were a private agreement between unequal parties whereby the master (employer) controlled the servant (employee) and the imposition of penal sanctions (for example, whipping, imprisonment, forced labour, fines and forfeiture of wages) for breaches of the employment agreement.[8] Admittedly, the working arrangement between a master and a servant was not contractual wherein the parties are 'free' to exchange under conditions of equality. The master's control over the servant was total, and such control was enforced through punitive sanctions. Workers were mere tools in the production process, their choice and agency having been denied by law. Workers' freedom was subservient to the master's property rights.

In early modern England, the master–servant agreement took varied forms depending on the nature of specific trades.[9] Exchange of labour adhered to different rules depending on whether workers were servants in husbandry, artificers, workmen, mining workers, seamen, domestic servants, highly skilled covenant servants, indentured servants and workers hired for specific tasks (or 'gig'), hired for the day, hired annually or for other periods in between.[10] While some common elements were present in these divergent employment relationships in different trades, a unified theory of employment contract capturing the essence of these agreements in abstraction did not emerge until the nineteenth century.[11] By the mid-nineteenth century, a common theme of employment contract, which partly abandoned penal sanctions for the breach of contract, emerged in England.[12] It is during this time that the characteristics of employment contract were articulated at a conceptual level. In addition to this conceptual account of employment contract, then articulated as the master–servant law, a range of other civil and criminal laws regulated collective labour relations in England.

The common law of employment contract, based on *freedom of contract* and *respect for private property*, strongly emerged with the Industrial Revolution in England.[13] This modern idea of employment contract has been shaped by the master–servant law, the nature of industrial organisation and the emergence of the welfare state.[14] On the one hand, maintaining a permanent workforce with direct employment contracts appeared more attractive to industries at this time; on the other, such organisation appeared to the state to be an effective basis for efficient regulation and taxation.[15] Because of the convergence of these two interests – that is, industrial capitalism and state bureaucracy – long-term, open-ended employment contract emerged as *the legal model* of labour relations, subsuming previous heterogeneous (waged) labour relations under the model.[16] While this unitary, modern formulation of employment contract was an expression of individual autonomy in contractual freedom, the traditional master–servant jurisprudence kept exerting an opposite pull.[17] What followed was a disjuncture between the basis of the law of contract (as expression of equal autonomous will) and employment contract (legally unequal bargain).[18] State action in the form of legislative intervention, including the enactment of social welfare legislation, later helped bring employment contract closer to the law of contract.[19]

The process of turning employment relationship into the contractual model began through the dismantling of the (maximum and minimum) wage-fixing system and the apprenticeship requirements for employment that were the prominent characteristics of the master–servant model.[20] While the legislative wage-fixation (with strict enforcement of maximum wages) regulated the supply and demand of labour, the apprenticeship system maintained the corporatist structure of the labour exchange (and, to a lesser extent, controlled labour supply).[21] Dismantling the wage-fixation system removed the regulatory capacity of the system to control the supply and demand of labour in the market. Ending the apprenticeship requirements ended the capacity of the guilds (that is, masters) to set the terms of labour exchange in the market. By deregulating market supply and demand, including the control of the guilds over the worker, these measures facilitated the transition to the capitalist system of *free* labour exchange unencumbered by the control of the guilds.[22] These deregulatory measures were later supplemented by a gradually expanding social provisioning framework through the poor law, which supplemented the wage-labour of the market.[23]

Collectively, these legislative interventions ensured the move from the corporative guild-based system to a market-based model of labour exchange on the ideal of freedom of contract.[24]

In England, with the repeal of the master–servant laws, and the gradual relaxation of stringent disciplinary codes and criminal sanctions, employment contracts were brought closer to the formal (classical) contractual model.[25] Although market freedom and capacity to contract were the ideals behind the move from a guild-based system to the market-based model of labour exchange, the juridical conceptualisation of the employment contract relied on the nature and extent of 'control' in the exchange relationship to distinguish an employment contract from other contracts. Control, of course, is a relic of the pre-Industrial Revolution period wherein masters, on account of their superior knowledge of the trade, engaged and controlled apprentices and journeymen to the completion of their venture.[26] This juridical imaginary of control had the backing of the legislature and the judiciary and was strictly enforced against the servants.[27] Simon Deakin and Gillian Morris add:

> A contractual model of employment only began to emerge in the case of middle class, salaried workers, whose position placed them outside the scope of the Master and Servant Acts. Thus, although a modern-style contract of employment can be seen developing in the nineteenth century, the scope of its application was limited by clear notions of social and economic status. One indication of this is the terminology used by the courts; the terms 'employee' and 'servant' denoted different forms of work relationship at this time.... *It is only in decisions of the early twentieth century that the courts can first be seen applying the contractual model, which they had developed for the middle classes, to industrial workers, agricultural labourers and domestic servants.* [28]

The collectivisation of labour relations – with the recognition of collective bargaining – further consolidated the formal equality between an employer and an employee.[29] The recognition of the validity of collective action, which signified limiting criminal culpability (for example, conspiracy, restriction of trade and tort) for action in concert, furthered the idea that workers are able to 'negotiate' with an employer with the ability to constrain the employer's choice of operation if they act in concert. This legally protected ability to negotiate took away the enormous power of the employers (that is, masters) from labour relations.[30] Formally, then, an employee could be regulated by a *negotiated contract* rather than the *unequal 'employment' relationship*. Legislative interventions during the 1960s and 1970s, by specifying basic entitlements of employees and mandating written contracts, further consolidated the contractual model.[31] These statutory interventions conceptually understood employment relationship as a contractual exchange and therefore aimed at curbing employers' (that is, masters') prerogative by mandating minimum standards for the exchange of labour. Although a complete equality between the negotiating parties was (*is*) impossible to achieve (in view of employers' proprietary rights), these basic standards minimised the power difference between the contracting parties, bringing employment relationship closer to the contractual model.

However, although employment relationships came to be conceived as contracts in common law, they have always been different from the classical contractual model. While law imagines the employment relationship to be a contract, parties are not completely free to decide the terms of the contract, many of which are spelled out by legislation.[32] The minimum standards legislation, in fact, recognises the inequality of the employment contract and seeks to address the sui generis nature of the latter. Common law employment contracts are not only unequal in their constitution, they are also hierarchical in their execution.[33] Inequality in the constitution of the employment contract means that the parties to the contract (employer and employee) accept that the terms of the contract will be dictated by the employer and the employee is not free to negotiate the entirety of the contractual terms. Hierarchy in execution signifies the day-to-day subjection of the employee to the control of the employer. Although for certain purposes this distinction between the two stages of freedom-inhibition may be important, we do not have to overwork this distinction. For our purposes, these two stages of the employment contract go on to show the legally recognised unfreedom of the employees in the contract.

As noted earlier, seeing employees primarily as instruments in executing an employment contract per se is freedom inhibiting since it ignores the other motivations that an employee may have in undertaking an employment. In this conceptual sense, the employment contract is a narrow lens that does not capture the total import of the freedom of trade or occupation. Even within that narrow common law contractual lens, employees' freedom to contract is substantially curbed because of the superior market position of the employer. Since this unfreedom is a defining characteristic of the common law employment contract, common law jurisdictions have aimed at removing this unfreedom through statutory intervention. Statutory interventions have generally adopted two simultaneous approaches: first, curbing the employer's freedom of contract and, second, expanding the employees' freedom of contract. While statutory protection of basic employee entitlements (such as minimum wages, maximum hours and limits on dismissals) caters primarily to the first approach, legal safeguard of trade unionism and collective bargaining addresses mainly the second.

Thus, statutory safeguards of basic employee entitlements and collective action are preconditions to the realisation of contractual freedom of employees. While statutory safeguards for employees seek to counterbalance the employer's market power and create conditions for a more equitable operation of the freedom of contract, striking this balance between curbing and expanding freedom is a context-specific exercise. The balance between the common law of employment contract and statutory entitlements is, then, a matter of degree, which eludes categorical evaluation. While the balance needs to be justified in the context of specific jurisdictions, what seems clear is that, in isolation, the employment contract per se does not signify an employee's real freedom to participate in the market (that is, trade, business, occupation or profession). In evaluating this balance between individual autonomy and state action in employment contract, the following section discusses the historic nature of the employment contract in India.

## The Nature of Employment Contract in India: Balancing Individual Autonomy and State Paternalism

The Constitution of India safeguards freedom of conscience, individual liberty, right to occupation and trade, and equal protection of law as *fundamental* rights.[34] Thus, the Constitution secures the foundation of individual autonomy-based freedom to engage in market exchanges – contracts – which is the foundation of trade and commerce in a liberal society. However, the constitutional mandates on individual freedom and legal equality are not articulated in a formal fictive sense – that is, it is not assumed that market participants are de facto equal and autonomous and that, as a result, their bargained contract will lead to an efficient resource distribution. Legal equality and contractual freedom in a constitution are aspirational ideals. What underscores the constitutional narrative of individual freedom and market exchanges is that unless market participants possess approximately equal negotiating power, markets should function under state paternalism.[35] In other words, the state shall actively promote conditions under which trading partners – individuals and businesses – are able to bargain on a more equitable footing. In this narrative, on the one hand, the prerequisite to contractual freedom is state action; on the other, state action also seeks to promote the broader freedom of trade for workers (by also addressing the non-contractual bases of work[36]), which is a more expansive idea of freedom than the more limited freedom of contract. This paternalistic constitutional narrative is part of the broader conceptual realm that regards markets (or 'freedom of contract') as instrumental – and, thus, ancillary – to the requirements of public interest, including 'freedom of trade' and the mandate of justice.

In no other market exchange this constitutional narrative unfolds as extensively as it does in the context of the labour market or employment contract-based exchanges of labour. State paternalism in employment contract is unsurprising since the employment contract is de jure an unequal relationship of exchange in common law. One of the foundational characteristics of the employment contract is the ability of the employer, partly because of her proprietary rights over her business, to 'control' employees.[37] The Indian Supreme Court noted that the idea of employment contract should be informed by the characteristics of the master–servant relationship.[38] Although the Supreme Court has moved away from control of the manner of doing work as the exclusive determinant of employment contracts, it has employed the principle of control to demonstrate the employer's ownership of workplace, machines and tools; performance of service by employees at owner's premises; owner's right to removal of an employee from service; and owner's right to reject the final product.[39] In *Hussainbhai v. the Alath Factory Tezhilali Union and Others*,[40] acknowledging the economic reality of the employment relationship, the Supreme Court remarked that, in India, employment contract cannot be understood in the same dogmatic common law contractual sense characterised by free choices of autonomous individuals under laissez-faire market conditions. In this judgment, the court recognised the inherent 'exploitative situations' of the labour market in contrast to the classical contractual model.[41] In successive decisions, the court had developed a more expansive idea of employment contract.[42]

Although the idea of employment contract has been gradually expanded by the Supreme Court, the uniform characteristic underlying all judicial articulations of the contract remained that of an unequal dependence – superior–subordinate relationship – wherein the rules of (labour) market exchange between the parties is the prerogative of the employer. If the terms of employment contracts were to be left completely to the negotiating power of the respective parties, such terms (that is, workers' rights) will invariably reflect the inequality of market power between the parties. This potential outcome is unsurprising because markets are per se spaces of private exchange, not social justice. Such exchange works on the basis of the rules of demand and supply. While, in general, workers barely possess any market power to influence their employment contract, in a labour-intensive country such as India, workers' market power is significantly more diminished.[43] Effective market participation and negotiation power demand some skillsets – that is, workers should possess skills that are valued, in demand, by the market. These skillsets are the result of education, training, nutrition, healthcare, physical capacity and socio-cultural circumstances. In absence of these preconditions – including public provisioning of these factors – to market participation, workers' formal freedom to market access is, in fact, a constrained freedom.[44] What follows is that while a laissez-faire market is in fact a space of legally recognised expansive freedom of the employer, it is a space of potential unfreedom (subjugation) of workers.

Indian labour law tackled this de facto disparity of contractual freedom under conditions of laissez-faire market exchange – including the lopsided ownership-backed freedom of the employer – by imposing reasonable limits on the employers' freedom to run their businesses. Accordingly, the Indian labour relations regime has historically been highly determinate and state-centred. For example, in industrial undertakings where at least 100 workers (sometimes less) are employed, law mandates that employment contracts must incorporate certain substantive provisions (called 'standing orders').[45] Every employment contract is required to enumerate classification of workers (such as permanent, temporary, apprentice and probationer); manner of communicating hours of work, holidays, paydays and wage rates to workers; shift-working rules; rules on attendance and late arrival; manner and conditions of leave grant; specific rules on entering business premises and body-searches; entitlements and obligations for temporary work stoppages and closing of sections of businesses; termination and notice requirements; employee misconduct and disciplinary action; means of contesting unfair and wrongful treatment by employer; and others issues that may be prescribed by the government.[46]

While the government may exempt certain industries from the application of these mandatory contractual clauses, these substantive entitlements constitute the foundation of a valid employment contract, upon approval by relevant authorities.[47] Government-appointed authorities, or 'certifying officers', are not only empowered to approve the substantive provisions of employment contracts, but they are also to adjudicate the 'fairness' and 'reasonableness' of the contractual clauses.[48] By subjecting negotiated employment contracts to scrutiny on the basis of fairness and reasonableness, the legal regime limits the operation of contractual autonomy. What the legal regime conveys is that although the parties – employer and employees – are free to decide their contractual obligations, the eventual validity of such contract will depend on the fairness of contractual terms as assessed by executive-appointed statutory authorities. This state paternalism achieves two simultaneous goals: first, by limiting the employer's freedom in the contractual exchange, it seeks to situate both parties at a rough negotiating equality; second, by retaining the power to validate employment contracts, it ensures that such contracts further (not hinder) 'freedom of trade' and align with the constitutional social justice narrative.

There have been other features that further consolidated the role of the executive in the Indian industrial relations regime. In addition to scrutinising the formation of employment contract on the principle of fairness, the government (or its designated authority) historically had substantial power to influence the continuation and termination of the contractual relationship, including by closure of the business. The Industrial Disputes Act, 1947 (hereinafter, 'ID Act'),[49] aimed at settling contractual ('industrial') disputes and employment-related matters, had historically entrenched the government in employment contracts. Employers had limited power to disrupt or terminate the employment contract. Depending on the nature of disruption in the employment contract, various degrees of governmental intervention were contemplated under the ID Act.[50] Although law required employers to serve prior notice to workers if they wanted to change conditions of service after contract formation, the government was empowered to dispense with such requirements in public interest.[51] The government was also required to be kept informed if a strike action was imminent in a public utility service.[52]

Industries employing 100 workers or more have been required to obtain prior governmental permission to lay off (with some exemptions, where post-lay-off approval was allowed) and terminate workers, and to close down industries.[53] An employer needed to explain reasons for her aforementioned actions to the government. The government was empowered to assess the genuineness of the employer's reasons for her actions, essentially scrutinising the motive of the employer for her actions. Thus, there was an implied condition of good faith in employment contracts insofar as the above actions are concerned. Additionally, for industry closures, the government needed to take public interest into account in arriving at their decision. Although businesses employing 50–100 workers were not required to seek prior governmental approval for laying off, terminating or closing down, they were required to serve prior notification to the government when terminating services of employees and closing down their businesses.[54] For business closures, employers were also required to explain reasons for such closure to the government.[55] In addition to determining the limits of employment contracts, the government had the power not only to refer contractual disputes to quasi-judicial authorities, but also to modify, reject or withhold enforcement of an award and have it examined in the legislature.[56] Even awards from voluntary arbitral processes had to be submitted to the government.[57]

In addition to the extensive governmental control of the contractual employment relationship, there have been other statutory limits on substantive aspects of employment contracts. Foremost among those are statutory minimum wage, including an express prohibition on contracting out of minimum wages, maximum hours (and overtime), pay equity and non-discrimination (on the basis of gender).[58] The government had been entrusted to fix and revise minimum wages and determine maximum working hours under the Minimum Wages Act, 1948.[59] In addition to these statutory limits to contractual freedom, a range of industry-specific health and safety standards (and other conditions at work) had been mandated for factories, mines, plantations, docks, transportation and other industries.[60] In all of these industries, it was the government, through (appointed) labour inspectors and inquiry committees, that oversaw the implementation of the health and safety standards through periodic inspections. Upon inspection, the inspectors (including 'certifying surgeon' and medical practitioners) were empowered to advise specific industries to improve their safety practices in order to meet the statutory mandates. The government was also empowered to exempt industries from the mandate of some of the health, safety and working conditions standards. Another interesting aspect of regulation of the market forces could be seen in the Payment of Bonus Act, 1965, which mandated businesses to pay bonuses to employees, including at a minimum rate, from their annual profits.[61] Thus, historically, on the one hand, workers were shielded from the risks of the market by means of statutory minimum safeguards in their employment contracts; on the other, they stood a chance to benefit from the profits of the business. While dissociation of minimum wages and conditions at work from industry performance (losses or profits) secured the foundations of distribution, the mandatory entitlement to bonuses sought to make workers enjoy the benefits (that is, efficient outcomes) of the market.

From the overview thus far it is clear that just as there has been supervisory and direct legal 'control' of employer over employees, the government has historically exercised direct control over an employer's action to a significant extent. For many of the business decisions that affected workers, employers needed to either inform or seek prior permission from the government and then subject themselves to inspection and course correction. Government supervision of the employment contract, however, did not (and does not) contravene either freedom of trade or individual liberty. Instead, government oversight sought to tackle the preconditions of the laissez-faire market – that is, the assumption of contracting parties' autonomy and equality of negotiating power. In enabling the market to operate for distribution purposes (rather than perpetuating social inequities), the government adopted two simultaneous strategies: first, the expansion of workers' real freedom (by means of minimum contractual entitlements) and, second, the contraction of the employer's extensive freedom (by imposing limits on her decision-making capacity). By so strategizing through myriad legislative interventions, the government aimed at creating suitable conditions for effective market participation – under conditions of real freedom – by the respective parties. Furthermore, this interventionist approach to understanding contractual freedom is consistent with the reasoning that the role of the market is instrumental, not per se important; it is a tool for furthering social justice and public interest. Thus, externally (that is, outside the internal market operations), government oversight of employment relationship has traditionally sought to formulate these freedoms (of trade and to individual liberty) in a manner that is compatible with social justice and public interest. The internal and external reasonings are consistent with – and underlie – the juridical framework of the Indian Constitution.

Jurisprudentially, then, the Indian labour law regime had never envisaged a total laissez-faire market model for labour relations. An unregulated free-market model is a model of unfreedom for the workforce. Both the narrower freedom of contract and the broader freedom of trade are constrained under laissez-faire market conditions. An employer is legally and materially the superior party to the employment contract. Without state intervention, employees will have to submit to the terms and conditions of employment unilaterally offered by the employer. In this backdrop, the Indian labour law regime has historically crafted a market order wherein the employer's market freedom is curbed and the employees' market freedom is expanded, as noted earlier. The legal recognition of trade unionism (a justiciable fundamental right) and collective bargaining (a legal right) further adds to the workers' negotiating freedom. In addition to this approach to equalising real freedom of the respective parties, the contract of employment is scrutinised by the government for its overall fairness. Following the constitutional mandate, this balance between individual autonomy and state paternalism is a carefully crafted balance that developed over the years after independence. Any attempt to disturb this balance will have direct implications on contractual freedom and, more broadly, the freedom of trade of the Indian workforce. It will be shown later in this chapter that this balance has actually been disturbed by the recent labour law reforms in the country, which ends up diminishing the market freedom of workers, thereby challenging the constitutional premise on individual liberty and freedom of contract.

Historically, however, the Indian labour law regime has largely left the so-called informal workers – unorganised workers – outside the purview of this juridical balance between individual autonomy and state paternalism and has subjected them to the inequitable and uncertain laissez-faire conditions of the market. The exclusion of informal workers from the formal legal mandate of state protection for market participation particularly stands in contrast to the elaborate legal protection afforded to formal industrial workers. Informal, or unorganised, workers are defined as those workers who are excluded from the purview of legislative safeguards.[62] Since the very definition of this group of workers is their exclusion from legislative safeguards, it is unsurprising that their existence and activities persist without state intervention. Without state intervention, informal workers only have the benefit of the formal, fictitious individual liberty and freedom of contract, which stands uneasily with the richer constitutional ideals, as will be emphasised in the following section.

## Informal Workers, Market Freedom and State Paternalism

The history of the Indian labour law regime narrated in the previous section collapses when we assess the situation of the so-called informal workers in the country. The very ideas of informal economic activities and informal workers are constructed on the basis of their exclusion from the aforementioned legal framework. In fact, informal workers are defined on the basis of their contrast from the formal industrial workers who historically remained the principal subject matter of labour laws in India. Informal workers are defined as workers working without any employment-related or social security benefits.[63] Exclusion from employee rights and social security benefits often occur when economic activities are not registered or licensed with the state authorities – that is, when they operate without legal affiliation. Such exclusion also occurs when economic activities are either directly or indirectly exempted by statutes. While direct exemption happens when a statute exempts a specific category of economic activity, such as domestic work, from its coverage, indirect exemption of certain economic activities takes place when a statute is made inapplicable to economic activities that engage a small number of workers (for example, ten or less).

An example will be instructive. As discussed, the ID Act established state paternalism in labour relations by restricting the scope of the market freedom of the employer. Even though an employer had a proprietary interest in her business and was free to further her business interests, she was not free to lay off or terminate her employees as she deemed fit. The employer's actions were controlled and scrutinised by the government in recognition of the constrained nature of contractual freedom of the workers. This state paternalism existed alongside statutory minimum safeguards (such as minimum wages, maximum hours, and so on), which also aimed at expanding the employees' market freedom. Together, these measures aimed at balancing contractual freedom of the parties. However, informal workers have traditionally been left outside this carefully crafted balance of market (that is, contractual) freedom of the parties. Since the legally mandated governmental intervention on the employer's (or other intermediaries and contractors', for self-employed informal workers) freedom applied above a given (numerical) employee threshold, such intervention excluded informal workers who mainly worked in smaller businesses. In the absence of the government-mediated limitations on the employer's market freedom, informal workers have been exposed to a contractual regime that is unilaterally determined by the employer. What follows is that informal workers' contractual freedom has been historically constrained because of their exclusion from labour law.

Other prerequisites to curb the employer's superior market freedom and expand informal workers' real contractual freedom also remained largely unmet. Legally safeguarded entitlements on minimum wages, maximum working hours, pay equity and unfair dismissal, all of which could reasonably restrict an employer's contractual freedom, have also been uncertain for informal workers. These entitlements have been uncertain because while some of these entitlements could possibly be extended to informal workers, others would not cover their specific circumstances.[64] For example, statutes such as the Equal Remuneration Act, 1976; the Bonded Labour System (Abolition) Act, 1976; and the Trade Unions Act, 1926, were (are, when some of these statutes are not repealed) applicable to all workers, including informal workers. However, statutes such as the Minimum Wages Act, 1948; the Child Labour (Prohibition and Regulation) Act, 1986; the Inter-State Migrant Workmen (Regulation of Employment and Condition of Service) Act, 1979; the Motor Transport Workers Act, 1961; and the Sales Promotion Employees (Conditions of Service) Act, 1976, were (are) only applicable to certain categories of informal workers. Some other statutes such as the Contract Labour (Regulation and Abolition) Act, 1970; the Building and Other Construction Workers (Regulation of Employment and Conditions of Service) Act, 1996; and the Maternity Benefit Act, 1961, could be extended to informal workers under certain circumstances. Some of these statutes did not apply to informal workers because of the numerical threshold (that is, ten or twenty workers) required for the applicability of the statutes. This situation was further complicated by regional initiatives wherein state legislatures had enacted minimum standards statutes (such as on minimum wages) and welfare schemes (such as on provident and welfare funds) for specific categories of informal workers.[65]

On the other hand, even when informal workers had legal entitlements to collective action, informal workers' trade unionism had faced significant obstacles until workers found innovative ways to overcome such obstacles by collectively organising and mounting successful challenges to interpretation of statutes (such as the Trade Unions Act, 1926).[66] Thus, although freedom-expanding prerequisites have not completely been outside the reach of informal workers, such prerequisites have only been sporadically available to only select categories of informal workers. As a general category, however, informal workers have traditionally been deprived of conditions necessary for the expansion of their real freedom of contract. Thus, traditionally, in spite of constituting the majority of the workforce in the country, informal workers' contractual freedom – and, as a consequence, freedom of trade – has been constrained, thereby falling short of the constitutional ambition of expanding such freedom. Under these conditions, informal workers' choice and agency at work have been systematically undermined by the labour law regime in the country.

An attempt was made by the Supreme Court to incorporate as many workers as possible within the purview of the ID Act by defining the term 'industry' expansively as including even smaller establishments, presumably those that remain excluded from the purview of the different labour welfare statutes.[67] The court defined the term 'industry' as *any systematic activity* organised through the cooperation between the employer and the employee, except single simple ventures where workers are employed only for minimal matters. While this definition would still have left a range of self-employed workers, own-account workers and employees of smaller undertakings outside the purview of the Act, it would have allowed the government to play the balancing role for a much broader group of workers in the country. While an amendment to the definition of 'industry' was introduced on the basis of this definition, the amendment was never operationalised until the enactment of the IR Code.[68] Unfortunately, however, as will be discussed in the following section, this expansion of the definition of 'industry' in 2020 did not in fact end up expanding contractual freedom of more workers or eventually promoting their freedom of trade because the new code has simultaneously undermined the ability of the government to counterbalance the superior market freedom of the employer, which is starkly contrary to the intention of the Supreme Court when it articulated the expansive definition of 'industry' in 1978.

## The Labour Law Reforms: The Withdrawal of State Paternalism

In evaluating the recent reforms in their ability to expand market-based freedom of workers – the freedom of contract in its narrow sense and the freedom of trade in its broader version – this section argues that the IR Code fails on both of these accounts. It fails to promote workers' freedom of contract by failing to maintain the carefully developed long-standing balance among different factors underlying the freedom; and relatedly, it fails to promote the broader freedom of trade by failing to secure the bases of such freedom. This section also analyses the Code on Wages, 2019 (hereinafter, 'Wage Code'), and the Occupational Safety, Health and Working Conditions Code, 2020 (hereinafter, 'OSH Code'), in their collective ability to promote workers' freedom of contract and their freedom of trade. To be sure, the bases of the broader version of freedom of trade also require social security entitlements and collective action in addition to work-based rights. The analysis of social security entitlements and their role in promoting freedom and dignity of workers will be tackled in the next chapter (Chapter 3). Workers' collective action will be analysed in Chapter 4.

As noted, the IR Code defines industry in a much broader manner than was done previously. This broader conceptualisation of the idea was proposed by the Supreme Court with the intention of expanding the application of the legal employment relations framework to a much wider group of workers who were originally excluded from the scope of the legal framework. In this sense, such an expanded definition is a cause for celebration for workers because it would signify extending the state-mediated facilitation of contractual freedom of workers under market conditions. As argued earlier, without reasonably restricting the employer's freedom, workers' real contractual freedom under market conditions could not be achieved. Since the common law already recognised proprietary rights of the employer and conceptualised employment relationship with reference to the master–servant model, it is only by means of limiting the employer's freedom that workers' real freedom to negotiate an employment contract could be realised. The other factors expanding such freedom are the statutorily enumerated minimal contractual terms (that is, floor of rights such as minimum wages, maximum hours, health and safety standards).

However, the Supreme Court has lately questioned the validity of this balance struck between unconstrained market freedom and state paternalism. The court emphasised that the industrial relations law (that is, the pre-reform ID Act) should not be seen only as a worker-welfare law.[69] An interpretation of the idea of industry focused on worker interest is an inequitable approach that ignores the interest of the employer and the public. The court further reasoned that an expansive definition of industry that brings a larger set of employment relationships under legislative coverage 'might be a deterrent to private enterprise in India' and hinder self-employment.[70] Sole emphasis on workers' rights and restrictions on employer's contractual freedom might result in financial hardship for the employer, resulting in the employer's exit from the market, which in turn will adversely affect workers. A range of other decisions on labour flexibility and the employer's market freedom, including the validation of temporary employment of workers without statutory benefits of a regular employee even when such workers were temporarily employed for ten or more years, have been issued by the court.[71] The Supreme Court also offered an ideological critique of the historical understanding of labour law, when it noted:

> [Formerly] [t]his Court seems to have been swayed by the idea that India is a socialist republic and that implied the existence of certain important obligations which the State had to discharge.[72]

It is indeed true that India *is* constitutionally a socialist republic. It is also true that everyone, including the judiciary, in the country must *act and decide in a manner compatible* with the aforementioned ideal. However, even without any dogmatic adherence to socialism, the state does have responsibilities to discharge towards its citizens as a mandate of social justice, as emphasised earlier in this book (see Chapter 1). Thus, the court's suggestion that the judiciary must not be 'swayed' by the ideal of state interference in employment relationships rests on a faulty understanding of the Constitution and precarious interpretation of the freedom of trade.

By showing allegiance to this faulty premise of judicial reasoning, in spite of adopting the expansive conceptualisation of the term 'industry', the IR Code ends up eventually narrowing the contractual freedom of workers by weakening the bases of such freedom. The benefit of an expansive definition is undercut by the substantial withdrawal of the state's role from employment contracts, which has historically consolidated the bases of freedom of contract (and trade), under the new code. Prominently, the IR Code does away with the requirement of seeking prior governmental permission that existed under the ID Act, to lay off and terminate workers and close down businesses wherein 100 or more workers have been employed. Such precondition to lay off, terminate or close business is now only required of larger industrial establishments. It is only the larger (in terms of number of employees) businesses that are required to justify their business decisions to the government. These businesses have more extensive oversight from the government.

Larger businesses employing 300 or more workers must also adhere to the government-issued standing orders – delineating the terms of the employment contract (or working conditions) such as the nature of a worker, working hours, wage rates, paydays, holidays, suspension, dismissal, process of termination of employment and grievance resolution – as minimum standards.[73] Although the employer and the employees (and their representatives) are free to negotiate a standing order for their respective businesses, the government sets the basic standards of such order. The government-appointed certifying officer is empowered to assess the 'fairness or reasonableness' of a negotiated standing order.[74] The benchmark for adjudicating the fairness of a standing order is the government's model standing order. An unfair or unreasonable standing order will not be certified by the certifying officer and, therefore, will not be deemed to be the employment contract between the parties. Thus, the government has direct and substantial control over the employment contract in large businesses, so much so that unconscionable employment contracts, in theory, will not pass the review by the certifying officer.

As noted, the IR Code requires the employer to seek governmental approval for laying off, terminating the services of employees and closure of the business, but the requirement for prior approval is limited only to non-seasonal workplaces (factories, mines and plantations) where 300 or more workers are employed.[75] In such businesses, the employer requires the prior permission from the government to lay off her regular employees, unless such lay-off is the result of unavoidable circumstances including force majeure.[76] Where lay-off results from unavoidable circumstances, the employer is to obtain ex post facto permission from the government. Similarly, employers cannot terminate services of employees unless prior permission has been obtained from the government.[77] While closing down a business, an employer is also required to seek prior permission from the government.[78] In contrast, an employer employing less than 300 workers is generally required only to serve a sixty days' notice, not to seek prior permission from the government but of her intention to close the business.[79]

While deep and direct governmental intervention in employment relationships is contemplated for bigger businesses, for mid-sized businesses employing 100 or more workers (but less than 300), the focus of the IR Code is on facilitating bipartite labour relations. The government would require the establishment of works committees and grievance redressal committees constitutive of employer and employee representatives in order to operationalise the continuing employment contract for these businesses.[80] Constraints on the employer's (and employees') contractual freedom are exercised in a more indirect form – that is, by means of statutory floor of rights. The Wage Code secures the legal right to government-mandated minimum wages for different categories of employees and different geographical locations, pay equity between different genders, maximum working hours, weekly holiday and overtime pay.[81] Although the Wage Code addresses a range of wage-related issues, including pay equity, Santanu Sarkar has pointed out the ambiguities, contradictions, exclusions and fallacies that have crept into the Wage Code because of conceptual confusions in characterising various categories of workers.[82] The lack of nuance in conceiving specific entitlements under the Wage Code is somewhat mitigated by the decentralised law-making delegation mandated under it. While the modus operandi in actually determining minimum wages for different categories of employees and workers remains underspecified under the Wage Code, the responsibility to actually determine minimum wages has been delegated to the state governments who are expected to contextually decide (floor wage and) minimum wage for different categories of workers.[83]

Additionally, the OSH Code[84] provides for daily maximum working hours, overtime pay, weekly holidays and entitlement to annual leave for specific categories of workers.[85] The OSH Code also stipulates contractual obligations of the employer in providing a safe, hazard-free and healthy workplace for employees.[86] These obligations of the employer must be mentioned in the written employment contract.[87] Employees have the right to information on health and safety measures and the right to make direct representation to the employer on unsatisfactory health and safety conditions.[88] Employees are also duty-bound to comply with the required health and safety guidelines and take reasonable care at work.[89]

The OSH Code empowers the central and state governments to specify safety and health standards for specific workplaces such as factories, mines, docks, plantations, *beedi* and cigar manufacturing, and construction businesses and enumerates safety and health standards for specific categories of workers such as contract labour, inter-state migrant workers and audio-visual workers.[90] State governments have the power to modify some of these standards within their jurisdictions.[91] The OSH Code contemplates a detailed standard-setting function of the central government, wherein the government may specify standards ranging from the general cleanliness of the workplace to the treatment of effluents and monitor the implementation of such standards through inspector-cum-facilitators.[92] The government is entrusted with special responsibilities for the employment of women workers and may require the employer to provide additional safeguards to women workers in employment that the government considers dangerous for their health and safety.[93] The aim of the government is to secure conditions that the government understands to be necessary for a *decent standard of life of the employees* in the specific context of their workplaces.[94] Remedy for the contraventions under the code is punitive, not compensatory, signifying that the code is a public policy document rather than a purely contractual baseline.[95]

It is important, however, to note that although employees' minimum standards (such as minimum wages, maximum hours, safety and health) in employment contract are dissociated from the loss or profits of the business or market fluctuations, employees are not kept completely isolated from the benefits of market efficiencies. In addition to statutory minimum pay (minimum wages and overtime pay), employees are legally entitled to receive a share of the business profits as bonus pay.[96] For employees who earn less than a government-specified threshold wage, this bonus is a mandatory entitlement that does not depend on the employer's profits (or 'allocable surplus').[97] The bonus amount increases proportionally with the employer's profits.[98] Parties to the employment contract cannot contract out the minimum standards, including entitlement (and obligation) to the payment of bonus.[99]

In spite of these carefully crafted fundamental employment standards, through which the government exercises an indirect influence on the parties' freedom of employment contract, the scheme of the OSH Code does end up simultaneously granting substantial discretionary power to the government to relieve businesses from meeting the minimum standards under the code. The government may exempt businesses, including new factories, from the application of the OSH Code.[100] The justificatory basis of such exemption is the classic neoliberal deregulatory rationale: that the (state) government is satisfied that such exemption is necessary 'in the public interest ... to create more economic activities and employment opportunities'.[101] An extension of such logic could also be found in the government's power to suspend the operation of the OSH Code during emergencies.[102] As has been seen during the COVID-19 pandemic, some state governments are not hesitant in exercising their power to suspend labour laws in their respective jurisdictions.[103] What these discretionary powers suggest is that in spite of the legally guaranteed minimum standards, the government retains the ultimate authority to directly impact employment relationships in a manner that takes away the basis of the contractual freedom of workers, thereby exposing them to the inequities of the laissez-faire market.

Thus, governmental intervention is most extensive in the case of larger businesses. Such intervention pertains to specifying fair (that is, model) contractual terms as minimal entitlements of workers, seeking justification for the employer's business decisions affecting workers and approving or declining to approve laying off and termination of employees and the closure of businesses. As noted earlier, these interventions in employment contracts do two things: first, they limit the contractual freedom of the employer by not allowing them to use their superior market position to dictate the terms of the contract including its termination; second, they expand the contractual freedom of employees by not only stipulating minimal working conditions including health and safety guarantees but also mandating a share of the business profits. This combined strategy not only expands the contractual freedom of workers by securing the bases of such freedom, it also contributes to facilitating the broader freedom of trade. Unfortunately, however, this balance between individual autonomy and state paternalism does not extend to the vast majority of the Indian workforce. The majority of the Indian workforce works in mid-sized and smaller businesses and (informal) economic activities. By not extending state paternalism to those market-based relationships (employment contract or dependent relationships), the reforms expose the vast majority of Indian workers to the inequities of the market, thereby constraining their actual freedom of market exchanges.

It is true that the Wage Code and the OSH Code enable the government to indirectly influence employment contracts by specifying minimum contractual conditions in order to ensure a decent standard of life for workers. It is also true that many of these minimum standards have the potential to expand real contractual freedom of workers. However, the scope of some of these standards is, sometimes, more limited. For example, bonus provisions apply to workplaces employing twenty or more workers, thereby leaving the vast majority of informal workers outside its scope. Even when they cover smaller workplaces and divergent workers, these minimum standards only tackle one part of the problem of market freedom. They cater to expanding the freedom of contract of the workers by securing minimum preconditions to such freedom. These minimum standards are unable to constrain the employer's expansive market freedom more directly, which the state (that is, the government) is capable of doing in the context of larger businesses. The only time the law allows direct intervention from the government in employment relationships of mid-sized and smaller businesses is to exempt or suspend the operation of these minimum standards for some or all businesses for the purpose of promoting economic development and employment opportunities. Thus, when direct state intervention is contemplated, it is contemplated to accelerate the operation of the laissez-faire market conditions, which are freedom constraining for workers and contrary to how the governmental role is conceived for larger businesses.

In this scheme of things, it is the informal workers who remain at the risk of substantial unfreedoms. Informal workers constitute the vast majority of the workforce in the country. However, their market engagement may not always be conceived as employment relationships, although there are relationships of economic dependence. Accordingly, the statutory minimum standards may not apply to informal workers in ways that they do for formal workers in employment contracts. On the other hand, their working arrangements are also excluded from the scope of direct state intervention. While this dual exclusion makes their market condition particularly vulnerable, the scope of their freedom and dignity could not be properly assessed without analysing the social protection framework envisaged through the latest reforms. The next chapter will engage in such an analysis.

## Conclusion

The freedom to participate in market exchanges is primarily an instrumental freedom, important insofar as it promotes workers' freedom to lead a dignified life. Retraction of state paternalism from market exchanges prima facie creates a more expansive space for the operation of the freedom – in its narrow sense, the freedom of contract, and, more broadly, the freedom of trade. In this chapter, it is argued that this view on the expansion of contractual freedom is faulty and subverts the constitutional premise. It is argued that withdrawal of state paternalism from the vast majority of market exchanges results in a narrowing down of contractual freedom of workers. This constrained market freedom, in turn, affects workers' ability to use the market to lead a dignified life. The history of state paternalism – alongside contractual freedom – in labour relations aimed at consolidating the basis of the broader freedom of trade, thereby facilitating a dignified life through work. This historical narrative has been somewhat disturbed by the latest labour law reforms in the country.

For the vast majority of informal workers, contractual freedom is particularly constrained because statutory minimum standards may not be the most appropriate ones for their specific contexts, and direct intervention by the state is contemplated only in facilitating a laissez-faire market condition. Thus, informal workers may not have the bases of their contractual freedom guaranteed, and direct state intervention in their market-based relationships is denied by law. For formal workers in mid-sized to small businesses, although the minimum standards may create the bases of real contractual freedom, the reforms do not envisage direct state intervention in simultaneously constraining the employer's market freedom. It is only in the context of large businesses employing 300 or more workers that both – the bases (that is, minimum standards) of expansion of workers' freedom and state paternalism to constrain the employer's freedom – work together to create a more equitable market condition wherein the parties could realise their contractual freedom in taking advantage of market-based distribution of economic resources.

Thus, the latest labour law reforms substantially expose the Indian workforce to laissez-faire market conditions. This approach to expanding the scope of the deregulatory market, while it may not be ultra vires the Constitution, does misunderstand the ethos of the Constitution. Although individual autonomy (that is, individual conscience and personal liberty) and contractual freedom (that is, freedom of trade) are fundamental rights protected under the Constitution, these rights are not conceived as formal entitlements. In addition to being important per se, these rights are the bases of meaningful market participation by workers. Such participation requires that the preconditions to the actual expansion of these freedoms are met. The 2020 labour law reforms expand the operation of contractual freedom under market conditions without consolidating the preconditions for the real articulation of the freedom. By failing to create preconditions for de facto free market exchanges, the labour law reforms end up constraining such freedom. However, such constrained freedom of contract – or prominence of the laissez-faire market conditions – does not per se render the labour law reforms unjust in toto. To evaluate the justness of the reforms, the greater deregulation of market exchanges must be weighed against social protection – on the principle of solidarity – by the state. In the next chapter, the labour law reforms are evaluated on their approach to expanding social protection for workers who stand exposed to the risks of the laissez-faire market.

## Notes

1. Amartya Sen, *Development as Freedom* (New York: Alfred A. Knopf, 1999), 18, 74–75; Amartya Sen, *The Idea of Justice* (Cambridge, MA: Harvard University Press, 2009), 228–230.
2. John Gardner, 'The Contractualisation of Labour Law', in *Philosophical Foundations of Labour Law*, ed. Hugh Collins, Gillian Lester and Virginia Mantouvalou, 33–47 (New York: Oxford University Press, 2018).
3. Gardner, 'The Contractualisation of Labour Law'.
4. Vando Borghi, 'Transforming Knowledge into Cognitive Basis of Policies: A Cosmopolitan from Below Approach', in *Science and Scientification in South Asia and Europe*, ed. Axel Michaels and Christoph Wulf, 242–254 (Abingdon and New York: Routledge, 2020), 247–248.
5. See Gardner, 'The Contractualisation of Labour Law'.
6. Act no. 35 of 2020.
7. Douglas Hay and Paul Craven, 'Introduction', in *Masters, Servants, and Magistrates in Britain & the Empire, 1562–1955*, ed. Douglas Hay and Paul Craven, 1–58 (Chapel Hill [NC] and London: University of North Carolina Press, 2004), 9–10.
8. Hay and Craven, 'Introduction', 1–2.
9. Hay and Craven, 'Introduction', 6.
10. Hay and Craven, 'Introduction', 7. It might be worthwhile to remember that the judiciary excluded domestic servants from the purview of the master-servant laws in England from the late eighteenth century.
11. Hay and Craven, 'Introduction', 6.
12. Hay and Craven, 'Introduction'.
13. Simon Deakin and Frank Wilkinson, *The Law of the Labour Market: Industrialization, Employment, and Legal Evolution* (New York: Oxford University Press, 2005), 42.
14. Deakin and Wilkinson, *The Law of the Labour Market*, 43.
15. Deakin and Wilkinson, *The Law of the Labour Market*.
16. Deakin and Wilkinson, *The Law of the Labour Market*, 43–44. It is important to note that some English law scholars now argue moving to a more heterogeneous conceptual understanding of employment contract(s) (or labour exchanges) in order to make sense of a range of waged labour exchanges that are insufficiently explained by the contract model. For a recent iteration, see Mark Freedland, 'The Legal Structure of the Contract of Employment', in *The Contract of Employment*, ed. Mark Freedland (general

editor), Alan Bogg, David Cabrelli, Hugh Collins, Nicola Countouris, A. C. L. Davies, Simon Deakin and Jeremias Prassl, 28–51 (New York: Oxford University Press, 2016), 28.
17. Deakin and Wilkinson, *The Law of the Labour Market*, 43–44.
18. Deakin and Wilkinson, *The Law of the Labour Market*, 44.
19. Deakin and Wilkinson, *The Law of the Labour Market*, 44–45.
20. Deakin and Wilkinson, *The Law of the Labour Market*, 51–52.
21. Deakin and Wilkinson, *The Law of the Labour Market*, 52–53.
22. Deakin and Wilkinson, *The Law of the Labour Market*, 53–55.
23. Deakin and Wilkinson, *The Law of the Labour Market*, 46, 52–53.
24. Deakin and Wilkinson, *The Law of the Labour Market*, 51–52.
25. Simon Deakin and Gillian S. Morris, *Labour Law* (London: Butterworths, 2001 [1995]), 22–28.
26. Deakin and Wilkinson, *The Law of the Labour Market*, 46; Deakin and Morris, *Labour Law*, 22–23.
27. Deakin and Morris, *Labour Law*, 22–28.
28. Deakin and Morris, *Labour Law*, 23, 25 (emphasis mine; internal citation omitted).
29. Deakin and Morris, *Labour Law*, 25–26.
30. Of late scholars of common law have noted that with the decline of trade unionism, contractual inequality between the employer and employees has expanded. Employers (management) have gradually acquired more power in employment contracts, enabling them to unilaterally control the employment relationship. See Alan Bogg and Ruth Dukes, 'The Contract of Employment and Collective Labour Law', in *The Contract of Employment*, ed. Mark Freedland (general editor), Alan Bogg, David Cabrelli, Hugh Collins, Nicola Countouris, A. C. L. Davies, Simon Deakin and Jeremias Prassl, 96–123 (New York: Oxford University Press, 2016), 123.
31. Deakin and Morris, *Labour Law*, 27–28.
32. Otto Kahn-Freund, 'A Note on Status and Contract in British Labour Law', *Modern Law Review* 30, no. 6 (1967): 635–644.
33. Hugh Collins, 'Is the Contract of Employment Illiberal?' in *Philosophical Foundations of Labour Law*, ed. Hugh Collins, Gillian Lester and Virginia Mantouvalou, 48–67 (New York: Oxford University Press, 2018).
34. See Constitution of India, 1950, Articles 14, 19, 21, 25 (hereinafter, 'Constitution').
35. Constitution, Article 19(6), suggests the idea in the following manner: The state may, by law, impose reasonable restrictions on trade 'in the interests of the general public'.

36. By providing public goods such as education, health, nutrition, training, and so on, as legal entitlements, the state secures the bases of a worker's aspiration to work. In other words, it is because of their education, health, culture, tradition and a range of other factors that workers aspire to undertake one kind of work as opposed to another, and the state has a role in promoting some of these factors.
37. See, for example, *Dharangadhara Chemical Works Limited v. State of Saurashtra*, (1957) 1 LLJ 477 (SC), for one of the earliest articulations of the employment contract, wherein the Supreme Court of India noted that the 'right of control in respect of the manner in which the work is to be done' is the central component of the contract between an employer and an employee.
38. *Dharangadhara Chemical Works Limited v. State of Saurashtra*, (1957) 1 LLJ 477 (SC).
39. *Silver Jubilee Tailoring House and Others v. Chief Inspector of Shops and Establishments and Another*, AIR 1974 SC 37.
40. *Hussainbhai v. the Alath Factory Tezhilali Union and Others*, AIR 1978 SC 1410.
41. *Hussainbhai v. the Alath Factory Tezhilali Union and Others*, AIR 1978 SC 1410, para. 4.
42. See, for example, *Workmen of Nilgiri Cooperative Marketing Society Limited v. State of Tamil Nadu*, (2004) 3 SCC 514; *International Airport Authority of India v. International Air Cargo Workers' Union*, AIR 2009 SC 3063.
43. Max Weber, 'Freedom and Coercion', in *Max Weber on Law in Economy and Society*, ed. Max Rheinstein, 188–191 (Cambridge, MA: Harvard University Press, 1954), 188. For the range of workers' unfreedoms in employment relationship, see Jens Lerche, 'A Global Alliance against Forced Labour? Unfree Labour, Neo-Liberal Globalization and the International Labour Organization', *Journal of Agrarian Change* 7, no. 4 (2007): 425–452; Samanthi J. Gunawardana, 'Emerging Economies, Freedom of Association and Collective Bargaining for Women Workers in Export Oriented Manufacturing', in *The Routledge Companion to Employment Relations*, ed. Adrian Wilkinson, Tony Dundon, Jimmy Donaghey and Alexander Colvin, 372–386 (London: Routledge, 2018); Chiara Benassi and Milena Tekeste, 'Employment Relations and Precarious Work', in *The Routledge Companion to Employment Relations*, ed. Adrian Wilkinson, Tony Dundon, Jimmy Donaghey and Alexander Colvin, 307–320 (London: Routledge, 2018); Jimmy Donaghey and Juliane Reinecke, 'Global Supply Chains and Employment

Relations', in *The Routledge Companion to Employment Relations*, ed. Adrian Wilkinson, Tony Dundon, Jimmy Donaghey and Alexander Colvin., 342–356 (London: Routledge, 2018); Jean Jenkins and Paul Blyton, 'In Debt to the Time-Bank: The Manipulation of Working Time in Indian Garment Factories and "Working Dead Horse"', *Work, Employment and Society* 31, no. 1 (2017): 90–105; and Rina Agarwala and Shiny Saha, 'The Employment Relationship and Movement Strategies among Domestic Workers in India', *Critical Sociology* 44, nos. 7–8 (2018): 1207–1223.

44. Sen, *Development as Freedom*, 6–7, 25–26, 112–129. To be sure, existing structures of market participation and social biases are also responsible for workers' market-centred unfreedoms (see the references cited in note 43). However, public provisioning – social welfare – of the aforementioned factors, including programmes to alter the bases of socio-cultural biases is a prominent step towards expanding workers' real freedom to participate in market exchanges. As will be demonstrated in Chapter 3, social welfare entitlements under the latest reforms are insufficient in strengthening the basis of workers' unconstrained participation in the market. The inadequacy of social welfare is particularly conspicuous when compared with the increased risks introduced in the labour market by the 2020 reforms. While facilitating workers' market participation is not the only function of social welfare entitlements, it is an important precondition to promoting an agency-based well-being of workers. Questions on the functions of social welfare will be taken up in the next chapter.
45. Industrial Employment (Standing Orders) Act, 1946 (Act no. 20 of 1946) (hereinafter, 'Standing Orders Act'), sections 1, 2, 3, 4 and The Schedule ('Matters to be Provided in Standing Orders under This Act'). The 2020 reforms continue with these requirements.
46. Standing Orders Act, sections 2(g), 3(20) and the Schedule.
47. Standing Orders Act, sections 3, 14.
48. Standing Orders Act, section 4.
49. Act no. 14 of 1947.
50. See, inter alia, the Industrial Disputes Act, 1947 (hereinafter, 'ID Act'), sections 9D, 10, 10A, 12–15, 17–17A, 19, 22, 25A, 25F, 25FFA, 25K, 25M, 25N, 25O, 34, 36B.
51. ID Act, section 9B.
52. ID Act, section 22.
53. ID Act, sections 25K, 25M, 25N, 25O.
54. ID Act, sections 25A, 25F, 25FFA.

55. ID Act, section 25FFA.
56. ID Act, sections 10, 12–15, 17A, 34.
57. ID Act, section 10A.
58. See the Minimum Wages Act, 1948 (Act no. 11 of 1948). Also see Equal Remuneration Act, 1976 (Act no. 25 of 1976 as amended by Act no. 49 of 1987).
59. Minimum Wages Act, 1948 (Act no. 11 of 1948). Also see the Working Journalists (Fixation of Rates of Wages) Act, 1958 (Act no. 29 of 1958); Working Journalists and Other Newspaper Employees (Conditions of Service) and Miscellaneous Provisions Act, 1955 (Act no. 45 of 1955).
60. See the Factories Act, 1948 (Act no. 63 of 1948); Plantations Labour Act, 1951 (Act no. 69 of 1951); Mines Act, 1952 (Act no. 35 of 1952); Motor Transport Workers Act, 1961 (Act no. 27 of 1961); Beedi and Cigar Workers (Conditions of Employment) Act, 1966 (Act no. 32 of 1966); Contract Labour (Regulation and Abolition) Act, 1970 (Act no. 37 of 1970); Inter-State Migrant Workmen (Regulation of Employment and Conditions of Service) Act, 1979 (Act no. 30 of 1979); Dock Workers (Safety, Health and Welfare) Act, 1986 (Act no. 54 of 1986); Building and Other Construction Workers (Regulation of Employment and Conditions of Service) Act, 1996 (Act no. 27 of 1996).
61. See the Payment of Bonus Act, 1965 (Act no. 21 of 1965).
62. Supriya Routh, *Enhancing Capabilities through Labour Law: Informal Workers in India* (Abingdon and New York: Routledge, 2014), 36–40.
63. Routh, *Enhancing Capabilities through Labour Law*, 38–40, 60–63.
64. Routh, *Enhancing Capabilities through Labour Law*, 59–69.
65. For a discussion, see Routh, *Enhancing Capabilities through Labour Law*, 68–69, 190–195.
66. Supriya Routh, 'Informal Workers' Aggregation and Law', *Theoretical Inquiries in Law* 17, no. 1 (2016): 283–320.
67. See *Bangalore Water Supply and Sewerage Board v. A. Rajappa and Others*, AIR 1978 SC 548.
68. See the Industrial Disputes (Amendment) Act, 1982 (Act no. 46 of 1982). The definition of 'industry' as enacted – but not brought in force – through the Industrial Disputes (Amendment) Act, 1982, formed the basis of the current definition of 'industry' under the Industrial Relations Code, 2020 (hereafter, 'IR Code'), albeit in a modified manner. See IR Code (Act no. 35 of 2020), section 2(p).
69. See *State of UP v. Jai Vir Singh*, 2005 MANU 0360 SC.
70. *State of UP v. Jai Vir Singh*, 2005 MANU 0360 SC, paras. 40–41.

71. See *Secretary, State of Karnataka and Others v. Umadevi and Others*, 2006 (4) SCC 1. Also see, generally, Supriya Routh, 'Developing Human Capabilities through Law: Is Indian Law Failing?' *Asian Journal of Law and Economics* 3, no. 1 (2012): Article 4 (1–20), for a discussion on the Supreme Court's neoliberal turn; Ramapriya Gopalakrishnan, 'Labour Jurisprudence of the Supreme Court: Recent Trends', in *Labour, Employment and Economic Growth in India*, ed. K. V. Ramaswamy, 292–318 (Delhi: Cambridge University Press, 2015), for an analysis of the prominence of economic reasoning – as opposed to constitutional or legal reasonings – in the Supreme Court's decisions after liberalisation of the Indian economy. Gopalakrishnan notes that in spite of other judicial articulations on the basis of social justice, equity and non-discrimination, the economic rationale has become the dominant approach of the apex court.
72. *Secretary, State of Karnataka and Others v. Umadevi and Others*, 2006 (4) SCC 1, para. 16.
73. IR Code, sections 28, 29, 30.
74. IR Code, section 30(7).
75. IR Code, ch. 10.
76. IR Code, section 78.
77. IR Code, section 79.
78. IR Code, section 80.
79. IR Code, section 74. For a broader critique of the IR Code, see Aishwarya Bhuta, 'Imbalancing Act: India's Industrial Relations Code, 2020', *Indian Journal of Labour Economics* 65 (2022): 821–830.
80. IR Code, sections 3, 4.
81. Code on Wages, 2019 (Act no. 29 of 2019), sections 3, 5, 6, 8, 9, 11, 13, 14 (hereinafter, 'Wage Code').
82. See Santanu Sarkar, 'The 2019 Code on Wages: Truth versus Hype', *Indian Journal of Industrial Relations* 57, no. 1 (2021): 1–12, for a detailed critical discussion of the Wage Code.
83. Sarkar, 'The 2019 Code on Wages'.
84. Contract Labour (Regulation and Abolition) Act, 1970 (Act no. 37 of 1970).
85. Occupational Safety, Health and Working Conditions Code, 2020, sections 25, 26, 27, 28, 29, 30, 32 (hereinafter, 'OSH Code').
86. OSH Code, sections 6, 23, 24.
87. OSH Code, section 6(1)(f).
88. OSH Code, section 14.
89. OSH Code, section 13.

90. OSH Code, sections 18, 45, 47, 60, 62, 66, 68, 74, 78, 79, 81, 82, 86, 87, 92, 93. For a critique of the recent reforms from the point of view of migrant workers, see Somanshu Shukla and Aryan Bhat, 'Migrant Workers in Unorganised Sector: Socio-Legal and Policy Analysis', in *Labour Law Reforms 2021*, ed. Jeet Singh Mann, 387–416 (Delhi: Centre for Transparency and Accountability in Governance, 2021).
91. OSH Code, section 18(4).
92. OSH Code, sections 23(2), 24(1), 34, 35.
93. OSH Code, sections 43, 44.
94. OSH Code, sections 24(1)(viii).
95. See, generally, OSH Code, ch. 12. The general nature of damages in breach of contract is compensatory, not punitive.
96. Wage Code, section 26.
97. Wage Code, section 26(1).
98. Wage Code, sections 26(3), 31, 32, 33, 34, 40.
99. Wage Code, section 60.
100. OSH Code, section 127.
101. OSH Code, section 127(2).
102. OSH Code, section 128.
103. The state governments' attempts to suspend labour laws will be discussed in Chapter 3.

# 3

# Solidarity and Social Welfare

## Introduction

The Constitution of India promises equality of status and opportunity to the citizens.[1] It entrusts a specific duty on the state to *minimise* inequalities in income and *eliminate* inequalities in status, facilities and opportunities through social welfare.[2] The aim of the social welfare provisioning by the state is to promote equality of opportunities – with a view to rectifying opportunity gaps of particularly disadvantaged citizens and groups – so that their wealth and earning inequalities are kept to a minimum.[3] Such provisioning has to be secure and sustainable to meet the mandate of equality contemplated under the Constitution.[4] In fact, the state is mandated to secure a decent standard of life, including social and cultural opportunities, for *all workers* through their work.[5] It is, thus, the state's constitutional duty to pursue *equitable outcomes* for all workers irrespective of the nature of their work and their organisation. This is a broader mandate than the achievement of a decent life through market-based employment relationships. It is a mandate of equity wherein no worker should be left behind in achieving a fulfilling life through work. At the same time, this constitutional mandate is not a guarantee of work. The aim is the achievement of the *decent life* by means of work. If work – that is, *human agency* – should be the basis of an equitable decent life, the state must also secure social provisioning linked to work in order to facilitate the decent life of workers when work (including opportunities to work) falls short of delivering such a life. This specific constitutional concern for workers is an instance of the more general concern for the equitable treatment of disadvantaged citizens and groups through social welfare.

As discussed in Chapter 2, the Constitution creates a space for the operation of workers' individual agency through market exchanges. This is important from the constitutional perspective because individual agency is the basis of the ideal of worker-citizens, as analysed in Chapter 1. However, as noted earlier, the worker-citizen is not an exclusively individualistic ideal. The ideal also signifies a deep relationship with the state. The Constitution entrusts the nation-building initiative to worker-citizens and expects them to be industrious in this collective undertaking. Thus, in spite of the prima facie focus on individual agency, there exists a deep social relationality to the idea of the worker-citizen. Worker-citizens are bound to the state and fellow citizens through their industriousness and contribution. They are part of the social collective rather than merely isolated market participants. This social, non-market, relationality is the foundation of 'fraternity', or solidarity, under the Constitution. The idea of solidarity – social connectedness – signifies that society is under an obligation to support worker-citizens' constitutional claim to a decent, dignified life. Just as individual agency is necessary for such dignified life, public services through social support are also essential for such life.[6] The complementarity of individual agency and social support is also foundational to the Constitution, as expressed through the principle of the basic structure (see the discussion of the basic structure in Chapter 1). The provision for social support recognises that market access is often inequitable and that power relationships in market exchanges frequently impede the realisation of an agency-focused, dignified life. Legal entitlement to social welfare, while recognising the contribution made by worker-citizens, consolidates their ability to achieve a decent life.

Social welfare in the Indian Constitution has two roles. It is both intrinsically important for the well-being of workers and instrumental in expanding opportunities for workers to enable their successful market participation. These roles of social welfare – social security – are well recognised by the Supreme Court. Social security has been declared as an integral part of the justiciable right to life by the court.[7] The very identification of social security as a component of the fundamental right to life signifies that social support is considered intrinsically important for individual workers. That individual workers can enforce their right to social security means that it does not have to be justified on another ground except that it is important for the well-being of every worker. The nature of justiciable rights also means that social security provisioning does not depend on the discretion of the state. Instead of being an executive policy choice, secure social provisioning is an obligatory duty of the state. Additionally, as noted in Chapter 1, social security provisioning is constitutive of the idea of dignity under the Constitution.[8] The ideal of solidarity, practically realised through public support for health, nutrition, education, disability, sickness, unemployment, maternity benefits, employment injury, old age, and so on, consolidates the deep account of dignity under the Constitution.[9] Leading a dignified life by relying on an expansive range of social support is important by itself, an 'expression of the human-self'.[10]

Social security provisioning is also instrumentally important for creating conditions wherein workers are able to successfully employ their agency – personal labour – to benefit from the market. Public provisioning of health, nutrition, education and training helps workers develop their marketable skills. These skills enable them to successfully participate in the market, eventually contributing to their well-being through market-based resource distribution. This opportunity-promoting role of social security as a means to enable (that is, empower) citizens for autonomous action has also been emphasised by the Supreme Court in its understanding of human dignity.[11] As noted, it is also important to recognise that by so participating in the market, worker-citizens also contribute to national development, as the Constitution envisages (see Chapter 1). In this respect, social security is not only important for a worker's individual benefit but also eventually supports the development of the nation.

Social security entitlements should occupy a particularly prominent position in India in view of the sheer heterogeneity of market-based employment relationships and non-market working relationships in the country. This need for prominence sits uneasily with the way social security is conventionally conceived. Although social security is central for workers who do not work under stable employment contracts, the very nature of the conventional imagination of social security as a long-term contributory scheme tied to an employment relationship does not function for workers who work under insecure conditions with low pay and face periods of unemployment.[12] Since the significant majority of workers in India work under informal working relationships, often characterised by insecure and unstable working conditions, the conventional social security framework remains inoperable for their situation. Yet informal workers are the ones who need social security the most. Accordingly, social security entitlements must be conceived differently for informal workers without compromising the comprehensiveness of such social security protection. In addition to the range of informal workers, newer technology-induced forms of working relationships such as online platform-based on-demand work (that is, gig work) and increasing automation in work also require comprehensive social security protection for workers. Although social security entitlements should be differently organised for these heterogeneous categories of workers, the comprehensiveness of such entitlements must be assessed with reference to the existing entitlements for formal workers. It is through this comparative evaluation that equal treatment – equal potential to a decent and dignified life – of formal and informal workers (that is, *all* workers) could be assessed (recall that the Constitution promises all workers equitable opportunities to lead a decent life).

While the Constitution does not specify the exact meaning of the fundamental right to equality, it is the basis for the comparative evaluation of social security entitlements among various categories of workers, falling under the two broad classificatory groups of formal and informal.[13] It will, however, be unreasonable to expect that both formal and informal workers receive identical social security entitlements because of Article 14's mandate ('equal protection of the laws'). What is reasonable is to expect that in its comprehensiveness social security entitlements should be roughly comparable between the two groups even when specific entitlements are adapted to their respective contexts. In evaluating legislative entitlements on the ground of equality, the Supreme Court has mostly favoured a formal understanding of equality that analyses legal entitlements in their ability to satisfy the 'classification test'.[14] The classification test examines whether an impugned law's classification (distinction between coverage and exclusion from entitlements) is based on an understandable difference and whether such classification is reasonable for the purpose of the law.[15]

In examining the law, what the classification test ignores is the *discriminatory effect* of laws and legal inaction (that is, omission to enact laws) on specific groups even when such laws satisfy the aforementioned test (of including or excluding specific groups for particular entitlements).[16] Thus, state inaction to offer social security entitlements for certain groups of workers will not attract the scrutiny of the court.[17] But preferential treatment of particularly disadvantaged workers (to minimise inequality) may end up drawing the scrutiny of the court.[18] However, the Indian judiciary (including the Supreme Court) is gradually taking note of the drawbacks in its understanding of equality and offering occasional reflections on a more substantive approach to equality.[19] Substantive equality scrutinises 'actual impact of the law' on individuals and groups rather than the internal logic of legal entitlements.[20] On this evaluation, legal entitlements meet the equality mandate when they are able to eradicate 'actual inequality of disadvantaged groups in society'.[21] Failure of a law to take cognisance of specific needs of disadvantaged groups amounts to discrimination.[22]

The following section discusses social security entitlements of the formal workforce in the country. This section emphasises that even though social security entitlements are expansive for formal workers, because of the numerical threshold for their applicability to a workplace and restrictive judicial interpretation of formal employment relationships, the benefits of such protection traditionally only reached a small minority of workers. The second section examines social security entitlements of informal workers. Social security entitlements of informal workers are analysed in the backdrop of the constitutional ambition to 'minimise inequality' by means of social welfare. This section compares social security entitlements of informal workers with those of formal workers employing the conceptual lens of substantive equality. The third section shows the restrictive nature of social security protection under the latest reforms. By drawing attention to the fact that the relationship between market freedom and social solidarity is integral under the constitutional social justice framework, this section examines how the latest reforms fail to complement increased labour market insecurities with an extensive and stable social welfare framework for both formal and informal workers. The conclusion leads to the next chapter.

## Social Security for Formal Workers

Formal workers have traditionally been entitled to an expansive range of social security provisions in India. Social security entitlements included social insurance, contributory savings (provident fund), compensation for employment-related injury, gratuitous payment at retirement, and so on.[23] Additionally, there have been sector-specific social security entitlements such as the *beedi* workers' welfare scheme, building and construction workers' welfare fund, journalists' gratuitous pay and cine workers' contributory savings and gratuitous payment provisions.[24] These parliamentary statutory entitlements have been supplemented by a range of state-level social security programmes.[25] These programmes primarily operated on the conventional logic of contributory social security provisioning, which is dependent on long-term stable employment relationships. Therefore, it is unsurprising that in spite of the significant social security coverage, a formidable number of workers have been left without any meaningful social protection because of their exclusion from the conventional model.[26]

Social security provisions have largely excluded the majority of the workers in the country who work under various working arrangements that do not fit the conventional employment model. The very category of informal economic activity, defined mainly for its characteristic differences from formal employment contracts, consists of workers working through divergent and often insecure work-based relationships. And since informal workers constitute the overwhelming majority of the Indian workforce, social security entitlements stayed limited to a small group of formal workers. The scope of social security has been further limited by the judiciary's narrow understanding of formal employment contracts. In interpreting employment contracts for the purpose of social insurance entitlement, the judiciary had sometimes resorted to an unduly restrictive understanding of the employment contract characterised by the employer's control and continuous monitoring of an employee.[27] This narrowing of the definition excluded certain formal workers – those who were not continuously monitored by employers – from the scope of some social security entitlements. Additionally, some social security entitlements were explicitly made applicable to workplaces employing at least ten or twenty workers, even if such workers were on long-term employment contracts.[28] Further, with increasing engagement of contract workers at the expense of regular long-term employees, the number of formal workers actually receiving social security entitlements dwindled.[29] As a result, some studies indicate that it is a small minority of the Indian workforce who de facto receive social security protection.[30]

If this small minority of the Indian workforce is taken to represent the well-protected formal workforce, they have had access to the most extensive set of social security entitlements. This extensive set included retirement savings funds, pension schemes, life and health insurance, employment injury benefits, disability benefits, dependants benefits, maternity benefits, limited unemployment benefits and post-employment gratuitous payment.[31] Of course, this range of social security entitlement for formal workers existed under the pre-reform labour law regime. As discussed in Chapter 2, one of the prominent features of the 2020 labour law reforms is the significant withdrawal of the state (that is, the government) from labour relations. By relieving most industries from having to seek governmental permission to lay off, terminate employment of workers or shut down industries, the reforms expose the Indian workforce to the uncertainties of the labour market in an unprecedented manner. As noted earlier, while this exposure to the market is not ultra vires the Constitution and remains within the scope of the permissible limits of the constitutional social justice rationale, it does disturb a long post-independence balance between capital and labour in the country. Under these circumstances, the mere coverage of social security entitlements (in absolute terms) through the current reforms cannot offer a proper evaluation of the reforms.

It is by comparing the social security entitlements under the current reforms with the earlier (pre-reform) regime and by contextualising such comparison in the backdrop of the state's retraction from labour relations that we can arrive at a fair evaluation of the current social security regime. With the retraction of the state, the labour law reforms not only allow an enlarged space for the operation of workers' autonomy, but also expose workers to the risks, uncertainties, inequities and power differentials of the labour market. This elevated exposure to market vulnerabilities must be complemented by a comparable social safety network in order to balance the contract-led and solidarity-based well-being of the workforce, which is the basis of the constitutional social justice programme. The following survey of the social security entitlements under the reforms shows that the reforms have largely failed to complement the added vulnerabilities of the workforce.

The Code on Social Security, 2020, aimed at extending social security to 'all employees and workers either in the [formal] or [informal] or any other sectors'.[32] Although the code fulfils this promise by offering informal and self-employed workers some social security coverage, the substantive entitlements offered under the code do not recompense the uncertainties of the market exposure introduced by the reforms. When the social security entitlements for formal workers are assessed, it becomes clear that the code merely continues the pre-existing (that is, pre-reform) entitlements. Workers in stable employment relationships are entitled to provident fund (retirement savings), pension (retirement benefits), medical and life insurance (coverage extended to families), maternity benefits, employment injury compensation and gratuitous payment at termination.[33] Legislative exclusions too are the continuation of the former regime. For example, workers are excluded from provident fund coverage if they are employed in a smaller workplace of fewer than twenty workers.[34] The threshold of provident fund coverage becomes fifty employees if the workplace is a cooperative operating without electricity. Legal entitlements to medical insurance and gratuitous payment on termination of employment are only available if a workplace has at least ten employees.[35] Unless a workplace is a factory, mine or plantation, access to maternity benefits is unavailable if there are fewer than ten employees.[36] Moreover, the government is empowered to exempt workplaces from the scope of some social security obligations.[37] These exemptions mean that even when workers are part of the formal employment contract, they may not always have access to a comprehensive social security framework.

One aspect of social security that requires specific attention is the legal entitlement to unemployment insurance. This evaluation has become particularly necessary because of the wider market exposure and expansion of formal contractual freedom initiated by the reforms. Since the reforms largely leave it to the workers and their employers to privately bargain their respective rights and obligations, the Constitution demands that workers' bargaining capacity be simultaneously improved and their (potentially) weak contractual entitlements be supplemented by a comprehensive social security protection. This is an exercise in legislative balance that the Constitution imposes on the legislature. A larger scope for freedom of contract must be complemented with an expansive social safety network. Unfortunately, however, Parliament failed to strike this balance through the labour law reforms. The market insecurities that workers are exposed to are disproportional to the security offered through unemployment insurance conceived under the reforms. The reforms merely continued the existing (that is, pre-reform) unemployment insurance programme instead of expanding on it.

Since 2005, the authority under the Employees' State Insurance Act (that is, the Employees' State Insurance Corporation) had initiated an unemployment insurance programme, namely the Rajiv Gandhi Shramik Kalyan Yojna, for workers who are insured under the Act.[38] Under the programme, workers could only receive unemployment insurance if they had made contributions under the Act for at least five years before receiving the insurance benefits. Unemployment benefits were available for a maximum period of twelve months during the entire period of insurable employment of a worker. While unemployment benefits could not be claimed in combination with sickness, maternity or disability benefits, workers and their families remained eligible for healthcare services from the Employees' State Insurance hospital (including doctors' and clinics' services). Workers were also entitled to reskilling benefits under the programme during their unemployment period. However, insured workers had access to this training only once in their entire working life. It is also important to note that this unemployment insurance was not available to workplaces with less than ten formal employees.[39] The Code on Social Security, 2020, continues this unemployment insurance entitlement for formal workers.

A second *experimental* unemployment insurance programme devised under the Act was the Atal Beemit Vyakti Kalyan Yojana.[40] This programme assured 50 per cent of daily average wage earned by insured workers in their employment during the period(s) of unemployment. To be eligible for the unemployment insurance, workers must have been in an insurable employment for a period of two years and in good standing with respect to their contribution to the programme for a specified period immediately before their unemployment. Workers were entitled to unemployment insurance only for three months during their period of unemployment (howsoever long the unemployment period may be). This was a one-time unemployment entitlement in a worker's entire working life. This programme began as a pilot project to be implemented for two years, from July 2018 to June 2020, but was later extended for another year in order to address the COVID-19-induced mass unemployment in the country.

In fact, the inadequacy of unemployment insurance – and social security protection in general – was exposed during the challenges posed to workers by the COVID-19 pandemic. Workers across the country faced a remarkably extreme version of market insecurities resulting from the interruption of economic activities induced by the pandemic.[41] Workers lost their work and source of income en masse; many were not paid by their employers; migrant workers struggled to feed themselves and to return home in the absence of work; some workers had to assume debt-bonds in order to survive and some others did not survive.[42] The government (that is, the Ministry of Home Affairs) ordered all employers to continue paying wages to their employees even when industrial activities were shut down because of the pandemic. Employers successfully challenged the governmental order in court until it ceased to remain operational (the government's order lasted for less than three months). While the Supreme Court denied a plea to enforce payment of wages during the industry closure (instead asking employers and employees to settle through renegotiation), the government (including state governments) announced cash support for certain categories of workers and increased wages for the Mahatma Gandhi National Rural Employment Guarantee Scheme workfare programme.[43] However, state support was remarkably inadequate to address the insecurities of unemployed workers, evident in the impoverishment, distress and death of workers during this time.[44]

During this time, the state's intervention was expansive but ad hoc. That the state needed to intervene extensively on an ad hoc basis – through cash transfers and income supports – to protect the Indian workforce during an acute period of market uncertainty (albeit with unsatisfactory results) goes on to demonstrate the very inadequacy of the existing social security entitlements. As discussed in Chapter 2, by means of the labour law reforms Parliament exposes the Indian workforce to increased risks of the market by withdrawing governmental monitoring and supervision. It is true that COVID-19 presented an extreme version of market insecurities, which is unlikely to be a regular phenomenon. However, it is also true that risks and uncertainties are inherent in market-based exchanges. And when such risks materialise, the private contractual framework (that is, market freedom) is inadequate to promote fairness and justice for workers, as is evident in the failure of the governmental order to compel private employers to keep paying wages during industry closure.

Although the latest reforms expose workers to increased market risks, they fail to complement such risks with elevated social security entitlements for workers, instead choosing to continue the existing limited social security entitlements for formal workers. Except for the temporary extension of unemployment insurance during the COVID-19 pandemic, pre-reform social security entitlements have not been expanded for formal workers alongside the substantial changes introduced through the labour law reforms. Accordingly, the current social security regime – unemployment insurance in particular – in combination with the market-promoting reforms, fails to strike the constitutional social justice balance. While this lack of balance exposes formal workers to increased insecurities, the lopsidedness of the reforms has a particularly adverse effect on informal workers, as will be noted in the following section.

## Social Security for Informal Workers

If the purpose of social welfare provisioning by the state is to 'minimise inequalities' among the citizenry, there are two levels of inquiry to examine social security entitlements.[45] The first is whether such entitlements are able to promote equality among all citizens (workers). This is a question of adequacy that seeks to know whether legal entitlements to social security are comprehensive and substantial enough to realise socio-economic equality. The previous section engaged in this analysis in reference to formal workers. The second level of inquiry involves a comparison of social security entitlements between different groups – formal and informal workers – in order to assess the equity of their entitlements. This second level of inquiry, then, involves asking questions about 'substantive equality', whereby, instead of comparing the legal entitlements, its effect on minimising inequality (between the groups) is compared.[46] In order to meet the demand of substantive equality, the state needs to do more for more vulnerable groups in order to minimise the inequality between the more vulnerable groups and other less vulnerable groups. Translated in the present context, social security entitlements may need to be more expansive for informal workers than they are for formal workers if inequality between informal and formal workers is to be actually minimised. This section evaluates social security entitlements of informal workers by following this second level of inquiry.

The Code on Social Security promises to extend social security to all workers irrespective of the formal or informal nature of their working arrangements, thereby aiming to achieve the constitutional mandate of equality.[47] The code continues and consolidates the existing substantive social security entitlements for informal ('unorganised') workers, developed under the Unorganised Workers Social Security Act, 2008 (even though the Act itself is repealed).[48] The code directs the central and state governments to create 'suitable welfare schemes' on life insurance and disability coverage, health and maternity benefits, old-age benefits, provident fund support, employment injury benefits, housing support, educational support (including for children), skill upgradation, funeral assistance and old-age homes for informal workers.[49] However, the code leaves it to the discretion of the central government to devise suitable social security schemes for on-demand ('gig') and (online) platform-based workers on subject matters such as life insurance and disability coverage, accident insurance, health and maternity benefits, old-age protection and childcare facility.[50] In devising the various schemes, the governments are to act under the advice of the (national and state) social security boards for informal workers.[51] In pursuance to the objective of the code, the central government as well as the state governments have formulated various social security schemes for informal workers.[52] Although some measures of life and disability insurance, old-age insurance and pension security are provided through these governmental programmes, a prominent deficiency is the absence of any unemployment insurance for informal workers (just as in the situation with formal workers).

However, informal workers are far more vulnerable to market insecurities compared to formal workers. Even after the significant governmental withdrawal from formal workers' employment relationships, they still benefit from governmental oversight and protection if they work in a larger workplace. On the contrary, informal workers never had (nor do they now) much governmental oversight or intervention in their market-based exchange relationships. There had never been a legal minimum standard in labour exchange-based relationships involving informal workers. Informal workers' market relations are overwhelmingly 'private' in the sense that parties to exchange relations (employer, employee, intermediary, on-demand worker, unwaged worker, dependent worker, debt bonded worker, own-account worker and self-employed worker) – howsoever unequal their bargaining positions are – interact only on the basis of their respective strengths (of labour and capital). Historically, the state's almost complete absence in these labour exchanges turned these exchanges into exploitative relations. Since the state's traditional regulatory emphasis has been on shaping formal employment contracts in miniscule details in order to promote fairness in employment relationships, it becomes incumbent that the state significantly expands its social security protection for informal workers, not only to meet the constitutional standards of fairness (social justice) but also to rectify the historical wrong of turning a blind eye to the well-being of informal workers.

Overcoming the lack of capacity and power of informal workers to participate in market exchanges and supporting them when they encounter market insecurities would, then, require substantially more resources than currently available to formal workers. Informal workers' deep-rooted insecurities were laid bare during the COVID-19 pandemic. An International Labour Organization (ILO) report pointed out that about 400 million workers in the informal economy in India were at the risk of slipping into abject poverty because of the COVID-19-induced lockdown of the country.[53] Another ILO report noted that the predominant 'coping strategy' of small and medium-sized enterprises, engaging mostly informal workers, was to temporarily or permanently lay off workers.[54] Although governments at various levels offered some makeshift support to informal workers, this support was neither adequate nor popular among the workers and enterprises.[55] Instead, workers preferred to rely on their kinship and social network for support, including by accepting credit from friends, relatives and banks; migrating back home; resorting to farming and using savings to cover the cost of living.[56] What the pandemic has shown is the complete lack of a comprehensive social security benefit, including unemployment insurance, for informal workers in the country, which relegated informal workers to a particularly precarious position. The most vulnerable groups were the informal workers who had to migrate to another region or state in search of work.[57] The absence of an unemployment insurance was particularly damaging for these informal workers.[58]

However, during this particularly precarious time, informal workers received some innovative, even though sporadic, support at the local administrative level, including the declaration of their work as 'essential services' and special permission to undertake their work during the lockdowns.[59] Even if scant, these instances indicate that often additional – and innovative – entitlements need to be carved out in order to address extreme vulnerabilities suffered by certain groups such as informal workers. There is a valid justificatory basis to advocate a more extensive social security protection for informal workers compared to that of formal workers. As noted earlier, the Constitution values minimising inequalities among the citizenry through law as well as equal protection of laws to all citizens. However, the predominant judicial understanding of the idea of equal protection of laws, as the laws' ability to make valid distinctions with respect to the aims of the law, somewhat limits the judiciary's ability to examine the failure of laws to minimise (de facto) inequality among citizens and groups.[60]

That minimising inequality cannot be achieved merely by questioning the internal logic of law (that is, the idea of formal equality) must be understood by the judiciary. It is the idea of substantive equality – which recognises that differential entitlement to legal rights among different groups may, in effect, result in a more equal outcome – that should be employed to evaluate social security entitlements of informal workers. That informal workers receive similar social security protection as formal workers even though they are a more vulnerable group is, in fact, contrary to the idea of substantive equality. The quest for equal protection of laws in a formal sense (discussed earlier) hinders the realisation of social welfare-based minimisation of inequalities. Although the Supreme Court understands the right to equality mainly in a formal sense, the concept of substantive equality is inherent in constitutional safeguards on non-discrimination and equal opportunity to public employment, wherein the state is expected to expend additional resources for particularly vulnerable populations.[61] What follows is that the principle of substantive equality necessitates that the state formulate a more expansive social security entitlement for informal workers that includes a secure unemployment insurance to reduce inequalities between informal and formal workers. The following section offers a fuller evaluation of social security protection under the reforms.

## Restricted Scope of Social Security under the Reforms

One would expect that when workers are exposed to scantly regulated market conditions, in order to meet the constitutional mandate of social justice that seeks to strike a balance between individual liberty and social solidarity, legislative reforms would correspondingly expand social security protection for such workers in order to facilitate their overall well-being.[62] As noted, although the latest labour law reforms liberalise the labour market, they fail to correspondingly expand social security protection for the Indian workforce. With respect to formal workers, the reforms merely continued the social security entitlements that existed earlier. However, prior to the reforms, social security entitlements existed alongside a labour market framework that operated under the close watch of the government. If the coverage of social security remained constant before and after reforms, and if the post-reform period is characterised by increased exposure of workers to market insecurities, the only conclusion that could be drawn is that the social security coverage under the reforms is weak and falls short of meeting the constitutional balance.

By the same logic, social security coverage of informal workers fails to meet the constitutional burden. Having continued the social security entitlements of formal workers from the former regime, the reforms empowered the government (and the social security boards) to create social welfare schemes for informal workers with coverage that is similar to those for formal workers. The social welfare schemes – on life insurance, old-age benefits, accidental death insurance and pension plans – designed by the government for informal workers generally tried to replicate what existed for formal workers before the reforms. This reasoning in formulating social security entitlements for informal workers suffers from an inherent flaw – namely, it completely ignores the fact that even when formal workers received governmental oversight in their market relations (that is, employment contracts), informal workers' heterogeneous market-based relationships operated without any governmental monitoring.

This absence of monitoring resulted in prolonged exploitation and marginalisation of informal workers. By further reducing the role of governmental oversight, the reforms exacerbate the vulnerabilities of informal workers. The additional risks and insecurities of informal workers are discounted and are not seriously addressed through the reforms. In absence of governmental oversight, any possibility of fairness in informal working relationships could be introduced only through comprehensive social security entitlements. However, informal workers' social security coverage cannot be a replication of the coverage offered to formal workers because of the enormous heterogeneity in informal working relationships. Such coverage should be sensitive to the contextual needs of informal workers.

The social security regime under the reforms is also problematic with respect to its adequacy. The idea of adequacy is different from that of coverage discussed earlier. While coverage means whether or not an aspect is *addressed* by social security entitlements, adequacy signifies whether or not resources offered as entitlements are *reasonable* for the specific purpose for which it is offered. That the social security regime is inadequate is evident from the weak safeguards it offered against increased insecurities of workers. Prominently, that unemployment insurance is available to formal workers for only one year in their entire working lives is astounding. Equally inadequate are the reskilling benefits, which could be accessed only once in a worker's lifetime.

That the state had to create a range of temporary benefits for the entire workforce during the pandemic is itself an acknowledgement that the statutorily enumerated permanent social security entitlements were not 'secure' enough to safeguard workers from the insecurities of loss of work and income. The ad hoc unemployment insurance secured 50 per cent of wages for workers for only three months irrespective of the duration of their unemployment. These unemployment benefits are grossly insufficient compared to the risks faced by workers. Additionally, as an ILO report noted, governmental support programmes created for informal workers and enterprises were not extremely popular among the workers and enterprises.[63]

Instead, informal workers relied on their personal support system of relatives and friends. This lack of worker interest in accessing governmental programmes may have been a reflection of the inadequacy of these programmes. In any case, none of these ad hoc measures are comparable to a secure unemployment insurance that can counterbalance the increased market insecurities of both informal and formal workers.

The latest reforms are also problematic at two further levels. First, the 'legal right' to social security offered by the reforms is the right to the various social security organisations (boards and corporations), not substantive claims to resources (or support). Although this is largely true for both formal and informal workers, because of the long history of substantive social security protection for formal workers and a history of exclusion of informal workers from social security entitlements, formal workers' entitlements are on a more secure legal ground and are often also statutorily enumerated. Second, although the reforms create a deliberation-based social security provisioning (through the boards), which should be ideal for understanding informal workers' heterogeneous contextual needs, they simultaneously narrow the deliberative space and weaken the scope for collective action by workers (as will be discussed in the next chapter). There is a predominance of governmental control in the social security organisations, thereby stunting the possibility of a truly embodied, experience-based formulation of legal entitlements. The weakening of the deliberative space, in turn, dilutes social security entitlements, particularly for informal workers. These two issues are discussed in turn.

There exists some level of formal equality before the law insofar as the social security entitlements of formal and informal workers are concerned. For both of these categories of workers, the Code on Social Security establishes various social security organisations, which are to create (with governmental support) substantive social security entitlements. In practice, however, one of the prominent differences between social security entitlements of formal workers and those of informal workers is that while substantive social security entitlements have become legal claims for the former, substantive entitlements are subject to governmental discretion (and the board's advice) for the latter. Informal workers' only legal right is to the constitution of the social security boards.[64]

Although the language of the Code on Social Security allows some discretion to the central government to formulate social security schemes on employees' (that is, formal workers) provident fund, pension and insurance, as we have seen from the discussions earlier, formal workers are already legally entitled to these schemes since they have been in operation for a while.[65] In keeping with the character of legal entitlements, formal workers' entitlements are specific and detailed. An instance of a specific legal entitlement (as distinguished from a duty imposed on the government to create a scheme) for formal workers under the code is as follows: 'every employee in an establishment ... *shall be insured*'.[66] Further, the code specifies how the employees' state insurance fund should be generated and managed and what benefits to insured workers are to be offered through such a fund.[67] Comparable specific and detailed statutory entitlements are absent for informal workers, who must depend on the government's willingness and ability to create an executive scheme. For example, compare the insurance entitlement of informal workers with that of the formal workers mentioned earlier: 'the Central Government *may ... frame [an insurance] scheme* for unorganised workers, gig workers and platform workers and the members of their families for providing benefits.'[68]

This inconsistency is as far away from any idea of substantive equality as it is possible. As noted earlier, the role of social security is to facilitate roughly equal outcomes for workers irrespective of their engagement in formal or informal working arrangements. In this sense, social security entitlements of informal workers should compare with those of formal workers in their outcome. If formal workers are legally entitled to provident funds, pensions, health insurance, unemployment insurance, maternity benefits, gratuities, and so on, informal workers should require a broader set of legally secured resources to be less unequal with formal workers. Although governmental schemes have been created under the code for informal workers, they are less comprehensive and, therefore, fail the test of substantive equality. Additionally, the indeterminate nature of the legal right to social security fails to 'secure' the basis of potential equal outcome for informal workers.

There is, however, a reasonable justification for the indeterminate nature of the social security protection for informal workers. As discussed, informal workers are designated on the basis of their difference from formal workers. At the same time, informal working arrangements are heterogeneous and abundant. Accordingly, social security protection for informal workers cannot possibly function on the same model that is conventionally used for formal employment relationships. The heterogeneity of informal working arrangements means that contextual insecurities and, correspondingly, welfare needs of various categories of informal workers are bound to be widely different. It makes sense, then, to allow substantive social security entitlements to emerge from contextual participatory deliberation by informal workers themselves. What follows is that the social security board-based creation of contextual legal entitlements should be more effective in addressing the market insecurities of informal workers since they will emerge from embodied experiences of such workers.

This rationale is consistent with the function of the social security boards under the Code on Social Security. The boards' functions include recommending the government(s) suitable social security schemes for different categories of informal workers, including on-demand and online platform-based workers.[69] The boards are also to monitor the implementation of the social security schemes formulated under the code, advise the governments on the administration of the code, review funding and records related to the social security schemes and perform other functions assigned by the government(s). However, membership of these statutory boards consists of government ministers (for the central and the state governments) of labour and employment, public service officers and representatives of informal (and gig or platform-based) workers, employers in the informal sector, eminent individuals from the civil society, various legislators and other government officials.[70] The various representative members of the boards are also nominated by the government, and the government retains the power to remove members from the board.[71] Board members' tenure, thus, continues at the pleasure of the government. The government also controls the functioning and decision-making capacities of the social security boards by retaining the power to authenticate 'all orders and decisions' of the board.[72] Thus, although the board could have institutionalised grassroots deliberative law-making for informal workers, in its constitution it ended up becoming a de facto bureaucratic front for the government under the reforms. Both the constitution of the board and the narrowing of the deliberative space, then, end up being detrimental to the interests of workers.

## The Social Security Boards and the Potential for an Expansive Industrial Relations Framework

As we have seen, instead of legal rights to extensive social security safeguards, informal workers are legally entitled to the constitution of social security boards under the Code on Social Security. Informal workers' social security is to be mediated and facilitated by the boards. In spite of the shortcomings of the board-centred mechanism to social security provisioning identified earlier, if reflectively put into practice – without the governmental attempt to pre-empt workers' dialogical space – the boards may serve as models for institutionalised dialogue bridging formal electoral democracy with organic and differently structured contextual deliberation. The institutionalisation of contextual deliberation integrates informal workers into the broader scheme of industrial democracy without subsuming their capabilities and agency into the conventional legal structure of industrial relations. Such institutionalisation may lead to decentralised deliberative law-making, thereby facilitating the formulation of informal workers' aspirations as valid legal claims. To be sure, this imagination may not be the natural trajectory of the boards as conceived under the code, but the potential for the boards to reinvigorate industrial democracy for informal workers in the country does exist in principle. In this section of the chapter, I focus on this potential.

As we have seen, during the pandemic, instead of taking advantage of government-created social security programmes, informal workers preferred to rely on their kinship- and friendship-based social support systems. This reliance on (informal) social solidarity could be predominantly seen in practices of temporary credit systems and farming and agricultural practices of unemployed workers. The use of non-state social support systems during an emergency (such as the COVID-19 pandemic) is not an aberration. In fact, informal workers are often more familiar with these types of 'informal' (familial or organic) social support systems. Informal sources of credit often include local moneylenders, friends, relatives, traders and shopkeepers and employers or landlords.[73] Institutions of social identity such as gender, caste, religion, ethnicity, language, locality and life cycle have been known to have developed social support entitlements for informal workers on the basis of such identities.[74] Informal entitlements secured through these social institutions cover situations such as temporary and permanent unemployment, skilling and reskilling (or credentialisation) of workers and temporary aid provisioning during emergencies.[75] Households and kinship are often the basis of help during emergencies.[76]

Frequently, undervalued and unpaid care work performed by households constitutes the unrecognised conditions of social security for informal workers. Care work includes provisioning for fuel, fodder, forest produce, land care and animal care for the family, all of which go on to expand overall family (and community) resources and offer cushioning from the insecurities of market exchanges.[77] By expanding family (and community) resources, care work offers 'hidden subsidies' to the market economy.[78] However, care work largely remains framed as a private concern in spite of its role in supporting the foundational conditions of market exchange and social cooperation. In fact, unpaid care work, which is gendered and seen as a form of social assistance, often impacts the state's decision to spend less on social protection programmes.[79] This (unrecognised) social subsidy in the form of social assistance, offered primarily by women workers to the society and informal workers in particular, then, relaxes the obligation of the state to offer a comprehensive social assistance programme.[80] This relationship between care work and the state's obligation to provide social security has been noted by economists. Economists have shown the direct impact of austerity measures, whereby a state's public expenditure is substantially curbed, on the expansion and intensity of unpaid care work.[81] Informal women workers often supplement their paid work with unpaid care work of varying degrees of intensity.[82] More recently, there has been some recognition of women's unpaid work in workfare programmes such as the Mahatma Gandhi National Rural Employment Guarantee Act (MGNREGA), 2005, and in legal entitlements under the Forest Rights Act, 2006.[83]

In addition to the (broadly prevailing) household care-based social security provisioning, workers' collective action sometimes secures social security for informal workers. A prominent example of a gender-based collective action leading to extensive social security provisioning for informal workers is that of the Self-Employed Women's Association (SEWA), a trade union of women workers. SEWA-initiated social security programmes include provision for targeted savings for pensions, educational expenses, housing, wedding expenses and credit facilities through the SEWA Bank (SEWA Women's Cooperative Bank); life insurance; health and dental care insurance; childcare insurance; maternity benefits; insurance against loss of assets; and so on.[84] These social security provisions are developed in the unique circumstances of extremely poor heterogeneous informal workers. Accordingly, they employ novel strategies in guaranteeing entitlements. For example, the SEWA Bank's strategies for identifying creditworthiness of its informal worker clients are unconventional and contextually attuned, which takes into account factors such as a non-alcoholic husband as an asset and 'the goodwill of one's caste' as an asset.[85] SEWA has innovated a range of gender-based social security provisioning through the direct participation of informal women workers themselves. SEWA's founder, Ela Bhatt, emphasised: 'It is SEWA policy that all its services should be run, owned, managed and used by the worker-members themselves.'[86] Although SEWA is one of the most prominent women's organisations in the country, it is not the only one working towards furthering social security for women informal workers.[87] A range of other non-state organisations seek to further social security for informal workers in India. Like SEWA, the orientation of these organisations is to offer innovative and contextual social security entitlements for informal workers based on direct participation and continued engagement from such workers.

In addition to gender-based social security provisioning, a range of formal and informal religion- and caste-based social security opportunities are sometimes available to informal and migrant (formal or informal) workers.[88] These social security structures are accessed by workers on the basis of (religion-, caste- and place-of-origin-based) closed networks. 'While it divides so mercilessly, the caste system also unites.... Within the same caste, bonds between caste members are strong, providing unquestioned loyalty and *a great sense of security*.'[89] Some of these networks operate at the intersection of caste and gender.[90] These networks emerge on the basis of mutual recognition of social identities. Membership of these networks and the substance of social assistance received by workers depend on discursive practices among the providers and the beneficiaries of these networks. Some common social assistance programmes include credit provisioning, support for housing, emergency care, reskilling, access to jobs and unemployment assistance. While these are not always properly structured and are often not adequate, there are some useful substantive supports through these networks that many workers – particularly migrant workers – receive. Often, these unstructured and informal support systems are workers' stepping stones to more robust and better livelihood opportunities.

Some of the non-state social institutions offering social security are historically entrenched and predate the establishment of modern states in several parts of the globe, including India.[91] Accordingly, the bases on which these institutions offer social security predate the constitutional state and its secular institutions. Social institutions offering social security programmes often employ customary norms and non-institutional deliberative processes that remain outside the formal institutions of representative democracy.[92] These institutions often function on the basis of non-state social norms.[93] Citizens (particularly marginalised workers) are sometimes so accustomed to working with these social institutions that they find it difficult to navigate the formal institutions of the state. Therefore, even when citizens seek to access social security programmes developed by the state, they often rely on an intermediary – an individual or an informal organisation – to mediate their access to state-created social security entitlement. Thus, citizens' interaction with the state is often indirect and happens at the grassroots level without the direct engagement of formal institutions of governance.[94] Furthermore, there are sometimes contradictions between state-secured entitlements and non-state institution-promoted entitlements, which go on to complicate the state–citizen relationship on social security.[95]

In this backdrop, a general statement by the Code on Social Security on expanding social security coverage to promote inclusivity – integrating both formal and informal workers – will not suffice to meet the constitutional mandate.[96] The manner of such expansion, including how social security entitlements emerge from contextual deliberations and how ongoing engagement strengthen such entitlements, should be central in determining the strength of the social security framework. In this respect, the boards will need to learn how to engage with non-state social institutions and their deliberative practices. The boards will need to take cognisance of traditional rationales of social security. Relatedly, they should also take household and kinship-based social security provisioning seriously, acknowledging their significance for a substantial number of workers, even though the qualifying criteria for these social security entitlements are often non-secular and inegalitarian. This acknowledgement should begin also by the recognition of the role of unpaid care work in consolidating informal workers' overall social security. Since the nature of these engagements is complex and somewhat novel for formal state institutions, opening up deliberative space for a range of actors outside the formal industrial relations framework is essential for expanding the scope of social security provisioning for a diversity of workers. In particular, the social security boards are potentially useful in conceptualising and devising informal workers' social security programmes, meeting the demands of both the substantive scope and deliberative components of social security. The general principle of diversifying dialogue without domination by the government in creating social security entitlements for informal workers would go a long way in creating an effective social security framework for the country. And the diversification process needs to be mindful of the aforementioned complexities of informal workers' social security mechanisms.

To be sure, as important as they are for informal workers, the aforementioned social identity-based networks could sometimes be exploitative and extractive. Since they operate as closed networks, social relationship and kinship-based social security safeguards take advantage of workers' ignorance and their lack of wider connections to the institutions outside the networks. Provision for informal credit facilities is an area where exploitation is often visible in these networks.[97] Credit-recipient workers often remain bound to the moneylender (who is also often the employer) for a long term under conditions of high interest rates. These networks are mostly exclusive of other identities and discriminatory along identity lines.[98] They are also not egalitarian in their operation; often a strongman (the employer or moneylender) dictates the terms of the entitlements and obligations for the beneficiaries of his choosing. The terms of entitlements may change over time, and there is little that the beneficiaries can do for such uncertainties. Social norms dictating these relationships and, accordingly shaping the social security entitlements are predominantly based on inegalitarian principles. Social norm on care work is an example of the inegalitarian basis of social security. Deeply entrenched patriarchal social norms often compel women to offer unpaid care – social assistance – to workers for whom state-devised and non-state social security falls short.[99] Conversely, both state and non-state social security entitlements often operate with the assumption that informal workers are recipients of unpaid care-based support from their households, kin relations and friends.

The aforementioned problems, which often have historical roots, however, should also be seen in their proper context. One such context is the constrained access to governmental services and programmes (where they exist) by certain groups of workers. Access to governmental services is sometimes out of reach for some groups and individuals because of socially entrenched caste-based discrimination against them.[100] Government officials have been found to refuse to interact with and extend governmental entitlements to individuals from lower castes and minority religions.[101] While such refusal is formally illegal, there are rarely avenues that can aid such excluded workers or dissuade them from substantially relying on informal social support networks. As problematic as they may be, an engagement with these existing non-state structures of social protection and deliberation is essential to expand the horizon of conventional industrial relations. The rationale for such engagement is not to valorise social norms or non-state social security entitlements but to recognise that they operate alongside state laws and institutions of social security. The entanglement of formal and informal (that is, social) norms and institutions[102] should be recognised in order for the social security boards to become useful institutions for promoting social security by means of a more expansive industrial – deliberative – democracy for complex heterogeneous societies such as India. In this sense, the boards could embody a future of labour relations that is more diversified and exists beyond a single narrative of industrial relations.

Unfortunately, however, realising diversified labour relations and deliberative democracy engaging social norms through the boards, as they are now conceived, is improbable because of extensive governmental participation in the boards. Extensive governmental role in the boards forestalls participation from a range of actors embedded in the complex social security scenario in the country. Furthermore, one of the criticisms against some of the existing (pre-reform) state boards is that they are inactive in constituting deliberative committees and reluctant in allowing representations from workers for whom they develop social protection programmes.[103] If a similar trend persists in the new social security boards, the boards' potential to carry labour relations into the future will remain unfulfilled. Just as the governmental withdrawal from labour market relations under the reforms is problematic, governmental co-option of the deliberative space for social security is also unimaginative. The latter space should have been rightfully ceded to a range of informal workers and organisations of informal workers who could bring in their lived experiences of working informally under conditions of insecurity and precariousness, which could inform the policies and actions of the boards. Extensive participation from workers and their organisations is essential for developing nuanced contextual entitlements for heterogeneous workers. Often, a strong collective action is a precondition to such extensive participation in the law-making process. The next chapter examines the potential for workers' collective action under the post-reform labour law.

## Conclusion

During the economic and labour market upheavals caused by the pandemic, some state governments such as Uttar Pradesh, Gujarat and Madhya Pradesh decided to exempt businesses from the application of labour laws, including by suspending labour laws altogether.[104] While these attempts to bypass labour laws eventually failed, they now stand as a testimony of governmental attempts to undermine the Constitution.[105] In these attempts, the governments were making use of their legislative power (through ordinances) to intervene in the labour market, but their intervention was aimed at dispossessing workers of their legal (and constitutional) rights. These attempts demonstrate that there is no reason to remain optimistic about governmental intervention in labour relations (and lament governmental withdrawal from labour relations). By the same token, there is no guarantee that increasing governmental participation in devising social security entitlements is a sure mechanism for the efficacy of such entitlements. On the contrary, if the executive views labour laws with contempt, there are reasons to be alarmed of governmental interventions in the various social security organisations.

For reasons discussed in this chapter, the social security boards should primarily be led and run by workers' and employers' representatives (when they exist), in collaboration with civil society groups and some governmental participation. Until this arrangement is consolidated, there is good reason to advocate in favour of more concrete legal enumeration of social security protections for workers in the Code on Social Security, with some additional scope for the (representative) boards to nuance substantive social security safeguards for the specific contexts of heterogeneous workers. With increased risks in the labour market, social security has become a prominent and inseparable component of labour law. The long-term security and stability provided by the conventional labour relations framework must now be transferred to the realm of social security. It is by means of social security entitlements that the idea of solidarity finds practical expression in policymaking. Solidarity, of course, is an integral component of human dignity in India, which acknowledges the connectedness among worker-citizens in the nation-building enterprise. Unfortunately, the labour law reforms fail to balance the elevated insecurities of the labour market with a more expanded social security protection created on the basis of embodied experiences of various categories of workers. Emphasising embodied experiences as the foundational basis of law making would also mean a central position for institutions facilitating deliberations on the basis of lived experiences. This is where workers' collective action becomes a core component of the labour law narrative. In the following chapter, the scope of workers' collective action and participatory deliberation after the reforms will be discussed.

## Notes

1. See the Constitution of India, 1950, Preamble (hereinafter, 'Constitution').
2. Constitution, Article 38.
3. Constitution, Articles 38, 39, 41, 46.
4. Tarunabh Khaitan, *A Theory of Discrimination Law* (New York: Oxford University Press, 2015), 124–126, 130–131.
5. Constitution, Article 43.
6. Upendra Baxi, 'The Place of Dignity in the Indian Constitution', in *The Cambridge Handbook of Human Dignity: Interdisciplinary Perspectives*, ed. Marcus Düwell, Jens Braarvig, Roger Brownsword and Dietmar Mieth, 429–436 (Cambridge, UK: Cambridge University Press, 2014), 430–431.
7. *Calcutta Electricity Supply Corporation (India) Limited v. Subhash Chandra Bose*, AIR 1992 SC 573; *Regional Director, ESIC v. Francis D'Costa*, AIR 1995 SC 1811; *Consumer Education Research Centre (CERC) v. Union of India*, AIR 1995 SC 922.
8. Baxi, 'The Place of Dignity in the Indian Constitution'.
9. See Constitution, Articles 38, 41, 42, 45, 46, 47.
10. *Francis Coralie v. Union Territory of Delhi*, (1981) 2 SCR 516, 529. Also see *Bandhua Mukti Morcha v. Union of India*, (1984) 2 SCR 67.
11. See, generally, Baxi, 'The Place of Dignity in the Indian Constitution' (analysing dignity as empowerment).
12. Vicki Paskalia, *Free Movement, Social Security and Gender in the EU* (London: Hart, 2007), 39–41.
13. Constitution, Articles 14, 15, 16; Ratna Kapur, 'Gender Equality', in *The Oxford Handbook of the Indian Constitution*, ed. Sujit Choudhry, Madhav Khosla and Pratap Bhanu Mehta, 742–755 (Oxford: Oxford University Press, 2016), 744.
14. See, generally, Tarunabh Khaitan, 'Equality: Legislative Review under Article 14', in *The Oxford Handbook of the Indian Constitution*, ed. Sujit Choudhry, Madhav Khosla and Pratap Bhanu Mehta, 699–719 (Oxford: Oxford University Press, 2016), 701–705.
15. Khaitan, 'Equality'. The other test, sometimes relied on by the Supreme Court is the 'non-arbitrariness' test, which assesses legal entitlements on the basis of their ability to offer a rational basis for their action. By its very nature, this test is non-comparative and does not compare legislative coverage and exclusion of different groups and individuals.
16. Khaitan, 'Equality', 702–703, 705–706, 709–711.

17. Khaitan, 'Equality', 707–708.
18. Kapur, 'Gender Equality', 748–749.
19. Kapur, 'Gender Equality', 744–745.
20. Kapur, 'Gender Equality', 745–746.
21. Kapur, 'Gender Equality', 745 (internal citation omitted).
22. Kapur, 'Gender Equality', 746. For a critical account of Indian jurisprudence in its ability to promote the principle of substantive equality in employment, see Deepti Shenoy, 'Courting Substantive Equality: Employment Discrimination Law in India', *University of Pennsylvania Journal of International Law* 34, no. 3 (2013): 611–640.
23. See Saurabh Bhattacharjee, 'Adapting Social Security to 21st Century Indian Economy: A Case for Universalisation', *NUJS Journal of Regulatory Studies* 1, no. 1 (2016): 1–15, 4. Also see the Employees' State Insurance Act, 1948 (Act no. 34 of 1948); Employees' Provident Funds and Miscellaneous Provisions Act, 1952 (Act no. 19 of 1952); Employees' Compensation Act, 1923 (Act no. 8 of 1923); and Payment of Gratuity Act, 1972 (Act no. 39 of 1972).
24. See the Beedi Workers Welfare Fund Act, 1976 (Act no. 62 of 1976); Building and Other Construction Workers (Regulation of Employment and Conditions of Service) Act, 1996; Working Journalists and Other Newspaper Employees (Conditions of Service) and Miscellaneous Provisions Act, 1955; Cine-Workers and Cinema Theatre Workers (Regulation of Employment) Act, 1981 (Act no. 50 of 1981).
25. Bhattacharjee, 'Adapting Social Security to 21st Century Indian Economy'.
26. Bhattacharjee, 'Adapting Social Security to 21st Century Indian Economy'.
27. For example, see *Managing Director, Hassan Co-Operative Milk Producer's Society Union Limited v. Assistant Regional Director, Employees' State Insurance Corporation*, (2010) 11 SCC 537.
28. See, for example, the Employees' Provident Funds and Miscellaneous Provisions Act, 1952, section 1(3) (enumerating twenty workers or more for the application of the Act). Also see the Employees' State Insurance Act, 1948, section 2(12) (specifying the application of the Act to factories employing ten or more workers); Bhattacharjee, 'Adapting Social Security to 21st Century Indian Economy', 5–6.
29. Bhattacharjee, 'Adapting Social Security to 21st Century Indian Economy', 7.
30. Ramgopal Agarwala, Nagesh Kumar and Michelle Riboud, 'Reforms, Labour Markets and Social Security Policy in India: An Introduction', in *Reforms, Labour Markets and Social Security in India*, ed. Ramgopal Agarwala, Nagesh Kumar and Michelle Riboud, 1–19 (New Delhi: Oxford

University Press, 2004), 2. Also see, generally, K. P. Kannan and Jan Breman (eds.), *The Long Road to Social Security: Assessing the Implementation of National Social Security Initiatives for the Working Poor in India* (New Delhi: Oxford University Press, 2013).

31. See the Employees' Provident Funds and Miscellaneous Provisions Act, 1952 (Act no. 19 of 1952); Employees' State Insurance Act, 1948 (Act no. 34 of 1948); Employees' Compensation Act, 1923; Maternity Benefit Act, 1961 (Act no. 53 of 1961); Payment of Gratuity Act, 1972; and Personal Injuries (Compensation Insurance) Act, 1963 (Act No 37 of 1963).
32. See the Code on Social Security, 2020 (Act No. 36 of 2020), Preamble (hereinafter 'Code on Social Security').
33. See Code on Social Security, sections 15–16, 21, 26, 28, 32, 34, 36, 38–40, 53, 59–61, 64–67, 74–75, 100. (In addition to the aforementioned entitlements, constructions workers are also entitled to a welfare fund under the code.)
34. Code on Social Security, First Schedule.
35. Code on Social Security, First Schedule.
36. Code on Social Security, chapters 4 and 6, First Schedule.
37. Code on Social Security, section 20(2).
38. See Employees' State Insurance Corporation, Circular No. N-11/12/2003-Bft. II/Vol.II, Sub. 'Rajiv Gandhi Shramik Kalyan Yojana', 9 February 2009.
39. Code on Social Security, First Schedule, sections 1(4), (8), 152(1).
40. See Government of India, Ministry of Labour and Employment, 'Atal Bimit Vyakti Kalyan Yojana', https://www.india.gov.in/spotlight/atal-beemit-vyakti-kalyan-yojana (accessed on 16 August 2023).
41. See, generally, Saurabh Bhattacharjee, 'COVID-19 and Labour Law: India', *Italian Labour Law e-Journal* 13, no. 1 (2020): 1–7; V. Sudesh, 'Domestic Worker Rights Violation during COVID-19 Lockdown: Need for Labour Law Protection', in *Labour Law Reforms 2021*, ed. Jeet Singh Mann, 86–94 (Delhi: Centre for Transparency and Accountability in Governance, 2021).
42. Bhattacharjee, 'COVID-19 and Labour Law: India', 2–3. Also see Stranded Workers Action Network, '32 Days and Counting: COVID-19 Lockdown, Migrant Workers, and the Inadequacy of Welfare Measures in India', 1 May 2020.
43. See *Ficus Pax Private Limited and Others v. Union of India and Others*, W.P. (C) Diary No. 10983 of 2020. Also see Stranded Workers Action Network, '32 Days and Counting'; Bhattacharjee, 'COVID-19 and Labour Law: India', 3–5.
44. Stranded Workers Action Network, '32 Days and Counting'. Also see Bhattacharjee, 'COVID-19 and Labour Law: India', 3–5; Jayati Ghosh, 'A

Critique of the Indian Government's Response to the COVID-19 Pandemic', *Journal of Industrial and Business Economics* 47 (2020): 519–530.
45. Constitution, Article 38.
46. This comparison does not mean that the question of adequacy of social security for the more vulnerable group – that is, informal workers for our discussion – is not an important question. However, before answering such a question in absolute terms, it is important to assess whether the more vulnerable group is *at least* able to reach the same level of well-being as the less vulnerable group (that is, formal workers).
47. Code on Social Security, Preamble. Also see the references in note 23. This constitutional mandate directly flows from Article 14 of the Constitution, which guarantees equal protection of the laws. Article 38 advises the state to minimise inequalities of outcome. Whereas there is a direct connection between these two mandates – one should lead to the other – as discussed earlier in this chapter, the Supreme Court's predominant understanding of the equality principle as a 'formal' doctrine stunts the potential of the Article 14 principle to assess state action under Article 38. In other words, challenges to laws on the ground of equality (a fundamental right) may be decided on whether the law's classification between different groups is justified or not, rather than whether such laws fail to minimise inequality in practice.
48. Act no. 33 of 2008. For a general overview of specific social security programmes for informal workers both under the Code on Social Security and outside the purview of the code, see Mridusmita Bordoloi, Mohammad Hamza Farooqui and Sharad Pandey, *Social Security for Informal Workers in India: Exploring India's Labour Market Policies on Provisioning of Social Security to Informal Workers in the Unorganised Sector* (New Delhi: Centre for Policy Research), November 2020 (Research Brief).
49. Code on Social Security, sections 109, 154, 155, 156. The law also contemplates social security benefits for self-employed workers, which is to be instituted by the central government (see Code on Social Security, section 15[1][d]). Specific categories of workers, such as construction workers, are also entitled to the constitution of the Building and Other Construction Workers' Welfare Board and the social security programmes created by the board (Code on Social Security, sections 7, 100, 106, 108).
50. Code on Social Security, section 114.
51. Code on Social Security, section 6; also see section 141, on funding of social security for informal workers.

52. For example, some of the social security schemes formulated for informal workers by the central government are the Pradhan Mantri Jeevan Jyoti Yojana (life and disability insurance), Pradhan Mantri Surksha Bima Yojana (accidental death insurance), Ayushman Bharat: Pradhan Mantri Jan Arogya Yojana (health and maternity benefits), Pradhan Mantri Shram Yogi Maan–Dhan Yojana (old-age insurance), and National Pension Scheme for Traders, Shopkeepers and Self-Employed Persons (pension plan). See Government of India, Ministry of Labour and Employment, 'Welfare Schemes for Unorganised Workers', 22 March 2021, https://pib.gov.in/PressReleaseIframePage.aspx?PRID=1706609 (accessed on 16 August 2023). For a state government-devised pension benefit scheme for informal workers see International Labour Organization, *India: A Provident Fund for Unorganized Workers (West Bengal)*, ILO Subregional Office for South Asia, https://www.ilo.org/wcmsp5/groups/public/---ed_protect/---soc_sec/documents/publication/wcms_secsoc_6581.pdf (accessed on 16 August 2023).

53. See International Labour Organization, 'ILO Monitor: COVID-19 and the World of Work—Updated Estimates and Analysis' (2nd edition), 7 April 2020, https://www.ilo.org/wcmsp5/groups/public/---dgreports/---dcomm/documents/briefingnote/wcms_740877.pdf (accessed on 16 August 2023). Also see International Labour Organization, 'ILO Monitor on the World of Work' (9th edition), 23 May 2022, https://www.ilo.org/wcmsp5/groups/public/---dgreports/---dcomm/---publ/documents/briefingnote/wcms_845642.pdf (accessed on 16 August 2023), noting that the pandemic has had disproportional adverse impact on informal workers, particularly women workers.

54. See International Labour Organization, *Situation Analysis on the COVID-19 Pandemic's Impact on Enterprises and Workers in the Formal and Informal Economy in India* (New Delhi: International Labour Organization, 2021), 51–53.

55. See International Labour Organization, *Situation Analysis on the COVID-19 Pandemic's Impact*, 74–76.

56. See International Labour Organization, *Situation Analysis on the COVID-19 Pandemic's Impact*, 68–70.

57. See, generally, International Labour Organization, *Situation Analysis on the COVID-19 Pandemic's Impact*.

58. International Labour Organization, *Situation Analysis on the COVID-19 Pandemic's Impact*.

59. Martha Chen, 'COVID-19, Cities and Urban Informal Workers: India in Comparative Perspective', *Indian Journal of Labour Economics* 63 (2020): S41–S46.
60. See Kapur, 'Gender Equality'. Also see Khaitan, 'Equality'.
61. See Constitution, Articles 15, 16.
62. The importance of this balance between labour flexibility and social protection has also been emphasised from a development perspective. See, for example, Anil Verma and Ana Virginia Moreira Gomes, 'Labor Market Flexibility and Trajectories of Development: Lessons from Brazil, India and China', *Indian Journal of Industrial Relations* 50, no. 1 (2014): 51–74.
63. International Labour Organization, *Situation Analysis*, 71–78. This observation is unsurprising since, as S. C. Srivastava notes, only 6 per cent of informal workers received some form of social security under the different social security programmes created for informal workers even after the enactment of the Unorganised Workers' Social Security Act, 2008 (Act no. 33 of 2008). See S. C. Srivastava, 'Labour Law Reforms on Unorganised, Gig and Platform Workers under the Code on Social Security: Issues and Challenges', in *Labour Law Reforms 2021*, ed. Jeet Singh Mann, 1–40 (Delhi: Centre for Transparency and Accountability in Governance, 2021), 39–40.
64. Code on Social Security, sections 6, 109. Compare this right with the more substantive social insurance entitlements of informal – domestic – workers in some jurisdictions in Mihika Poddar and Alex Koshy, 'Legislating for Domestic "Care" Workers in India: An Alternative Understanding', *NUJS Law Review* 12 (2019): 67–117, 109–113. In absence of legally binding substantive social security entitlements, Srivastava argues that the code fails to offer a universal social security safeguard for informal workers. Srivastava, 'Labour Law Reforms on Unorganised, Gig and Platform Workers', 35.
65. Code on Social Security, sections 15, 16, 114.
66. Code on Social Security, section 28(1) (emphasis mine). Also see Code on Social Security, sections 32, 33, for the enumeration of specific entitlements.
67. See Code on Social Security, sections 25, 26, 27, 29.
68. Code on Social Security, section 45 (emphasis mine).
69. Code on Social Security, section 45.
70. Code on Social Security, sections 28(1), 114(6).
71. Code on Social Security, section 8; also see section 149, on the government's power to direct the different welfare boards.

72. Code on Social Security, section 9; also see section 11, on the government's power to reconstitute the various welfare boards.
73. Anjani Kumar, Ashok K. Mishra, Sunil Saroj and P. K. Joshi., 'Institutional versus Non-institutional Credit to Agricultural Households in India: Evidence on Impact from a National Farmers' Survey', *Economic Systems* 41, no. 3 (2017): 420–432, 422–423.
74. Barbara Harriss-White, 'Work and Wellbeing in Informal Economies: The Regulative Roles of Institutions of Identity and the State', *World Development* 38, no. 2 (2010): 170–183, 171–174; Ranajit Das Gupta, 'A Labour History of Social Security and Mutual Assistance in India', *Economic and Political Weekly* 29, no. 11 (1994): 612–620.
75. Harriss-White, 'Work and Wellbeing in Informal Economies'.
76. Harriss-White, 'Work and Wellbeing in Informal Economies'; Das Gupta, 'A Labour History of Social Security and Mutual Assistance in India'.
77. Ritu Dewan, Indira Rani, Ravi S. K., Radha Sehgal, Aruna Kanchi and Swati Raju, *Invisible Work, Invisible Workers: The Sub-Economies of Unpaid Work and Paid Work—Action Research on Women's Unpaid Labour* (New Delhi: ActionAid, 2017), 13–14. Also see Mubashira Zaidi, 'Work and Women's Economic Empowerment in Tribal Rajasthan, India', in *Gender, Unpaid Work and Care in India*, ed. Ellina Samantroy and Subhalakshmi Nandi, 147–164 (Abingdon and New York: Routledge, 2022), 147, 150.
78. See Jayati Ghosh, 'The Uses and Abuses of Inequality', *Journal of Human Development and Capabilities* 20, no. 2 (2019): 181–196; Dewan, Rani, Ravi, Sehgal, Kanchi and Raju, *Invisible Work Invisible Workers*, 17. Also see Indira Hirway, 'Unpaid Work and the Economy: Linkages and their Implications', *Indian Journal of Labour Economics* 58, no. 1 (2015): 1–21, 3–4, 9.
79. Hirway, 'Unpaid Work and the Economy', 3–4; Zaidi, 'Work and Women's Economic Empowerment in Tribal Rajasthan, India', 147; Ritu Dewan, 'Contextualising and Visibilising Gender and Work in Rural India: Economic Contribution of Women in Agriculture', *Indian Journal of Agricultural Economics* 71, no. 1 (2016): 49–58, 52.
80. Dewan, Rani, Ravi, Sehgal, Kanchi and Raju, *Invisible Work Invisible Workers*, 16; Zaidi, 'Work and Women's Economic Empowerment in Tribal Rajasthan, India', 151–152; Ghosh, 'The Uses and Abuses of Inequality'.
81. Jayati Ghosh, 'Gendered Labour Markets and Capitalist Accumulation', *Japanese Political Economy* 44, nos. 1–4 (2018): 25–41; Hirway, 'Unpaid Work

and the Economy', 10; Dewan, Rani, Ravi, Sehgal, Kanchi and Raju, *Invisible Work Invisible Workers*, 17.

82. Zaidi, 'Work and Women's Economic Empowerment in Tribal Rajasthan, India', 152–154. Accordingly, independent policy research institutions had asked Parliament to be mindful of the complexities and fluidities of women's work in undertaking the reforms. See, for example, Shraddha Chigateri, *Labour Law Reforms and Women's Work in India: Assessing the New Labour Codes from a Gender Lens* (New Delhi: Institute of Social Studies Trust, 2021).

83. See the Scheduled Tribes and Other Traditional Forest Dwellers (Recognition of Forest Rights) Act, 2006 (Act no. 2 of 2007). Also see Zaidi, 'Work and Women's Economic Empowerment in Tribal Rajasthan, India', 154–157.

84. See, generally, Ela R. Bhatt, *We Are Poor but So Many: The Story of Self-Employed Women in India* (New Delhi: Oxford University Press, 2006).

85. Bhatt, *We Are Poor but So Many*, 105–106.

86. Bhatt, *We Are Poor but So Many*, 125.

87. For example, the Working Women's Forum also offers micro credits to informal workers through its own cooperative bank. See, generally, Jaya Arunachalam and Brunhild Landwehr (eds.), *'Structuring a Movement and Spreading It On': History and Growth of the Working Women's Forum (India) 1978–2003* (Frankfurt and London: IKO – Verlag für Interkulturelle Kommunikation, 2003).

88. Das Gupta, 'A Labour History of Social Security and Mutual Assistance in India'; Jayshree P. Mangubhai, *Human Rights as Practice: Dalit Women Securing Livelihood Entitlements in South India* (New Delhi: Oxford University Press, 2014), 1–5, 41–42; Bhatt, *We Are Poor but So Many*, 35–36.

89. Bhatt, *We Are Poor but So Many*, 32 (emphasis mine).

90. For example, see Dalit women's organisations and networks mentioned in Mangubhai, *Human Rights as Practice*.

91. Melani Cammett and Lauren M. MacLean, 'Introduction', in *The Politics of Non-State Social Welfare*, ed. Melani Cammett and Lauren M. MacLean, 1–16 (Ithaca, NY: Cornell University Press, 2014), 1. Also see Das Gupta, 'A Labour History of Social Security and Mutual Assistance in India'.

92. Das Gupta, 'A Labour History of Social Security and Mutual Assistance in India'; Anirudh Krishna, 'The Naya Netas: Informal Mediators of Government Services in Rural North India', in *The Politics of Non-State*

*Social Welfare*, ed. Melani Cammett and Lauren M. MacLean, 175–192 (Ithaca, NY: Cornell University Press, 2014), 175–176.
93. Ellina Samantroy and Subhalakshmi Nandi, 'Introduction', in *Gender, Unpaid Work and Care in India*, ed. Ellina Samantroy and Subhalakshmi Nandi, 1–9 (Abingdon and New York: Routledge, 2022), 3.
94. Krishna, 'The Naya Netas'. Also see, generally, Indrajit Roy, *Politics of the Poor: Negotiating Democracy in Contemporary India* (New Delhi: Cambridge University Press, 2018); Sanjeev Routray, *The Right to Be Counted: The Urban Poor and the Politics of Resettlement in Delhi* (Redwood City, CA: Stanford University Press, 2022).
95. Mangubhai, *Human Rights as Practice*, 41–42.
96. See Kamala Sankaran, 'Emerging Perspectives in Labour Regulation in the Wake of COVID-19', *Indian Journal of Labour Economics* 63, no. 1 (supp.) (2020): S91–S95.
97. See, generally, Kumar, Mishra, Saroj and Joshi, 'Institutional versus Non-institutional Credit to Agricultural Households in India'. Also see Bhatt, *We Are Poor but So Many*, 36–37, 99.
98. Mangubhai, *Human Rights as Practice*, 42–46.
99. Zaidi, 'Work and Women's Economic Empowerment in Tribal Rajasthan, India', 147–148.
100. See Archana Kaushik, 'From Hunger Deaths to Healthy Living: A Case Study of Dalits in Varanasi District, Utter Pradesh, India', *Contemporary Voice of Dalit* 10, no. 2 (2018): 173–181.
101. Kaushik, 'From Hunger Deaths to Healthy Living' (noting that some government officials refuse to serve people from lower castes because of deeply held prejudice against such lower-caste citizens). For discrimination on the basis of religion, especially against Muslims, see Routray, *The Right to Be Counted*, 272–279.
102. Mangubhai, *Human Rights as Practice*, 13.
103. For example, see Dewan, Rani, Ravi, Sehgal, Kanchi and Raju, *Invisible Work Invisible Workers*, 58–59.
104. See Atul Sood and Paaritosh Nath, 'Labour Law Changes: Innocuous Mistakes or Sleight of Hand?' *Economic and Political Weekly* 55, no. 22 (2020): 33–37; K. R. Shyam Sundar and Rahul Suresh Sapkal, 'Changes to Labour Laws by State Governments Will Lead to Anarchy in the Labour Market', *Economic and Political Weekly* 55, no. 23 (2020), https://www.epw.in/engage/article/changes-labour-laws-state-market-anarchy-labour-market (accessed on

19 November 2023); S. Anuja, 'Lifting the Veil through Judicial Activism: Access to Justice Model during COVID-19', in *Labour Law Reforms 2021*, ed. Jeet Singh Mann, 185–200 (Delhi: Centre for Transparency and Accountability in Governance, 2021).

105. See *Gujarat Mazdoor Sabha and Another v. State of Gujarat*, (2020) 13 SCR 886, where the Supreme Court quashed the Gujarat government's notification exempting all registered factories from several of the welfare provisions of the Factories Act, 1948 (Act no. 63 of 1948). Also see Anuja, 'Lifting the Veil through Judicial Activism', for an analysis of the aforementioned Supreme Court judgment.

# 4

# Industrial Democracy and Republican Citizenship

Collective Action in Resource Redistribution*

## Introduction

The Constitution of India specifies the subject matter of distribution (social goods or the measuring standard of social justice) – consisting of individual freedoms (Part III) and material resources (Part IV) – in furtherance of the social justice agenda. While the Constitution equally safeguards individual freedoms of all citizens, it does not specify a rule – a method – for the redistribution of material resources except for noting that 'weaker sections' of the population should receive 'special care' as the state seeks to minimise and eliminate inequalities.[1] With this general guidance, the Constitution leaves the specific rule of redistribution to be determined through the political 'governance' process.[2] This approach to redistribution means that constitutionally mandated redistribution must take place through direct citizen participation in governance. Participatory democracy, as the third

---

* Parts of this chapter – the second section, 'Collective Participation in Market-Based Distribution', and the fourth section, 'Combination, Coalition and Participatory Law-Making' – originally appeared in the following publication: Supriya Routh, 'Workers and Competition Law in India: Workers' Associations Are Mostly Not Cartels', in *The Cambridge Handbook of Labor in Competition Law*, ed. Sanjukta Paul, Shae McCrystal and Ewan McGaughey, 193–207 (Cambridge, UK: Cambridge University Press, 2022). All rights reserved.

component of the social justice agenda, is particularly appropriate as a basis for a redistributive framework given the nation's exceptionally diverse and large population. Operationalising a specific, singular, functional redistributive method, albeit with contextual modifications, is bound to be difficult, if not impossible, for a country as heterogeneous as India. The Constitution subjects redistributive entitlements to a participatory decision-making process to make room for contextual sensitivity in diverse circumstances.

Liberal theories of justice based on individual autonomy widely recognise the significance of this process in shaping the nature of the economy (and polity). The role of democratic deliberation in workplaces has been underscored from the perspectives of workplace democracy and workplace republicanism.[3] Workplace democracy sees participatory decision-making as the right to collective governance of enterprises, and workplace republicanism defines it as a worker's right to contest arbitrary management decisions.[4] It is, thus, argued that democracy in workplaces is important in both conferring control of productive assets on workers and protecting them from the management's caprices.[5] These perspectives emphasise the participatory process operating within the capitalist relations of production based on private contract and property relationships and are thereby consistent with the Indian Constitution's scheme of social justice.[6] As noted earlier (in Chapter 1), the Constitution conceives of worker-citizens as autonomous self-interested actors in market exchanges. The Constitution supports the foundation of this mode of market participation without interfering in the outcome of individual exchanges.

Autonomy (at work) is the basis of market-based relationships when contractual exchanges occur without state interference.[7] Although market-based private exchanges are premised on individual autonomy, mere autonomy cannot ensure fair market exchanges. Market exchanges are fair – more equitable – when parties possess rough equality during negotiations (that is, at bargaining). As Elizabeth Anderson notes, some level of equality (between workers and employers) is the prerequisite to facilitate freedom of contract.[8] Securing this (approximate) equality of bargaining power is the role of the state. Since the state determines the framework of private contractual relationships through law, such a 'baseline against which any bargaining takes place' should be subject to democratic deliberations within the state.[9] In this sense, democracy in the workplace advances the 'fair distribution of the *goods of work autonomy*', which constitutes the foundation of market-based contractual relationships (or employment relationships).[10]

Worker control (by management) and claims against non-arbitrary interference, as emphasised in the aforementioned accounts of democracy in the workplace, offer justifications for worker involvement in the workplace.[11] However, while workplace control and independence from management are important goals due to the outcomes they can secure for workers, continuous worker involvement in the broader industrial relations process (that is, beyond specific workplaces) has both intrinsic and instrumental significance. Worker involvement generally signifies that workers participate in the law-making process that creates the market rules governing private contracts. While worker participation attests to the intrinsic importance of the democratic process, such participation is also instrumentally significant when the process leads to other valuable outcomes (such as securing bargaining equality in the labour market). The very nature of this participation is collective, not individual – not as private citizens but as the *workplace public*. The workplace public is the public – collective – that has a legitimate interest in fairly organising labour relations. What follows is that if autonomy is the basis of market participation, fair distribution of autonomy is the function of democratic participation by the worker collective. In this sense, even within the framework of capitalist market exchanges, it is plausible – even essential – that workers engage in industrial democracy. Industrial democracy is, therefore, a precondition to promoting an effective and fair market-based distribution of material resources because it helps guarantee relative equality between the parties to labour exchanges.

As noted, worker involvement in the industrial process is a broader concept than democracy in the workplace. The perspectives of workplace democracy and workplace republicanism have the 'management' (or the employer) in mind. When they situate workers' democratic participation in workplaces, they understand it as a method of limiting employers' property rights and constraining managerial power.[12] The Indian Constitution, on the other hand, envisions worker democratic involvement as collective participation in industrial policy beyond employment contracts between labour and management. Industrial policy beyond the employment contract consists of all socio-economically productive work arrangements and economic relationships not captured in a bipartite contractual framework. In particular, in the Indian context, it consists of workers' involvement in policymaking in informal (or unorganised) economic relationships.

In this broader participatory role, it is true (at least theoretically) that workers – trade unions – participate in the law-making process so that a more equitable distribution results from labour market exchanges. However, they also participate to ensure that state-led redistribution of material resources is fair and contextually sensitive. In this case, worker-citizens' participation and engagement would contextually establish the rules of redistribution, which should better respond to the specific needs of differently situated workers. To clarify, the justification for workers' democratic participation in industrial policymaking is not compensatory – democratic participation compensating workers for their subjection to workplace rules; instead, this participation is the prerequisite for the formulation of rules of entitlement.[13] The constitutional principle of democratic participatory governance finds more concrete expression as a mandate for decentralised governance in self-governing village-level administrative units, worker participation in industrial management and democratic control and autonomous functioning of cooperative societies.[14] If our understanding of the Constitution's social justice scheme is to be guided by its preoccupation with decentralised governance, we should see workers' participatory law-making as a 'governance' issue broader than the employee–management collective decision-making process on labour market exchanges.

Understanding worker participation in the law-making process as a governance issue is particularly important in the Indian context. As noted in the introduction, the Indian workforce is massive and diverse. Very few Indian workers (about 10 per cent) work under long-term formal contracts, which is still the predominant juridical basis of Indian labour welfare statutes. Most of the workforce (approximately 90 per cent) engage in informal livelihood activities, which the bipartite employment contract model does not fully capture. Furthermore, there are a diverse array of informal relationships and exchanges. Informal workers can be self-employed, work on their own account under conditions of constrained choices or work for their extended families without recognition as workers. They also work under obscure dependent relationships, imprecise contractual obligations, multiple employers under varying conditions, obligations of real and imagined kinship, debt-bond, and so on. The common theme in these diverse arrangements is that the workers undertake their livelihood activities without formal documentation or adherence to the rules legally structuring their work. Note that it is not the type of work that makes it informal, because the same kind of work – for example, transportation – might be carried on either informally (when the actors avoid registration and reporting) or formally (when the actors register their vehicles and workers with the state and pay taxes and licensing fees).

Because of this divergence in socio-economic contexts and variation in exchange relationships at work, centralised universal legal entitlements could scarcely meet the workforce's unique needs. While Parliament may create a general framework for redistribution, the de facto rules of such redistribution should remain the prerogative of decentralised participatory law-making.[13] In view of the heterogeneity of work, decentralised law-making is, in fact, essential if worker autonomy is to be respected and the redistribution of resources is to cater to varied lived experiences. If autonomy requires that workers are subject only to the legal mandate that they help formulate and if lived experience offers the most authentic revelation of the role of material resources in their lives, it is, then, workers working in their sui generis work arrangements that can offer the background knowledge for legislative entitlements. Law-making will only be legitimate and contextually authentic when it is done through the active participation of workers and their coalitions.

In the following section, the principal characteristics of legitimate and authentic law-making are analysed. In the second section, trade unions' role in law-making is discussed insofar as such collective participation relates to decision-making concerning market-based distribution of income, resources and opportunities for workers. In the third section, the significance of workers' collective action for state-based redistribution of resources is analysed. Slightly diverging from the immediate theme of collective action in law-making, the fourth section examines whether the competition law regime is an impediment for workers' collective action in the country. This examination becomes important especially in the context of informal workers, who could sometimes be seen as (self-employed) entrepreneurs instead of workers (for example, street vendors), a view which might pose a challenge to workers' collective action under the competition law regime, which prohibits anti-competitive combinations and coalitions. The chapter ends with a brief conclusion.

## Characteristics of Legitimate and Authentic Law-Making

In principle, legal standards cannot morally command a legal actor's obedience if such standards fail to respect their autonomy and self-determination. When a law respects an actor's autonomy and self-determination, it is legitimate. In this sense, legitimacy is the very essence of legal standards, the absence of which strips such standards of what makes them law, as opposed to mere command backed up by force. However, there is another practical sense in which self-determination – or, more specifically, active law-making participation – is central to developing (redistribution-focused) legal entitlements; it makes them more effective or authentic. Law is authentic when it achieves its normative aims, which normally include improving (that is, better ordering) some aspect of a legal actor's life. Legal entitlements are most efficient in this sense when the interventions they make are optimal for both the legal actor and society. This evaluation of efficiency should consider the uniqueness of a community's characteristics, nature of private interactions within the community, community members' interface with the local administration, actual delivery of public services, cohesiveness or disjuncture within the community, role of power (or the lack of it) within and outside community interactions, ease of community engagement with the state, legal exclusion of the community (such as in squatter settlements), and so on. These characteristics are merely indicative, not exhaustive. In fact, in view of the diversity of the (Indian) population, it is nearly impossible to comprehensively document the variables that one needs to consider when formulating efficient legal interventions.

In this context, self-determination, understood as active and inclusive participation in the law-making process, helps to highlight contextual variables that need to be taken into account when developing legal entitlements. These variables comprehensively emerge out of the lived experiences of community members, which offer 'a way of seeing, from where [legal actors] actually live, into the powers, processes, and relations that organize and determine the everyday context of that seeing'.[16] Using lived experience-based law-making allows legal actors to remark on which entitlements are needed (that is, substantive content) and under what circumstances such entitlements can be considered a success (that is, evaluative judgement). By means of decentralised participatory law-making, legal actors are given an opportunity to supply the reasonings for, and expressions of, legal standards rather than being forced to fit their actual lived experiences into the language of law (that is, legal categories and legal tests).[17] Allowing legal actors to use their everyday language to describe their work lives and their problems – and having it recognised by law – is both efficient from the legal entitlement perspective[18] and authentic from the social cohesiveness perspective.[19]

Due to the significance of lived experience, such a worker-centric approach to law-making is especially crucial in societies with very diverse socio-cultural environments and livelihood conditions. The Indian workforce interacts with remarkably distinct social spaces which shape and are shaped by multiple intersecting legalities. In the continuum of formal–informal working arrangements, workers occupy different legal statuses depending on the nature of their specific work relationships (for example, employee, independent contractor, self-employed, own-account, illegal squatter, undocumented worker, and so on). Sometimes their work and entitlements are structured by statutes, sometimes by social rules based on religion, caste, ethnicity, gender, locality, kinship, fictive kinship, migration status, and so on.[20] Because of this deep divergence in working conditions, it is crucial that legal policymaking processes refrain from generalising the experiences of even similar categories of workers (such as domestic workers or street vendors) unless their working contexts are also comparable.[21] Thus, the legal meaning of work, the extent of its social and market contribution, its relationality and the society's reciprocal obligations to workers should primarily emerge from the deliberations of specific groups of workers with shared, common work–life experiences.

Because of the necessity of contextual deliberations, law should actively promote independent worker representative organisations and facilitate collective worker action. Representative organisations, including trade unions, are often the non-state institutional platforms through which workers develop the assertiveness to, and habit of, engaging in policy deliberations. These representative organisations also often allow workers to achieve visibility and influence with state institutions (including the legislatures). Worker organisations create the channels of communication between the casual deliberations of worker groups and the formal institutional representatives of the group's position. In view of these preconditions for legitimate and authentic law-making, legal standards – labour law reforms, in our case – should also be evaluated on their capacity to consolidate collective worker participation in law-making, which eventually go on to inform the manner of redistribution of material resources by the state.

However, although legal entitlements – the substance and manner of redistribution – should emerge primarily from contextual lived experiences of heterogeneous workers, there are limits to the contribution of lived experience as the exclusive basis of law-making. Lived experiences, or the ways of making sense of the world through localised peculiarities, are invariably embedded in broader processes and relations of the socio-economy.[22] The very *context* in which experience-based knowledge emerges is invariably also constituted through processes and relations that largely remain outside the immediate peculiarities of a community. For example, in the context of work-based relationships, political ideology, macroeconomic policies, product market conditions, consumer preferences, land use patterns, criminalisation of certain economic activities, caste- and ethnicity-based discrimination, and policies and prejudices on workers' movements are just some of the factors that have a bearing on local circumstances and consequently on lived experiences. These aspects of the supra-community, although inherently informing community experiences, may remain unarticulated in exclusively lived experience-focused law-making. However, since the very purpose of law is to normatively pattern the behaviour of legal actors and delineate the principles of institutional engagement, relevant factors transcending specific communities must also be explicitly identified and deliberated on during the law-making process. Therefore, the law-making discourse must have some openness to outside inputs, whether it takes the form of expert opinion, coalition agenda or international solidarity.

Different kinds of knowledge and opinions have a varying degree of relevance in an experience-focused law-making process. While the opinions offered by coalitions and solidarity networks may emphasise justice and rights, independent 'expert' inputs may help (objectively to) consolidate the realities and relationalities of situated experiences. This difference results from the fact that whereas civic groups, to a greater or lesser degree, identify with the interests and preoccupations of a specific community, experts often seek to generate objective scientific knowledge. Both of these perspectives – interest representation and objective representation – should play a role in (re)distributional policies. The role played by these supra-community actors and institutions is limited to offering the wider context of community knowledge in the law-making process, but the law-making perspective should remain that of the specific community. What these supra-community engagements do is that they nuance and enrich the community perspective. Thus, participatory law-making should consider substantive perspectives from lived experiences, which one can find in the internal community deliberations and supra-community opinions on those experiences, with the former prioritised over the latter. The second and third sections evaluate whether the 2020 labour law reforms in India, in reality, facilitate participatory law-making.

Worker participation in (re)distributional decisions takes two forms in the industrial relations scenario. The first is the private contractual bargaining framework, and the second is the public entitlement programme. When workers collectively (or even individually) bargain with their employers through their trade unions, they determine the rules of their contractual relationship. The bargaining process integrates workers' voice in structuring the legal nature of their employment relationship, outlining their rights and obligations in their employment contract under conditions of market freedom. To participate in the 'private' law-making process is to participate in market-based distributional decisions with reference to their specific industries or employment. Here, law-making is private because it is largely free of state-imposed restrictions on contractual terms (unless, of course, any such position violates the laws and policies of the state).

On the other hand, workers also participate in the state's re-distributional decisions when the state allocates resources on the basis of the Constitution's promise of social justice. These redistributional decisions are largely political decisions involving specific worker constituencies. When they engage in the decision-making process, worker organisations fulfil a constitutional function. This is because ideally their participation leads the state to act more in line with the Constitution's vision of social justice in redistributing material resources through legal entitlements (as noted in Chapter 3). By participating in the political 'governance' process, leading to the prescriptions of welfare entitlements, worker collective action constitutes the third component of the social justice framework of the Constitution. This decision-making process should be decentralised so that lived experiences of workers under sui generis conditions can inform their (private and public) entitlement agenda. In both forms of participation, it ought ultimately to be *actual workers that make their own decisions* on their own behalf in their interest that informs substantive legal entitlements. This participatory agenda, then, constitutes the normative standard for evaluating the reforms of labour law. While evaluating the 2020 labour law reforms, the legal scope of workers' law-making participation in both private and public law-making contexts will be evaluated in the second and third sections respectively.

## Collective Participation in Market-Based Distribution: Trade Unionism and Law-Making

Traditionally, the government has played a significant role in industrial relations in India. From deciding whether an issue amounts to a dispute between labour and management to recommending such dispute to conciliation or adjudication, the government has been a significant actor in what is essentially a tripartite industrial relations model.[23] While the freedom to engage in bipartite industrial relations exists, it is substantially limited. Government permission (or at least prior notification to the government) is required to make decisions about layoffs, retrenchment, industry closure, lockout and strike.[24] This entrenched, legally mandated dependence on the executive – and thereby the broader polity – has impeded the development of an independent and strong trade union movement in India. It is not surprising, therefore, that major trade unions in India seek to further their agenda by affiliating to – swearing allegiance to – a parent political party. Consequently, parent political parties often set the parameters of trade union agendas.[25]

Although the juridical framework for an independent and strong trade union movement is present, the reach and influence of independent collective action of workers remain weak in practice. Neither has the gradual evolution of the contours of the constitutionally safeguarded right to association helped their cause. As we discussed earlier, justiciable fundamental rights (Part III) and non-justiciable directive principles of state policy (Part IV) safeguard worker rights. Article 19(1)(c) of the Constitution, a justiciable right, states: 'All citizens shall have the right to form associations or unions or cooperative societies.' Although a mere right to form associations could have covered the right to trade unionism without much interpretive difficulty, the Constitution has expressly safeguarded the *right to unionisation* and, recently,[26] *the right to form cooperatives* in order to emphasise the particular relevance of these specific forms of organisations.

In spite of this express constitutional emphasis, judicial development of the right to trade unionism has resulted in a constrained articulation of the right with limited potential. In one of the most significant judgments on the subject – one that pre-empted (which is only clear to us now with hindsight) other possible approaches on the topic – the Supreme Court of India asserted that a citizen's right to unionisation is exhausted once they form a trade union.[27] Due to how the right is exhausted once a trade union (or a cooperative society) is formed, entitlements to collective bargaining or coercive bargaining strategies such as strikes are not components of the fundamental right to trade unionism. Thus, the Supreme Court cannot guarantee the right to the said bargaining or bargaining strategies as part of the right to association.

## Collective Bargaining

The Supreme Court undermined a basis of the Constitution's social justice agenda when it concluded that collective bargaining and strikes do not flow from the justiciable right to trade unionism. These rights facilitate effective worker participation in the industrial law-making process. However, although collective bargaining and strikes are not part of the constitutional right to trade unionism, they are statutory entitlements safeguarded under the Industrial Relations Code (hereinafter, 'IR Code').[28] The IR Code promotes collective bargaining between the employer and the recognised trade union(s).[29] It requires that an employer – in consultation with a recognised trade union or a negotiating council of trade unions – shall prepare the terms and conditions of employment, called the 'standing order', which will regulate the employment relationship between the employer and the employees.[30] Absent such a collective agreement (that is, the standing order) being in force, the IR Code makes the federal government responsible for issuing model terms and conditions of employment for an establishment until a standing order, or a collectively bargained agreement, is adopted and approved by the certifying officer under the IR Code.[31]

According to the IR Code, workers have the right to 'engage in concerted activities for the purposes of collective bargaining or other mutual aid'.[32] If an employer refuses to bargain collectively in good faith with recognised trade unions, they shall be guilty of unfair labour practice.[33] Likewise, a recognised trade union's refusal to engage in collective bargaining in good faith with an employer also constitutes an unfair labour practice.[34] Thus, a duty to bargain in good faith is statutorily mandated. The IR Code consolidates the duty to bargain in good faith by mandating the recognition of a bargaining unit, either in the form of a single trade union or as a negotiating council consisting of representatives from different trade unions.[35]

Thus, the dominant characteristic of the Indian industrial relations framework is to assign a role for collective worker participation in the market-based distributional agenda, albeit to a limited extent and under governmental vigilance. Trade unions are legally conceived as representative organisations of employees engaged in industrial bargaining and generally promoting the interests of their members. Although the scope of trade unions is now seen in a slightly broader light (as representatives also of informal or unorganised workers), the traditional way of seeing trade unions as employee representatives at the bargaining table is still the predominant industrial relations narrative. A registered trade union is the bargaining agent (that is, the 'negotiating union') of the employees, and an employer is obligated to recognise such a trade union as the workers' bargaining agent.[36]

Although there is no fundamental right to collective bargaining, the IR Code secures bargaining rights for workers. However, the multiplicity of trade unions (as worker wings of political parties) not only fragments (ideologically and numerically) and substantially weakens (by undermining independent unionism) the trade union movement in India, it also gives rise to a complex industrial relations scenario. In India, each union is entitled to bona fide collective bargaining rights and may undertake collective action, including strikes, to increase its bargaining power. This complexity and the power dispersed among numerous trade unions (without any cohesion among them) can adversely impact production relations, which presumably made the Supreme Court conclusively declare in 2003 that trade unions do not possess a right to strike.[37]

*Strike*

An industrial strike is a collective worker action to assert their combined market power. Strikes attempt to counterbalance the employer's superior economic strength and bargaining leverage under laissez-faire market conditions. The potential inherent in the right to strike (or, more specifically, the threat of strike) is partly instrumental in facilitating substantive worker participation in the contractual law-making process. It is true that under the IR Code, an employer 'shall recognise' collective worker representations in the bargaining process. However, such legal recognition merely secures a passive space – a legal formality – at the bargaining table for workers; it does not ensure that workers will be able to fairly – free of economic constraints – advocate for their interests. Furthermore, it does not guarantee that their lived experiences will be recognised in the contractual agreement, which, as previously mentioned, is essential to a just entitlement structure. In reality, the ability of workers to negotiate contractual clauses flows just as much from their ability to strike as it does from the formal recognition of their union as bargaining agents. Thus, the right to strike safeguards against unconscionable contractual law-making[38] in a relationship that legally conceives of the employer as the superior party with the ability to 'control' the relationship as an historical legacy of the master–servant imagination.[39] In other words, when legal fiction places the employer in the superior position with the ability to control workplace relationships, the right to strike becomes the precondition for ensuring fair law-making participation by the worker.

However, the Supreme Court seemingly ignored the enormous significance of the right to strike in facilitating worker participation in law-making, which furthers the constitutional social justice agenda, in a case involving Tamil Nadu government employees. In this case, there was a dispute in which the state of Tamil Nadu dismissed and suspended 170,241 government employees for going on strike. In its decision, the Supreme Court noted that government employees do not have any *fundamental, statutory, equitable or moral right* to strike.[40] The court noted that strike as a weapon is mostly misused and adversely affects society. It drew on the examples of a teachers' strike negatively impacting students, a doctors' strike hurting patients and a transport strike bringing society to a standstill. This reasoning not only applies to government employees but, taken to its logical conclusion, essentially denies any right to strike in a publicly oriented industry.

However, the decision only explicitly denies a legal (in contrast to a moral) right to strike to government employees. It reasoned that state statutes specifically prohibit government employees from going on strike. If government employees have a grievance, they should employ the grievance redressal mechanisms available under the applicable statutory regime. This suggestion shows the Supreme Court's inadequate understanding of the significance of strikes as an instrument for bargaining and protest. Strikes are the foremost manifestation of collective power that furthers worker interests rather than merely being a dispute resolution mechanism, which is how the court seems to understand strikes. The countervailing power of strikes helps keep a balance of power between labour and capital rather than resolving the dispute itself (which is a narrower by-product of the power). The court conflated these two issues when it denied the right to strike to government employees in particular and industrial employees in general.

While the Supreme Court denied a constitutional right to strike by government employees, the legal right to strike by industrial employees has a firmer foundation in the IR Code. According to the IR Code, workers can go on strike if they serve adequate notice.[41] However, workers cannot go on strike while a conciliation is pending, during tribunal or arbitration proceedings, or during the operation of a settlement award between the employer and the workers.[42] However, this requirement of a substantial notice period before a strike action, which used to only apply to public utility employees such as those working for railways and airlines, now extends to all employees.[43] By further limiting the scope of the right to strike, the latest reforms stunt the instrumental value of strikes in promoting de facto law-making participation by industrial employees.

## Informal Worker Market Participation

The juridical discourse on the right to association, collective bargaining and strike in India has narrowly revolved around the concerns of a minority of public and industrial employees. The juridical position on these issues for the vast majority of informal workers – ranging from 80 to 90 per cent of the workforce, on different accounts[44] – is still somewhat unsettled. It is, therefore, important to situate informal workers at the centre of these debates. A unique trait of most informal workers – those who are self-employed – is that they use collective action to bargain with the state (particularly the government) rather than an employer. Although they often organise as trade unions, these informal workers simultaneously facilitate their collective market participation through cooperative societies (and other legal forms, including that of a worker-promoted company).[45]

Informal workers, by definition, are workers who remain outside the industrial employment *form*. Due to this outside status, the legal frameworks built around the orthodox industrial employment model may not fit their situation. India's labour law regime for regulating industrial workers often excludes informal workers because it only applies to employers with more than a certain number of employees.[46] Ventures engaging informal workers through (mostly oral) employment contracts and other non-traditional exchange relationships (including family- and kin-based relationships) are mostly small-scale and thereby remain outside the purview of labour laws.[47]

The exclusion of informal workers from these regimes does not mean that informal workers are completely unregulated by law. Instead, municipal law (for street vendors), criminal law (for waste-recycling workers) and social security entitlements (including the social security statute for unorganised workers) often regulate informal working arrangements. Furthermore, in certain situations, traditional labour laws may apply to informal workers, but they operate differently in their specific contexts. For example, although registration as a trade union grants certain immunities to organisations of informal workers, such as the Self-Employed Women's Association (SEWA), insofar as collective bargaining or strike is concerned, the nature of their collective actions do not generally fit the conceptual categories created for industrial employees.[48]

A significant percentage of informal workers are self-employed (including own-account) workers; even when informal workers are engaged in waged employment, it is often difficult to discern a clear employment relationship. Given that they are explicitly excluded from statutory safeguards and in the absence of transparent employment relationships, informal workers generally cannot claim statutory entitlements to fair dismissal, workplace safety or strikes. Because of the heterogeneous working arrangements that informal workers are involved in, their associations often prefer to lobby the government rather than employers (even when they have one).[49] The rights to collective negotiation (or bargaining) and strike, in the context of informal workers, are then posed as demands against the state (primarily the government) by citizens, not exclusively against employers by employees.

Even when the IR code recognises informal worker trade unionism, it only legally secures rights to collective bargaining and strikes against *employers* rather than the government. Thus, it is unlikely that informal workers meaningfully possess statutory rights to collectively bargain or strike. According to the *All India Bank Employees Association* and *T. K. Rangarajan* decisions, in the absence of statutory rights to collective bargaining or strike, there is no constitutional (that is, fundamental) or moral right to collective bargaining or strike. Thus, in the context of informal workers – particularly the self-employed ones – there are no rights to collective bargaining or strike. That being said, they may negotiate with the government and undertake civil disobedience action as *citizens*[50] (that is, not exclusively as workers, but more explicitly as worker-citizens) employing their constitutional right to association. Thus, since the right to strike is only a statutory right under the IR Code, and since Parliament excluded (small-scale) businesses or individual employers engaging informal workers from the IR Code, informal workers only possess the right to organise (a constitutional right) but not the right to cease working (a narrower statutory right). What follows is that informal workers' collective action in the form of trade unionism is permitted primarily as an instrument of political negotiation with the government rather than collective bargaining with an employer. In fact, informal workers' trade unions often politically lobby the government rather than bargain with an employer.

However, trade unionism is not the only form that informal workers' collective action adopts. For example, although SEWA registered as a trade union, it undertakes diverse activities – from waste-recycling business to banking services – through numerous cooperative societies made up of their members.[51] These cooperatives allow informal workers, such as street vendors, waste recyclers, certain categories of agricultural workers and other groups of freelancers, to participate in market exchanges. Furthermore, this technique of using cooperatives to promote its members' aspirations is one that informal workers have used extensively across the world.[52] India's rich history of cooperatives can be traced back to agricultural and other workers.[53] It is the culmination of this history that the right to form a cooperative society is now a constitutionally safeguarded justiciable right.[54] While trade unionism promotes informal workers' political engagement with the government, the worker cooperative movement mainly aims at facilitating their effective participation in market exchanges.

Thus, in the Constitution's social justice scheme, participatory law-making is not limited to formal and informal employees' market distribution concerns. It is also central to the (re)distributive concerns of other workers (not merely employees), including those of informal self-employed workers. Collective action and its constitutive components of bargaining and strikes are traditionally conceived in the context of industrial employment relationships. However, before adjudicating the merits of the labour law reforms pertaining to the changes to collective action, it is important to evaluate the scope of participatory law-making, particularly by informal workers, in securing state-led legal entitlements for such workers. The state-led legal entitlements attain particular prominence for informal workers because of their limited opportunity to engage in formal market-based contractual exchanges. In the following section, workers' law-making participation in the redistribution agenda is analysed with an emphasis on participation by informal workers.

## Collective Participation in Redistribution of Material Resources: Worker Aggregations and Law-Making

The second facet of participatory law-making is worker participation in the delegated law-making process that affects social security entitlements in specific contexts. The nature of this participation is different from conventional collective bargaining in which workers aim to promote their 'private' (individual or group) interests within a given model, that of the industrial employment relationship, the characteristics (that is, rights and obligations) of which are well developed. In contrast, in redistributive law-making, workers participate in a 'communal' – not private – process which seeks to decipher elements of working arrangements and decide how social security entitlements might fit those contexts. Although it is true that social security entitlements often mechanically operate within formal employment models, nevertheless in order to be effective, collective deliberations involving the administration of social security still need to understand unique worker needs within the model. On the other hand, in the context of informal workers, this deliberative law-making exercise must, of necessity, decipher characteristics of specific groups of informal workers who do not conform to a model. In the latter situation, the participatory law-making exercise is primarily a contextual investigation into the lived experiences of heterogeneous informal workers. The Code on Social Security, 2020, does secure a legal right for formal and informal workers to participate in the social security decision-making process. While in the context of formal workers, such participation takes the form of tripartite decision-making bodies, in the context of informal workers, worker participation is integrated into broader representative forums (beyond tripartism), as will be seen later.

The Code on Social Security aims to expand social security provisioning by extending social security to both formal employees and informal workers.[55] The general approach of the social security statute is to specify the nature of social security for workers and then delegate decisions about their organisation and distribution to a decision-making body ('social security organisation') that has collective worker representation.[56] The social security organisations listed in the Code on Social Security are the Central Board of Trustees of Employees' Provident Fund, the Employees' State Insurance Corporation, the National Social Security Board for Unorganised Workers, the State Unorganised Workers' Social Security Board, the State Building and Other Construction Workers' Welfare Board.[57] The Central Board of Trustees administers provident, pension and insurance funds for employees and self-employed workers, and it must have an equal number of employee and employer representatives, which is finalised by the central government.[58] The Employees' State Insurance Corporation administers insurance funds for the purpose of health and medical treatment of employees and their family members (and related matters). This body also is required to have employee representatives approved by the central government.[59] The state-level Building and Other Construction Workers' Welfare Board formulates and administers welfare entitlements for construction workers, and it requires government-appointed tripartite representatives (of the government, employers and employees) in equal numbers.[60] The Code on Social Security also envisages the possibility of social security organisations at the state, regional and local levels.[61] Some welfare boards also have an equitable representation mandate to ensure that women, Scheduled Caste, Scheduled Tribe and other minority workers are included in the deliberation process. At a formal level, therefore, industrial employees are legally entitled – as part of a tripartite decision-making forum – to participate in the delegated law-making process, which now also includes informal workers.

The social security law recognises working arrangements outside the 'traditional employer–employee relationship', including informal self-employment. Accordingly, the Code on Social Security establishes national and state-level social security boards for informal ('unorganised') workers.[62] As discussed in Chapter 3, it is the responsibility of the national and state social security boards to help establish and monitor appropriate social security schemes for various categories of informal workers, including gig (on-demand) workers and online platform-based workers.[63] In addition to governmental representation, the code mandates that informal workers are represented in the National Social Security Board.[64] The national board also must have representatives of employers who operate in the informal sector. However, unlike the previous examples, the code not only mandates tripartite representation in the determination of social security entitlements for informal workers, it also opens up the possibility of participation from a broader coalition of actors.

This coalition includes 'eminent persons from civil society', 'members representing the [Indian Parliament]' and 'expert members'.[65] Members representing different constituencies must be 'persons of eminence' in labour welfare, management, finance, law and administration.[66] Thus, one would expect this broad coalition to bring in the outsider perspective to lived experience-based law making, thereby authenticating lived experiences in their relationship to the larger social, economic and political processes. However, in spite of this entitlement to law-making participation by a broad coalition, the government possesses significant control over the deliberation process, not only through its power to nominate representatives of different constituencies but also in securing direct participation from various levels of the government (see discussions in Chapter 3).[67] Additionally, the government possesses potentially unlimited power to direct social security organisations on how to implement social security entitlements under the code.[68] Thus, governmental mediation, which has historically been one of the central features of the formal industrial relations structure in India, has also been expanded to the social security framework for informal workers.

Informal workers' collective action, in their negotiations with the government and law-making participation, often also relies on networking with similar organisations and building broad coalitions. These coalitions are often an important precondition to their law-making participation that helps them generate political leverage and visibility in addition to situating their localised experiences in the global context. Accordingly, it is only fair that the labour law reforms be evaluated not only in their capacity to promote informal worker organisations but also in their ability to facilitate coalitions of such organisations. There is some legal recognition of the role of coalitions in informal workers' social security entitlements under the Code on Social Security, as noted earlier. However, the question remains whether this de jure recognition – of participation from civil society and experts – does de facto promote informal worker perspectives in delegated law-making. Since informal workers engage in collective action through both trade unionism and cooperative societies, and through networks of these organisations, these collective arrangements must be allowed to intervene in entitlement deliberations. However, as important as this collective intervention is, informal workers' collective action may sometimes constitute anti-competitive collusion, thereby making it illegal, under the competition law. Since a large percentage of informal workers are self-employed who may often be perceived to be in business on their own account (for example, street vendors and transportation workers), they could be legally understood as independent commercial entities. If some informal economic activities are understood as independent commercial entities, informal workers' collective action might appear to constitute anti-competitive combinations and agreements among businesses from the perspective of competition law and, thereby, legally restricted. In light of this apparent conflict between competition law and collective action, including participatory delegated law-making, the following section analyses the scope of the Competition Act, 2002, for workers' collective action.[69]

## Combination, Coalition and Participatory Law-Making: Is Competition Law an Impediment?

The Competition Act does not explicitly mention trade unions and worker associations. However, the wording of the statutory provisions clearly leads to the conclusion that workers and worker associations are prohibited from entering into anti-competitive agreements. The Act prohibits production, supply, distribution, storage and control of goods and services agreements by worker associations, including trade unions, when they potentially cause an 'appreciable adverse effect' on competition.[70] Likewise, the law also prohibits enterprises and groups from abusing their dominant position by imposing unfair conditions or prices in exchanges of goods and services.[71] Note that while the law prohibits predatory pricing, it encourages competitive pricing.[72] The competition law also prohibits combinations, including mergers and amalgamations of enterprises, capable of causing adverse effects on competition in India.[73] The thrust of this component of the law is on enterprises, which, after combining, occupy a dominant market position. For example, if a firm, after a merger, would have assets worth more than (approximately) USD 136 million (INR 1,000 crores) and also a turnover worth more than (approximately) USD 407 million (INR 3,000 crores), the law would prohibit the merger.[74]

Under the Competition Act, anti-competitive agreements are agreements that create barriers to new market entrants, drive out competitors, obstruct market-based competition, have an adverse impact on consumer interest and market efficiency, or hinder technical, scientific and economic development.[75] Likewise, while anti-competitive dominant positions can single-handedly distort efficient markets, anti-competitive combinations are those that adversely affect the market through their combined power, imports, prices, profit margins, market share, available substitutes, the ability to stunt innovation and the ability to force out competitors.[76]

Thus, the Indian competition law does not per se prohibit (collective) agreements or collusion on exchanges of goods or services. Instead, theoretically, the law will only intervene when such agreements have the potential to stifle competition. The Supreme Court of India, when it interpreted the normative goals of the Act, noted that the competition law primarily seeks to promote competition. However, it promotes competition for the purpose of long-term economic development and the promotion of consumer well-being by expanding 'adequate and affordable' consumer choice.[77] The court saw the Act as an instrument for promoting 'public interest' by limiting the 'freeplay [of] the private sector' in market transactions.[78] 'In fact, the ultimate goal of competition policy ... is to enhance consumer well-being'.[79] What follows is that if the objective of the Act is not limited merely to promoting competition at all costs but to eventually promote public interest, the scope of the law becomes expansive enough to be sensitive to trade union objectives of collective representation and negotiation. This is so even if such negotiation ends up imposing additional burdens (including costs) on conducting businesses.

Relevant to this discussion is the decision in *Competition Commission of India v. Co-Ordination Committee of Artists and Technicians of W.B. Film and Television and Others*.[80] In it, an artists' and film technicians' trade union coalition succeeded in forcing a television network to discontinue a Bengali-dubbed Hindi television series (on the Indian epic Mahabharata). The union took this action to prevent the harm it would cause to the Bengali film and television industry. Said harm stemmed from how the programme dispensed with the need to employ actors and film technicians from Bengal. However, the Supreme Court found that the coalition's actions violated the competition law, noting that 'agreement' under the Act also means an 'action in concert',[81] including the one undertaken by the trade union alongside an association and a registered company. The court concluded that, in this case, the Coordination Committee acted in its capacity of an 'association of enterprises' (that is, 'constituent members') seeking to restrain competition rather than acting purely as a trade union promoting the 'social function' of a trade union.[82] To further justify its decision, the court indicated that the Coordination Committee's action ultimately harmed consumers by depriving them of the pleasure of the show.[83]

Thus, the Supreme Court created a distinction between a trade union's role as a collective bargaining agent and a collective platform for freelancers and independent entrepreneurs (for example, technicians, producers, distributors and exhibitors of films). Briefly referring to European Union competition law, without any substantive engagement with its jurisprudence, the court seems to suggest that when trade unions perform a 'social function' on the 'principle of solidarity', they would be exempt from the scope of section 3 of the Act prohibiting anti-competitive agreements.[84] Thus, the court's interpretation of the Act underscored that when trade unions are merely engaged in collective bargaining, which also has a social function, their action is excluded from the purview of the Act. In addition to this trade union – or social function – exemption under the Act, the central government is empowered to exempt certain categories of enterprises or agreements. The government may do so in the interest of the security of the nation, in the public interest, to fulfil its obligations under an international treaty, or if it is performing a sovereign function.[85] The federal government can also supersede the Competition Commission of India (CCI) if it believes that the commission is either unable to discharge its function or has persistently failed to comply with government directions issued under the law.[86]

Although informal workers often employ robust collective action through trade unionism, their unionism is not geared principally towards the success of a collective agreement or a dispute resolution process, as is conceived under the IR Code.[87] Accordingly, the law does not support informal worker trade unionism on the basis of the IR Code as promoting collective bargaining or resolving industrial disputes (that is, the orthodox 'social function' of a trade union). Yet such unionism politically promotes informal worker interests. Are there bases to exempt informal worker trade unionism from the purview of the Competition Act? Possibly. The answer lies in the fact that informal workers' primary bargaining partner is the government. Since the Act empowers the government (that is, the central government) to exempt enterprises from the operation of the Act, bargaining with informal workers' trade unions, when the government does engage in such bargaining, will likely be exempt from the purview of the Act.[88] The federal government is not only empowered to supersede the CCI, it also has immunity for its actions taken in good faith.[89] Since the government is (that is, could possibly become) both the bargaining partner and the arbiter in this situation, collective bargaining with informal workers is, and will remain, less legal and more political in nature.

Similarly, in the context of informal workers, strikes are not only a tool employed for the success of collective bargaining with their employer. And as we have seen earlier, unless strikes are so employed, they are not a legal entitlement. However, informal worker trade unions participate in the cessation of work and disruption of economic activities, often alongside other trade unions.[90] If the collective cessation of work is not considered anti-competitive (agreements and combinations) under the Competition Act, it should be seen as an action in the public interest and, thereby, amenable to being exempted by the government.[91]

Strikes by Uber and Ola drivers are illustrative of the public interest aspects of these actions.[92] These strikes saw drivers in several cities withdrawing their services to force these companies to improve their pay structure to take into account increased operating costs (including increasing fuel costs).[93] In cities such as Mumbai and Delhi, these drivers organised under existing trade unions while also receiving widespread support from non-striking unions and political parties. Although the drivers placed their demands against the ride-hailing companies – Uber and Ola – their main leverage against the companies were their positions (claim) as worker-citizens of the state. The drivers' withdrawal of their services was not aimed at bipartite bargaining, despite how their demands targeted Uber and Ola. Instead, the strikes were aimed at forcing the government to negotiate with the companies on their behalf.[94] It is, therefore, unsurprising that the companies chose not to get involved with the striking drivers until the government intervened.[95]

How the drivers and the law understand the status of these drivers is complicated. An ethnographic study of Uber and Ola drivers in India showed that drivers 'don't view Uber/Ola as their employer but as a facilitator for their passengers and payments'.[96] These drivers also see themselves as independent small business owners rather than employees. Despite this, the nature of the demands that striking Uber and Ola drivers directed at the companies suggest that the drivers understand their economic dependence on the two companies. In spite of this underlying understanding, the drivers preferred to pressure the government to act on their behalf rather than engaging in direct negotiation with the companies.[97] Thus, even in the absence of a constitutional right to strike and the exclusion from the statutory right to strike, self-employed or dependent workers could still undertake a *political strike* to make the government a party to a negotiation process. Workers adopt this strategy on the strength of their worker-citizenship. And since the government enjoys discretionary power under the Competition Act, such political strikes will likely be exempt from the purview of the Act. Thus, collective action on the strength of worker-citizenship is simultaneously an effective strategy to circumvent restrictions under the Act.

To further their multidimensional collective agenda, informal workers negotiate with the government in lobbying their claims, on the one hand; on the other, they participate in market-based initiatives by organising themselves as cooperatives and registered companies.[98] Although the government may exempt their trade unionism, their more direct economic participation in the market – even if they are collective worker initiatives – will likely be regulated and, when necessary, restricted, under the Competition Act. In *Competition Commission of India*, the Supreme Court explained:

> [H]ad the Coordination Committee acted only as trade unionists, things would have been different.... However, ... [t]he Coordination Committee (or for that matter even [the] EIMPA [Eastern India Motion Picture Association]) are, in fact, association of enterprises (constituent members) and these members are engaged in production, distribution and exhibition of films. [The] EIMPA is an association of film producers, distributors and exhibitors, operating mainly in the State of West Bengal. Likewise, the Coordination Committee is the joint platform of [the] Federation of Senior Technicians and Workers of Eastern India and [the] West Bengal Motion Pictures Artistes Forum. Both [the] EIMPA as well as the Coordination Committee acted in a concerned and coordinated manner. They joined together in giving call of boycott of competing members ... and, therefore, [the] matter cannot be viewed narrowly by treating [the] Coordination Committee as a trade union, ignoring the fact that it is backing the cause of those which are 'enterprises'.[99]

Informal workers' trade unions may constitute cooperative societies, or the workers may organise themselves as cooperatives or companies to facilitate their market participation. But once such worker associations engage in economic activities, their associations will be treated similarly to other traditional enterprises, not as associations promoting worker solidarity – meaning that self-employed freelance workers, such as film technicians and artists, would likely be seen as economic entities rather than workers under the Competition Act. This leads to their associations being seen as anti-competitive cartels if they violate the Act's policy.

Since the objective of the competition law in India is to promote economic opportunity for businesses and consumers, it would be unwarranted to interpret the law to simultaneously constrain the economic opportunities of workers. Just as consumer choice is enlarged by the promotion of market competition, worker opportunities to benefit from the market are expanded by means of their collective action. While the competition law addresses the inequalities of the exchange relationships of the product and service markets, collective labour law attends to the inequalities of the labour market. Accordingly, one should see competition law and labour law as complementary rather than confrontational.

Moreover, if Indian competition law is intra vires the Constitution, it must recognise the justiciable fundamental right to association (in the legal forms of trade unions and cooperative societies). However, we should also recognise that the scope of the constitutional right to association is narrower than that contemplated under the IR Code. Whereas the IR Code recognises collective bargaining and strikes that further a trade union's economic agenda, the constitutional right to association aims at promoting worker agency – and dignity – through collective action (while not committing to facilitate workers' economic agenda through collective bargaining or strike). Additionally, if the competition law is to remain faithful to the Constitution's social justice agenda, it must not interfere with collective law-making participation – the third component of the constitutional social justice agenda – by workers' representative organisations.

Thus, in view of the central role of a worker's right to association in the country's social justice framework, the only possible interplay between competition law and the IR Code is that of harmonious coexistence. This would involve interpreting the Competition Act's overriding effect over other inconsistent laws as permitting workers' association rights, including the right to collective bargaining and strike unless they are *patently* market-distorting. To clarify, 'patently market-distorting' collective action is a high threshold, and in view of that threshold workers' collective action is hardly market-distorting per se. Furthermore, workers' collective action is a precondition to equitable market participation by workers and a production factor that is uniformly applicable to all varieties of (product and service) market participation. Collective action is, thus, not discriminatory (disfavouring one market participant over others) but a foundational characteristic of a just and functional labour market.

## Conclusion

The third component of the constitutional social justice agenda is direct citizen participation in the governance process. This involves citizens participating in an autonomous lived experience-centred deliberation process which allows them to help determine the scope of their legal entitlements. In the context of workers, this unfolds through their deliberative participation in market exchanges and in social security entitlements. By denying the right to collective bargaining and to strike as part of the constitutional right to association, the Supreme Court somewhat impedes the Constitution's social justice framework. In the absence of constitutional rights to collective bargaining and strike, the IR Code secures limited rights to collective bargaining and strike. However, the labour law reforms have narrowed the scope of the right to strike. In this sense, one can see the IR Code as somewhat curbing the precondition to market power that expands the potential of meaningful worker participation in the contractual law-making process while formally retaining the basis of participatory law-making.

Additionally, although the IR Code recognises trade unionism by informal workers, it is potentially relevant only for a minority of informal workers (including gig and online platform-based workers). Since the very basis of the concept of informal work is its divergence from the conventional industrial employment relationship, the conventional rights to collective bargaining and strikes are of little relevance to them. Informal workers primarily negotiate with the government, which is also the authority facilitating their participation in social security deliberations. Accordingly, the nature of informal worker participatory engagement in the law-making process should be understood as a political process – a public entitlement – to participatory democracy. When such collective participation takes the forms of cooperatives and companies (or entrepreneurial trade unions) of self-employed or own-account informal workers, it should fall within the exemptions of competition law – that is, not amounting to illegal anti-competitive agreements and combinations.

## Notes

1. Constitution of India, 1950, Articles 38, 46 (hereinafter, 'Constitution').
2. Constitution, Article 37.
3. Iris Marion Young, 'Between Liberalism and Social Democracy: A Comment on Tushnet', *Chicago Journal of International Law* 3, no. 2 (2002): 471–476; Nien-he Hsieh, 'Rawlsian Justice and Workplace Republicanism', *Social Theory and Practice* 31, no. 1 (2005): 115–142.
4. Hsieh, 'Rawlsian Justice and Workplace Republicanism', 116–117.

5. Barry Clark and Herbert Gintis, 'Rawlsian Justice and Economic Systems', *Philosophy and Public Affairs* 7, no. 4 (1978): 302–325, 303, 312–314, 324–325; Hsieh, 'Rawlsian Justice and Workplace Republicanism', 117, 121–127. For an overview of the reasonings for economic democracy – workplace democracy – in socialism, see Joshua Cohen, 'The Economic Basis of Deliberative Democracy', *Social Philosophy and Policy* 6, no. 2 (1989): 25–50, 25–30, 39–47.

6. See Clark and Gintis, 'Rawlsian Justice and Economic Systems', 311–315, for an argument on why workplace and political democracy, and in particular Rawlsian redistributive principle, allowing inequality when it benefits the least advantaged groups in society is inconsistent with a mixed-economy capitalism (and market socialism).

7. See Elizabeth Anderson, 'Equality and Freedom in the Workplace: Recovering Republican Insights', *Social Philosophy and Policy* 31, no. 2 (2015): 48–69, 48–49, 59, for a discussion of an extreme example of laissez-faire legal framing of the employment relationship in the United States on the basis of negative liberty (that is, non-interference). In contrast, the Indian Constitution's (non-laissez-faire) framing of the individual freedom-based labour market relationships is substantially narrow, leaving the scope of market interference by the state open.

8. Anderson, 'Equality and Freedom in the Workplace', 49–50, 59–60. (To clarify, in this essay, Anderson argues workplace relationships to be governance relationships – where employees are governed by their bosses once they accept a job – rather than contractual relationships between equal parties. Her observations are focused on the 'employment at will' in the United States.)

9. Anderson, 'Equality and Freedom in the Workplace', 64.

10. Chi Kwok, 'Work Autonomy and Workplace Democracy: The Polarization of the Goods of Work Autonomy in the Two Worlds of Work', *Review of Social Economy* 78, no. 3 (2020): 351–372, 364 (emphasis mine).

11. See Kwok, 'Work Autonomy and Workplace Democracy', 350, for the distinction between workers' 'control' of the workplace and their 'involvement' in firm-level decisions.

12. Hsieh, 'Rawlsian Justice and Workplace Republicanism', 116; Iris Marion Young, 'Self-Determination and Global Democracy: A Critique of Liberal Nationalism', *NOMOS* 42 (2000): 147–183. See, generally, Clark and Gintis, 'Rawlsian Justice and Economic Systems'.

13. Robert Mayer, 'Robert Dahl and the Right to Workplace Democracy', *Review of Politics* 63, no. 2 (2001): 221–247, 222, 236–241.
14. Constitution, Articles 40, 43A, 43B.
15. On a related note, see the discussion of universal rights and selective entitlements in Guy Davidov, 'Setting Labour Law's Coverage: Between Universalism and Selectivity', *Oxford Journal of Legal Studies* 34, no. 3 (2014): 543–566, 552–554.
16. Dorothy E. Smith, *The Everyday World as Problematic: A Feminist Sociology* (Toronto: University of Toronto Press, 1987), 9.
17. See Smith, *The Everyday World as Problematic*, 107, 160–161; Marjorie DeVault, 'Introduction', in *People at Work: Life, Power, and Social Inclusion in the New Economy*, ed. Marjorie L. DeVault, 1, 2, 5–6 (New York and London: New York University Press, 2008). Also see Marjorie DeVault, 'Mapping Invisible Work: Conceptual Tools for Social Justice Projects', *Sociological Forum* 29, no. 4 (2014): 775–790, 787–788; Ellen Pence, 'Safety for Battered Women in a Textually Mediated Legal System', *Studies in Cultures, Organizations and Societies* 7, no. 2 (2001): 199–229, 203.
18. Since legal actors already are aware of the tenets and concepts of the everyday language (or concepts), the disruption caused by legal acculturation and legal enforcement will be minimal.
19. Because of the linguistic community's (people speaking the same language) common social understanding of their living and working conditions, legal actors will better appreciate the specific role that law plays in validating their unique community preoccupations. See, generally, Supriya Routh, 'Examining the Legal Legitimacy of Informal Economic Activities', *Social and Legal Studies* 31, no. 2 (2022): 282–308.
20. Routh, 'Examining the Legal Legitimacy of Informal Economic Activities', 2, 9.
21. DeVault, 'Introduction'; Smith, *The Everyday World as Problematic*.
22. Smith, *The Everyday World as Problematic*, 8–9, 108.
23. See, generally, the Industrial Relations Code, 2020 (Act no. 35 of 2020) (consolidating several labour laws including the erstwhile Industrial Disputes Act, 1947) (hereinafter, 'IR Code').
24. See, generally, the IR Code, in particular chapters 9 and 10. By means of this recently enacted code, Indian Parliament sought to limit the government's role in the employer's decision-making on hiring and firing of workers in medium-sized establishments. This flexibility allowed to employers has been one of the more controversial aspects of the new labour code. It is, in fact,

the trade union federations in the country that protested against the partial governmental withdrawal from industrial relations in small and medium-sized enterprises.
25. See Mitu Sengupta, 'Economic Liberalization, Democratic Expansion and Organized Labour in India: Towards a New Politics of Revival', *Just Labour: A Canadian Journal of Work and Society* 14 (2009): 13–32.
26. Constitution (Ninety Seventh Amendment) Act, 2011.
27. *All India Bank Employees' Association v. National Industrial Tribunal & Others*, [1962] 3 SCR 269 (SC).
28. Apart from the coverage of the *IR Code* and three other prominent federal statutes, there are numerous state (provincial) amendments (and enacted statutes) that either modify federal laws or engage de novo (a rarity) with some aspects of the subject matters covered by some of these and other federal statutes. Legislative competence of the state legislatures and the federal Parliament is determined through the Constitution. See *the Constitution*: Articles 246, 254, for the scope of legislative power of Parliament and state legislatures.
29. IR Code, section 14. (As much as the IR Code safeguards collective bargaining, for an empirical evaluation of deteriorating trade union power to influence employment conditions through collective bargaining, see Anamitra Roychowdhury, 'Application of Job Security Laws, Workers' Bargaining Power and Employment Outcomes in India', *Economic and Labour Relations Review* 30, no. 1 [2019]: 120.)
30. IR Code, sections 14, 30, and the First Schedule. The collective agreement should inter alia include subject matters such as classification of workers; communication of wages, work shifts, holidays, and pay-days; nature of shift; attendance; conditions of leave; temporary work stoppages; details of termination of employment; liability for workers' misconduct; and available redressal mechanism for unfair treatment of workers.
31. IR Code, sections 29, 30.
32. IR Code, sections 2(70), 84, 86(5), 101(1) and Entry I (1) of the Second Schedule on 'Unfair Labour Practices'.
33. IR Code, Entry I (15) of the Second Schedule on 'Unfair Labour Practices'.
34. IR Code, Entry II (3) of the Second Schedule on 'Unfair Labour Practices'.
35. IR Code, section 14. Additionally, the federal and the state governments are empowered to recognise trade unions or federation of trade unions at the federal and the state levels respectively. See the IR Code, section 27.
36. IR Code, section 14.

37. *T. K. Rangarajan v. Government of Tamil Nadu and Others*, (2003) Appeal (Civil) 5556 of 2003 (SC).
38. *Black's Law Dictionary* defines 'unconscionability' as 'extreme unfairness. Unconscionability is normally assessed by an objective standard: (1) one party's lack of meaningful choice, and (2) contractual terms that unreasonably favor the other party.' See *Black's Law Dictionary* (11th edition) (2019), *sub verbo* 'unconscionability'.
39. See, for example, *Dharangadhara Chemical Works Limited v. State of Saurashtra*, (1957) 1 LLJ 477 (SC).
40. *T. K. Rangarajan v. Government of Tamil Nadu and Others*, (2003) Appeal (Civil) 5556 of 2003 (SC).
41. Strike is defined as 'cessation of work by a body of persons employed in any industry acting in combination, or a concerted refusal, or a refusal, under a common understanding, of any number of persons who are or have been so employed to continue to work or to accept employment and includes the concerted casual leave on a given day by fifty per cent or more workers employed in an industry'. See IR Code, section 2(zk).
42. IR Code, section 62.
43. See the now repealed Industrial Disputes Act, 1947, sections 22, 2(n), 2(n)(vi), First Schedule on 'Industries which may be declared to be Public Utility Services under sub-clause (vi) of clause (n) of section 2'. Public utility services included railway, port, other transportation, banking, postal, telegraph, telephone, electricity, water supplies, sanitation, coal industry, cotton textile industry, iron and steel industry, defence establishments, hospital services, fire brigade service, oil industry, airport services, government mints, and so on (while some of these industries were enumerated public utility services, the government was empowered to declare other industries as public utility services).
44. See International Labour Organization, 'Statistical Update on Employment in the Informal Economy', June 2012, http://www.ilo.org/wcmsp5/groups/public/---dgreports/---stat/documents/presentation/wcms_182504.pdf (accessed on 16 August 2023); National Commission for Enterprises in the Unorganised Sector, *Report on Definitional and Statistical Issues Relating to Informal Economy* (New Delhi: National Commission for Enterprises in the Unorganised Sector, 2008), 44.
45. See, generally, Supriya Routh, 'Informal Workers' Aggregation and Law', *Theoretical Inquiries in Law* 17, no. 1 (2016): 283–320.

46. In *Bangalore Water Supply & Sewerage Board v. A. Rajappa and Others*, 1978 AIR (SC) 548, interpreting the definition of 'industry' for the purposes of the then Industrial Disputes Act, 1947 (now integrated in the IR Code), the Supreme Court noted that while cooperation between the employer and the employee does qualify an undertaking as an industry, small to very small undertakings are not industries for the purposes of the Act. Similarly, the Code on Social Security, 2020 (Act no. 36 of 2020) permits access to certain entitlements, such as provident fund, medical insurance, gratuity and maternity benefit, on the basis of the size of an industry (employing at least ten or twenty employees for different entitlements). See the First Schedule of the Code on Social Security. The enormity of these statutory exclusions could be assessed from the fact that only about 1.37 per cent of commercial establishments in India employ ten or more employees. See Government of India, *All India Report of Sixth Economic Census, 2016*, ch. 2, 26–27, https://www.mospi.gov.in/all-india-report-sixth-economic-census (accessed on 16 August 2023).
47. Additionally, informal workers are also self-employed and, therefore, do not fit the labour law model based on employment relationship.
48. In fact, while seeking registration as a trade union, SEWA had to argue that even without engaging in collective bargaining (and strikes), a trade union could exist as a worker collective. For details of SEWA's registration and functioning, see Routh, 'Informal Workers' Aggregation and Law', 297–299.
49. Rina Agarwala, 'Reshaping the Social Contract: Emerging Relations between the State and Informal Labor in India', *Theory and Society* 37, no. 4 (2008): 375–408, 378, 393–396.
50. Agarwala, 'Reshaping the Social Contract', 378, 392–394.
51. See, generally, Ela R. Bhatt, *We Are Poor but So Many: The Story of Self-Employed Women in India* (New York: Oxford University Press, 2006), 16–22.
52. See, for example, the database on organising initiatives by informal waste pickers across different continents generated by the International Alliance of Waste Pickers. 'List: Waste Pickers around the World', https://globalrec.org/waw/list (accessed on 16 August 2023).
53. See, generally, Arun Kumar Ghosh, 'Cooperative Movement and Rural Development in India', *Social Change* 37, no. 3 (2007): 14–32; Sharit K. Bhowmik and Kanchan Sarker, 'Worker Cooperatives as Alternative Production Systems', *Work and Occupations* 29, no. 4 (2002): 460–482;

Ashok Gulati and Kavery Ganguly, 'The Changing Landscape of Indian Agriculture', *Agricultural Economics* 41, no. 1 (2010): 37–45; Rabi N. Patra and Mahendra P. Agasty, 'Cooperatives, Agriculture and Rural Development: Role, Issues and Policy Implications', *IOSR Journal of Humanities and Social Sciences* 13, no. 2 (2013): 14–25.
54. Constitution, Article 19(1)(c).
55. Code on Social Security, 2020 (Act no. 36 of 2020) (hereinafter, 'Code on Social Security'), Preamble. The code defines social security (section 2[78]) as follows:

> [T]he the measures of protection afforded to employees, unorganised workers, gig workers and platform workers to ensure access to health care and to provide income security, particularly in cases of old age, unemployment, sickness, invalidity, work injury, maternity or loss of a breadwinner by means of rights conferred on them and schemes framed, under this Code.

56. Code on Social Security, section 2(79).
57. Code on Social Security, sections 2(79), 4, 5, 6, 7.
58. Code on Social Security, sections 4, 16.
59. Code on Social Security, sections 5, 25, 26.
60. Code on Social Security, sections 7, 108.
61. Code on Social Security, section 12.
62. Code on Social Security, section 6.
63. Code on Social Security, sections 6, 109, 114.
64. Code on Social Security, section 6.
65. Code on Social Security, sections 6, 114.
66. Code on Social Security, section 6.
67. Code on Social Security, section 6.
68. Code on Social Security, section 149.
69. Competition Act, 2002 (Act no. 12 of 2003) (hereinafter, 'Competition Act').
70. Competition Act, section 3.
71. Competition Act, sections 4, 19. Section 4 defines a 'dominant position' as 'a position of strength' which enables an enterprise to function independently of market forces and influence its competitors and consumers to its advantage. Section 19 delineates detailed criteria for evaluating a dominant position.
72. Competition Act, sections 4, 19.
73. Competition Act, sections 5, 6.

74. Competition Act, section 5. It is improbable that any federation of trade unions in India would ever reach this high-assets threshold to be considered a threatening anti-competitive combination.
75. Competition Act, section 19.
76. Competition Act, sections 4, 20.
77. *Excel Crop Care Limited v. Competition Commission of India and Another*, (2014) Civil Appeal No. 2480 of 2014 (SC), paras. 21, 24–26, 29; *Rajasthan Cylinders and Containers Limited v. Union of India and Another*, (2014) Civil Appeal No. 3546 of 2014 (SC), paras. 70–71, 78–79, 89. Also see *Competition of India v. Steel Authority of India Limited and Another*, (2010) Civil Appeal No. 7779 of 2010 (SC). This approach, whereby consumer benefit becomes the ultimate benchmark for evaluating competition law, potentially differs from the United States' approach to competition law. Although the Indian competition law is based on the European Union and the United States antitrust regimes, the United States antitrust law seems to be focused on the ideal of competition rather than consumer harm (or benefit) resulting from anti-competitive agreements and practices. See Gregory J. Werden, 'Antitrust's Rule of Reason: Only Competition Matters', *Antitrust Law Journal* 79, no. 2 (2014): 713–759, 727–730, 743, 746, 756.
78. *Rajasthan Cylinders and Containers Limited v. Union of India and Another*, (2014) Civil Appeal No. 3546 of 2014 (SC), para. 72.
79. *Excel Crop Care Limited v. Competition Commission of India and Another*, (2014) Civil Appeal No. 2480 of 2014 (SC), para. 21.
80. *Competition Commission of India v. Co-Ordination Committee of Artists and Technicians of W.B. Film and Television and Others*, (2014) Civil Appeal No. 6691 of 2014 (SC).
81. *Competition Commission of India v. Co-Ordination Committee of Artists and Technicians of W.B. Film and Television and Others*, (2014) Civil Appeal No. 6691 of 2014 (SC), para. 39.
82. *Competition Commission of India v. Co-Ordination Committee of Artists and Technicians of W.B. Film and Television and Others*, (2014) Civil Appeal No. 6691 of 2014 (SC), paras. 39, 41.
83. *Competition Commission of India v. Co-Ordination Committee of Artists and Technicians of W.B. Film and Television and Others*, (2014) Civil Appeal No. 6691 of 2014 (SC), para. 42.
84. *Competition Commission of India v. Co-Ordination Committee of Artists and Technicians of W.B. Film and Television and Others*, (2014) Civil Appeal No. 6691 of 2014 (SC), para. 39.

85. Competition Act, section 54.
86. Competition Act, section 56.
87. See, generally, Rina Agarwala, *Informal Labor, Formal Politics, and Dignified Discontent in India* (New York: Cambridge University Press, 2013); Agarwala, 'Reshaping the Social Contract'; Routh, 'Reshaping the Social Contract', 314.
88. Competition Act, sections 54, 55.
89. Competition Act, sections 56, 59.
90. For example, SEWA participated in the nationwide strike alongside other trade unions in protesting the government's policies. *Hindu Business Line*, 'Trade Unions Go on Nationwide Strike against Centre's "Anti-People" Policies', 8 January 2020, https://www.thehindubusinessline.com/news/10-central-trade-unions-go-on-nationwide-strike/article30511129.ece (accessed on 16 August 2023).
91. Competition Act, section 54. Also see Constitution, Part IVA: Fundamental Duties.
92. Uber and Ola drivers are sui generis on the formal–informal spectrum. While they are sometimes considered 'formal' because they have to pay taxes since their engagement and app-based income are documented and accounted for, they are also 'informal' because they are largely excluded from labour law and social welfare entitlements. However, as noted, the recent labour law reforms conceive of social security for gig workers. See, generally, Aditi Surie, 'Tech in Work: Organising Informal Work in India', *Economic and Political Weekly* 52, no. 20 (2017): 12–15.
93. Aditya Ray, 'Unrest in India's Gig Economy: Ola–Uber Drivers' Strikes and Worker Organization', *Futures of Work*, 9 December 2019; *Hindustan Times*, 'Ola and Uber Taxis May Go on Strike in Mumbai Tomorrow', 27 February 2017.
94. Ray, 'Unrest in India's Gig Economy'.
95. *Hindustan Times*, 'Ola, Uber Strike: Who Gained and Who Lost', 27 February 2017.
96. Shantanu Prabhat, Sneha Nanavati and Nimmi Rangaswamy, 'India's "Uberwallah" Profiling Uber Drivers in the Gig Economy', paper presented at the Tenth International Conference on Information and Communication Technologies and Development (ICTD '19), 4–7 January 2019, Ahmedabad.
97. Prabhat, Nanavati and Rangaswamy, 'India's "Uberwallah"'.
98. See Supriya Routh, 'Constituting a Right to Association: A Postcolonial Exploration', *International Journal of Comparative Labour Law and Industrial*

*Relations* 36, no. 4 (2020): 523–552. Also see Routh, 'Informal Workers' Aggregation and Law', 318–319.

99. *Competition Commission of India v. Co-Ordination Committee of Artists and Technicians of W.B. Film and Television and Others*, (2014) Civil Appeal No. 6691 of 2014, para. 41.

# CONCLUSION

## Realising Labour Justice

The purpose of this concluding chapter is not merely to reprise the major arguments made in the book and condense its main thesis. Instead, building on the arguments made in the book, this chapter aims to be future-guiding and discusses a potential alternative approach to labour law, particularly from an Indian and more generally from a Global South perspective. It is hoped that some of the future-guiding reflections offered in this chapter will aid the way labour law is debated, practised and interpreted in the country, by both policy and legal practitioners, including the judiciary. Of course, some of the main arguments of the book are revisited here, but they occupy a limited part of this chapter. In revisiting the main arguments of the book, the intention is to emphasise the understanding of labour law in light of the specific requirements under the Constitution of India. In discussing an alternative approach to labour law, this chapter also indicates some potential areas for future scholarly explorations. After this more general introduction to the chapter, in the first section, the foundations of labour law in India, as conceived under the Constitution, are revisited. Drawing on this discussion, the second section offers a more general take on the alternative social justice based theorising of labour law. The third section is devoted to the discussion of the overall orientation of the 2020 labour law reforms. The chapter ends (fourth section) with a note on overcoming the dependent juridical mentality, which has historically constrained an alternative conceptual formulation of labour law in India, in view of the contextual realities of the country.

CONCLUSION

This book argued that labour law furthers the social justice mission of the Constitution, which is conceived in relation to social cooperation among worker-citizens of the country. Labour law is, then, an instrument to practically realise the constitutional commitment made to worker-citizens. In so realising the constitutional commitment, the challenge for labour law is to sustain the balance among the different aspects of the social justice mission envisaged under the Constitution. It is this balance among the three components of social justice – market freedom, social solidarity and participatory deliberation – that gives the idea of social justice its unique Indian character. In practically realising social justice for worker-citizens, if this balance – that is, the way the three aspects of the social justice agenda interact – is distorted, then the agenda does not merely lose its unique characteristics, the very agenda is jeopardised. This book showed that the amended labour law, after the comprehensive reforms of 2019–2020, jeopardises the constitutional social justice agenda insofar as its actual realisation is concerned. Whereas the new labour law in the country has made a heightened commitment to the laissez-faire labour market, it has failed to safeguard worker welfare by refusing to offer corresponding security to protect workers from additional risks resulting from the former. A greater commitment to market liberalisation would have required a significant expansion of statutorily guaranteed social security provisioning if the Constitution were to serve as a guide.

The book also showed that the problem of the current labour law is not limited to this distortion of the constitutional commitment alone. Additionally, the new labour law stunts the scope of collective action and participatory deliberation. Collective action and participatory deliberation are central to the social justice agenda. They are fundamental rights of worker-citizens and fundamental commitments of the state. Without robust collective action and participatory deliberation, the two other components of the social justice mission become untenable. In spite of this significance of participatory deliberation, it is astonishing that the entirety of the reforms were pushed through by Parliament against the near-complete objections of trade unions.

In addition to this general political deficiency, the new labour law fails on two more accounts. First, although trade unionism is an explicit fundamental right and, therefore, should naturally lead to collective bargaining and strike as its constituent elements, the reforms end up constraining the right to strike compared to the former regime, thereby failing to allow the right to unionisation its fuller expression. On the other hand, while the reforms recognise informal workers' right to collective action, their collective action is conceived only with reference to bargaining with an employer. This is a missed opportunity because it is primarily with the government rather than an employer that informal workers negotiate. Their non-traditional bargaining (that is, negotiation with the government) needed to be on a firmer ground. Both of these are problems relating to the scope of collective action.

The second problematic aspect of the reforms is that when it created institutional platforms for participatory deliberation, it simultaneously evicted workers' representations from such deliberative institutions, instead inserting representatives of the government in such institutions. The constitution of the social security boards, which are largely populated by government nominees, testifies to the aforementioned. Additionally, in view of the conflicting competition law regime for collective action by the self-employed, including informal workers, the reforms could have offered some guidelines clarifying the role of the competition law regime in this respect. Collectively, all of these shortcomings go on to establish the failure of the current labour law to discharge its constitutional burden. To be sure, the newly enacted labour law is intra vires the Constitution, but its ability to further the constitutional justice agenda is now substantially curbed.

Labour law's identity as an instrument for realising the constitutional social justice agenda is unique on account of the country's history and constitutional principles. Such identity is somewhat different from the conventional understanding of labour law. Although there are disagreements on the unique realm of labour law, the discipline has been conventionally understood as a special kind of contract in common law jurisdictions.[1] Labour law, broadly understood as including both individual employment and collective agreement, is integrally committed to the idea of contract. It operates on the premise that self-interested parties could negotiate between themselves in order to arrive at an agreement that is beneficial for both of them. This orientation of the discipline is seen more prominently in collective labour relations, where legal protection of bargaining attains centre stage, than in individual employment relationships. However, individual employment relationships are not devoid of this understanding of contractual relationships involving personal labour. Although labour law generally believes in the capacity of 'free' contract to fairly distribute income and wealth in a society, it is conscious of the de facto unfreedom in the bargaining process. As much as it operates with reference to the ideal of freedom of contract, it is cognisant of the disparity between the owner of capital and the owner of labour in market exchanges. In particular, it is cognisant that the special characteristic of 'labour' – as inseparable from the person of the worker and essentially a non-alienable commodity – constrains the capacity of the worker to freely negotiate the employment contract. The very nature of exchange of labour, combined with the employer's proprietary right over the production process, limits the worker's autonomy in the contractual process.

Because of labour law's ideological commitment to contractual exchanges, it seeks to operationalise the contractual process in a more equitable manner by removing constraints from workers' autonomy so that the reality of the market comes close to the ideal of the market. Labour law seeks to promote the contractual autonomy of workers by equalising the bargaining power between the contracting parties.[2] In the context of collective employment contracts, labour law does so by securing workers' right to collective action and, in the case of individual employment, by securing the floor of rights limiting the contractual freedom of the employer. By intervening in the negotiation process – in collective and individual contracts – labour law has an effect on the (labour) market outcome, which is assumed to be less inequitable between (owners of) capital and (owners of) labour at an aggregate level. Conventional labour law, thus, operationalises the labour market by seeking to remove the unfreedoms in market negotiations. It seeks to minimise inequality in the freedom of contract.

In the aforementioned sense, labour law's normative aim is to promote workers' contractual autonomy so that during the exchange of labour, workers could negotiate a fair agreement. What follows is that conventionally labour law has perceived – and continues to perceive – the worker as a *contractor*, someone capable of contracting.[3] Labour law seeks to strengthen this contractual capacity of the worker. Recognising the autonomy of workers, labour law leaves the worker to negotiate the worth of their labour. In other words, the law lets workers sell (exchange) their labour at a value that the workers consider appropriate insofar as they meet the minimum standards prescribed by law. The minimum standards are not the market value of labour; they are instead the foundation of workers' autonomy (without which a 'free' contract is impossible). In permitting workers (and employers) to determine (that is, negotiate) the *value of labour for the production process*, the caveat that labour law adds is that labour, even in exchange, should not be treated as any other commodity. Thus, the exchange value (that is, price) of labour goes beyond mere wages and includes aspects such as medical and health insurance and protection against discrimination. However, as discussed subsequently, this imagination of labour law is somewhat narrower than the conceptual foundation of the discipline in India.

## The Foundation of Labour Law in India

What the aforementioned conventional labour law perspective does not capture is the larger *contribution* that workers make beyond the *tasks* they are employed to perform. In contractual parlance, parties exchange goods and services. Workers undertake tasks in exchange for wages and perks. This isolated focus on tasks (performed in personal work relations[4]) obscures labour law's view of the social contribution that workers make as part of the collaborative production process.[5] In contrast to common law's narrow focus on the exchange of personal service, Indian labour law is premised on the recognition of the Indian workforce's broader social contribution. In this social contribution-centred recognition of Indian workers, workers are constitutionally obligated to excel in their individual and collective activities in order to catapult the nation towards 'higher levels of endeavour and achievement'.[6] This ideal of the betterment of society ('the nation') through the citizens' individual and collective activities underlies the notion of the worker-citizen as proposed in this book.

The worker-citizen, then, is not a mere contractor undertaking to perform personal service in exchange for wages. The worker-citizen is an agent 'striv[ing] towards excellence'[7] to contribute to social development and nation-building. Such social contribution cannot be captured by the narrow private contractual relation. Sensibly, the only way to understand such social contribution is to see it as part of social relationships among the citizenry. In this social relational manner of capturing work, the reciprocity inherent in the recognition of the workers' contribution permeates the private–public divide. Just as private employment relationships are part of the social contribution framework, public 'fraternal'[8] relationships are also part of the relational structure. While private exchanges compensate workers' tasks, public relationships reward their broader (social) contribution. Both of these aspects are, then, recognised and captured by the formulation of social justice under the Indian Constitution.

Social justice under the Indian Constitution, pursuing fairness for the workforce, unfolds through three components. First, through safeguarding fundamental rights, the Constitution secures workers' autonomy to engage in market exchanges, thereby enabling them to participate in market-based resource distribution processes. Second, in recognition of workers' social contribution and the ideal of solidarity underscoring such contribution, the Constitution, through directive principles, secures the basis of worker welfare. The first and second components are complementary and intertwined. One cannot exist without the other. Any change in one of these two components will require a corresponding change in the other in order to maintain the complementary nature of the two. As the third component of the social justice agenda, the Constitution safeguards collective action and participatory deliberation by workers as both fundamental rights and directive principles, so as to consolidate the democratic basis of the labour market and social welfare.

What follows is that the foundation of labour law in India is not contract but justice, a concern for the workers to be treated fairly for the social contribution they make. It is the responsibility of labour law to concretely realise the ideal of social justice conceived under the Constitution. If realisation of social justice is the task of labour law in India, the different components of labour law across the three dimensions of justice should fit together to coherently further the constitutional agenda. In this aggregative sense of the discipline, labour law extends well beyond the workplace and the employment contract. Beyond the labour market contract, social welfare is an integral part of the Indian labour law as is deliberative participation of workers (and other stakeholders). In fact, social welfare is destined to be an increasingly prominent part of labour law because of the challenges posed by the disintegration of the workplace and newer forms of structuring work (such as platform-based 'on-demand' work).[9]

Primarily, the challenge posed by newer forms of work is that they are not structured through the neat exchange rationale and contractual structure that characterise conventional labour law.[10] In the absence of such a rationale (and structure), strenuous adjudicative exercise seeks to fit disparate situations under conventional legal categories, resulting in conflicting interpretations and judicial outcomes in different common law jurisdictions.[11] Such inconsistency creates uncertainties for workers, sometimes resulting in the denial of their entitlements. Under such circumstances, relying solely on the structures of the market-based distribution framework may prove to be unsatisfactory in treating workers fairly. Unsurprisingly, a solidarity-focused redistribution framework might be more effective in extending more certainty to workers when their structures and experiences at work have the likelihood of excluding them from legal entitlements under the conventional employment contract model. It is by means of the redistributive logic that parts of corporate profits could be transmitted back to workers who helped garner those profits, even when the relationships at work obscure legal categorisation.

A focus on redistribution – social welfare – should also help tackle the increasingly prominent debate on the relationship between work and the sustainability of nature.[12] Under market exchange-based working relationships, labour and nature are often inseparable in their exploitation. Just as the employer (capitalist generally) benefits from workers' contributions, the former also exploits the environment to expand her profits.[13] Both labour and nature are (fictitious) market commodities catering to capitalist expansion.[14] However, just as with labour, fairness (that is, protection and reproduction) to nature cannot be pursued merely through market exchanges, as some scholars propose.[15] One such proposal is that employers should be under a mandate to fairly pay – that is, 'internalize the costs' of exploitation of both labour and nature.[16] However, the very character of capitalist market relations conflicts with the core of this proposal. The capitalist production process accumulates capital – makes profits – by externalising the costs (that is, exploiting) to labour and nature. If capitalist production processes are made to internalise additional costs (for environmental harm, for example), their profits are bound to shrink, which is unacceptable to the capitalist mode of production (because it goes against the very ethos of capital accumulation, the very foundation of capitalism).

If employers are made to pay for environmental degradation caused by production processes and fair compensation to workers, in order to keep their profit margin intact (and expanding), they will externalise such additional costs to consumers. An increased price of goods and services for the consumer will, in turn, exacerbate social inequality, thereby disputing the very rationale of the cost internalisation strategy. A potentially superior manner of addressing the exploitation of nature is by way of redistribution funded through corporate profits. Just as corporate profits could be transmitted back to workers through social welfare, such profits could also be transmitted back for the purpose of protection and reproduction of nature. It is true that this approach may also not negate employers' (businesses') quests for increased profits. However, in contrast to increasing the costs of businesses, corporate profits-funded social welfare has a better potential to address social (and environmental) inequality because of its broader redistributive capacity. This strategy of recognising social welfare as an inseparable component of labour law is consistent with the understanding of work as a socio-ecological[17] contribution made by the worker-citizen. Such socio-ecological imagination of work is also conceptually consistent with the solidarity-based redistribution agenda under the Constitution. This intersection of regulatory concerns relating to human labour and non-human nature is an area where further investigation ought to be made by employing a social justice lens.

Labour law as an instrument to further social justice is not unique to Indian jurisprudence. The expansive imagination of Indian labour law as inclusive of market exchanges and social welfare is somewhat (that is, juridically) similar to the imagination of social law in Europe.[18] This similarity lies not in how social rights are enforced (or the extent of resources they redistribute) but in how they are thematically imagined in a constitutional framework.[19] In continental European jurisdictions such as France and Germany, the social law furthers a social justice programme by safeguarding the citizens' economic security as a normative goal.[20] In furthering the social justice agenda, workers' market exchanges are not seen in isolation. Such exchanges are seen as part of the entire life cycle of workers, which also includes education, training, periods of unemployment, retirement and pension dependence.[21] Social law concerns itself with the 'unity of the goal' of individual workers' interests and the social interest.[22] Such social law draws its conceptual strength from an 'economic constitution', furthering fairness in market-based economic exchanges.[23] However, as Gautam Bhatia and Emilios Christodoulidis note, we should be careful not to overstate the similarities between the two jurisdictions.[24] While the position of social rights between the two jurisdictions has received some comparative attention, such comparison should be more fully explored through future research. What is, however, somewhat specific to India is the conceptualisation of the worker-citizens and their social contribution as a basis for the operationalisation of the social justice programme. In this sense, the legal arrangement uniting market exchanges, social welfare and participatory deliberation in India should be understood as labour law – not social law – organising regulatory principles on the basis of work (in contrast to strictly economic exchanges). Calls for similar expansive imaginations of labour law are increasingly heard from other jurisdictions too.[25]

## Theorising Labour Law

That conventional labour law needs conceptual reformulation has been extensively acknowledged by legal scholars across the globe. This scholarly preoccupation is a response to the inability of the conventional model of labour law – as individual and collective employment contracts – to satisfactorily explain the heterogeneous quasi-contractual and non-contractual working relationships and the plurality of norms surrounding work. A comprehensive theorisation of labour law is not only important to explicate heterogeneous relationships at work, but also central to explaining the relationship between work as a human activity and non-human nature (that is, socio-ecological significance of livelihood activities such as agriculture, animal husbandry, mining, waste recycling, and so on).

A social justice-based justification of labour law demonstrates the potential of a broadly conceived idea of regulation of work, one that promotes fairness through legal entitlements in varied concrete contexts of work-based relationships. The social justice rationale expands the scope of labour law in two fundamental senses. First, it understands work-based relationships beyond the confines of contractual relationships and situates work in its social relationships. Second, it understands work as a contribution to social development beyond private exchange, which entitles the contributors to an (appropriately defined) social citizenship (for example, worker-citizens) on the basis of their work. This idea of social citizenship is different from nationality, instead operating on the logic of reciprocal recognition of workers' social contribution. This expansive articulation of the law of work coherently explains the traditional ways of organising labour exchange through employment contracts, yet is able to account for the divergent forms of work that remain excluded from, or exist at the margins of, the traditional framework of labour law.

This book clarifies the justificatory basis of labour law in India. By clarifying the justificatory basis (justice or fairness) of regulation, it provides legal practitioners, scholars and policymakers with conceptual tools to better formulate – and understand – labour laws for heterogeneous forms of work and work relationships without remaining constrained by traditional legal categories (for example, employee or independent contractor). It is important to provide these conceptual tools in order to overcome the conventional narrow legal formulation of all work-based relationships only in terms of employment (including 'employment like') or independent contract, which often fail to capture the complexities of and motivations in divergent forms of work. The failure to capture these complexities and motivations often results in the disjuncture between juridical remedies (or the regulatory logic, more broadly) and the aspirations of workers in their specific contexts. A prominent example of this disjuncture could be seen in the conflicting judgments of various courts in common law jurisdictions characterising Uber drivers as either employees or independent contractors, resulting in either a complete range of employee entitlements or a complete exclusion from such entitlements. Alternatively, a social justice rationale might approach the same issue by recognising the drivers' contribution to social development (that is, mobility and transportation), entitling them to a range of resources and opportunities collectively provided by corporations and the state. This general formulation will result in different legal categories and institutions in divergent social contexts.

A social justice rationale to the law of work helps formulate regulation with a view to achieving the ends of justice, which is a fairer society for workers. As noted, the social justice narrative adopts a more comprehensive view of work as an ongoing social contribution made by a worker's personal labour rather than an instantaneous approach to value work on the logic of the labour exchange (that is, the moment of exchange or contract). This book understands social justice as fairness.[26] Applied in the context of the law of work, the social justice rationale focuses on the fairness with which workers should be treated because of their work-based social citizenship.[27] Such a mandate of fairness emerges from the ideal of reciprocity inherent in the concept of social contribution.

Some labour law scholars emphasise the importance of a theory of social justice to lend coherence to the discipline of labour law, which increasingly struggles to explain the empirical diversity of the real world.[28] This call requires expanding the justificatory basis of labour law beyond the general logic of market ordering.[29] Moving beyond the laissez-faire market model, these scholars indicate the significance of labour for society. This social significance of labour is more appropriately captured by the rationale of social justice.[30] Although these scholars agree that the conventional market efficiency-based justification of labour law is problematic, they diverge on the potential social justice model to guide regulation of labour.[31] These scholars not only diverge on the social justice model to justify labour law but also invoke social justice primarily to address one or other aspects of the discipline, such as its normative goal or its collective means.[32] A fuller account of the discipline of labour law based on the principles of social justice has generally been absent from legal scholarship. This book seeks to offer a preliminary step towards a fuller account of the discipline of labour law, albeit from a Global South perspective and contextualised in the backdrop of the comprehensive labour law reforms in India.

A social justice account, in the sense the idea is used in this book, both challenges the contractual model of labour law and introduces diversity as a central component of labour jurisprudence, with an emphasis on work-based relationships that have conventionally remained excluded from the scope of labour jurisprudence. As noted, since the contractual model of labour law imagines workers only as contractors, undermining their labour-based identity,[33] it sidelines the very contribution made through one's personal labour. To be sure, historically, the contractual model of labour law emerged as the exclusive model of labour regulation from among divergent work-based relationships that de facto existed across the globe.[34] The social justice perspective aims to explicitly recognise the de facto diversity of the real world and establish it as a central component of the regulatory ideal.

The social justice account also contests some of the alternative narratives of labour law. While, on the one hand, it finds the account of personal work relations too narrow and closer to the contractual exchange model,[35] on the other, it diverges from a specific constitutional narrative of labour law insofar as the latter limits its imagination of labour mainly as capitalist economic exchanges.[36] Even though these accounts usefully disturb the conceptual narrowness of labour law, they demonstrate an unwillingness to move beyond the private exchange model of legal regulation. By offering an expansive political narrative of the law of work (in contrast to a technical one), the social justice narrative shifts the gaze of labour law from interpretive manoeuvre (involving employee and independent contractor) to reconceptualising the basis of the regulation of work, including the legal institutions furthering the aim of such regulation. In particular, the social justice rationale of the law of work is useful in addressing some of the current debates involving the regulation of work, including where work does not have an immediate market exchange value (for example, unpaid care work).

In offering the political significance of work – work valued for its social contribution rather than its private exchange – as the rationale for regulation, the social justice narrative centralises values underlying such regulation (that is, the principle of reciprocity inherent in the work-based citizenship ideal).

A focus on values introduces a higher level of abstraction to regulatory debates involving work. This high-level abstraction is important as an expansive analytical perspective in making sense of the emerging issues at the intersection of work and regulation. The following examples are instructive of this importance.

As noted earlier, one of the prominent issues of our times is the challenge of sustainable development. The social justice perspective rearticulates this challenge as sustainability of livelihood activities. Such refocusing from 'development' to 'livelihoods' emphasises the values of an individual's work-based citizenship and well-being through such citizenship. This reorientation integrates individual agency (work) into the explanation of social justice, signifying the role of work for one's well-being and social development. Similarly, the social justice narrative analyses the 'transition' from fossil fuel- to non-fossil fuel-based economic activities to further sustainability with an eye on the effect of such transition on workers' agency-based well-being. The social justice conceptualisation also helps in evaluating another important question beyond national jurisdictions, which is the regulation of global value (supply) chains. As noted, since the conceptualisation is based on the recognition of work as a social contribution, which demands recognition of workers (as social citizens), its reasoning could be extended beyond political borders through supply chains. While the global justice literature recognises this supply chain-based relationship,[37] it needs further exploration in the theoretical context of labour law.

The social justice-based explanation of the law of work is also helpful in debates on newer working arrangements (for example, online platform-based work) and techno-managerial innovations (for example, automated decision-making and worker surveillance). This explanation helps us reimagine institutions of labour regulation without remaining fixated on the conventional imaginaries when working arrangements and labour relations take newer forms. By focusing on *values*, the justice-based narrative also supplies reasonings for regulation where some of the managerial, supervisory and labour functions are transferred from individuals and groups to automated mechanisms. While this book has not engaged with these questions, it may serve as a helpful starting point for some of these debates by raising fundamental questions on the viability of the worker-citizen idea and the scope of workers' participatory deliberation at work. The following has been the more immediate concern of the book.

## The Labour Law Reforms of 2020: Guiding Values

When the governments of several Indian states had initiated the suspension of, or exemption from, labour laws in order to ease economic and bureaucratic pressures on businesses during the pandemic, they were operating under a complete misunderstanding of the role of labour laws and a general disregard for the Constitution. The most extreme measure was taken by the state of Uttar Pradesh, which attempted to largely suspend the application of labour laws through a state ordinance. These governments assumed labour laws to be merely the laws of market exchange, regulating the contract of employment between the employer and the employee, and nothing more. They also misconceived governmental roles in labour relations. Such attempts, even in failure, show the risk posed by a narrow and piecemeal understanding of labour laws.

In the preceding situation, the (state) government(s) understood that they can interfere in the relationship between the employer and the employee under circumstances that they considered to be in the public interest (in this case, easing the burden on the employers so that they can continue operating their businesses, presumably in the public interest). Governmental interventions were made to secure the proprietary and business interests of the employers. Through their actions, while these governments acknowledged that market interventions may be acceptable (contrary to the laissez-faire ideal), the nature of the interference to be made was completely misunderstood. As mentioned earlier, labour laws exist in labour market exchanges because they secure the foundation of the market by (roughly) equalising freedom of contract between the employer and the employee. Labour law simultaneously expands workers' freedom and constrains employers' freedom. Markets can deliver on their promise to distribute income, wealth and opportunities only when these foundations (preconditions) are safeguarded through law. If these preconditions are removed, the market loses its character and authenticity.

It is true that during times of emergency, governments may impose additional conditions on the operation of the market in the public interest. However, such conditions cannot unilaterally prioritise property and business rights of the employer at the cost of the freedom (of contract) of the employee, which is what these state governments attempted to do. Labour laws as bases of the freedom of contract – a fundamental right – were sacrificed in order to protect the right to property of the employer, a constitutional but not fundamental right.[38] This is a constitutionally unacceptable position – ultra vires the Constitution. Under normal market conditions, workers are already at a disadvantage with respect to their freedom of contract because of their lack of proprietary rights and only the fictitious commodity of labour to exchange. At a time when workers are at their most vulnerable (such as during the COVID-19 pandemic), removing the vestiges of their real market freedom is unfair, and thus, such action also does not pass the social justice benchmark of the Constitution.

At the same time, however, governments are expected to intervene in labour relations in order to promote workers' welfare during an especially difficult period. In India, the government is obligated to assume this role in reciprocation to the contributions made by worker-citizens. Governmental intervention, as many governments practised in different jurisdictions across the globe during the pandemic, should have been to support market transactions through the introduction of additional resources (for example, easy availability of credits, tax exemptions, and so on) – that is, by providing additional social support for the operation of the market. Unfortunately, however, instead of allocating additional resources to the market, these governments' primary response was to remove the preconditions of market-based transactions, thereby exposing workers to further vulnerabilities during an extraordinarily uncertain time.

While, on the one hand, by interfering in the market in the aforementioned manner, these governments denied the very essence of the market, on the other, by not consolidating social protection during a difficult time, they failed to uphold the principle of solidarity. The government – the state – plays a more important role in formulating policies on social protection, especially during social upheavals. Social protection, operating on the principle of solidarity, introduces certainty and stability in the lives of workers. The need for social protection is acutely felt during periods of market turmoil. Even though the pandemic caused unprecedented market turmoil – often shutting down market interactions completely – as noted in this book (Chapter 3), the coverage of social protection during this time remained inadequate, driving workers to desperation and impoverishment. While sporadic unemployment insurance programmes could be seen, such insurance has not been generally a part of the social protection framework in India.

Thus, the proper governmental interference during the pandemic should have happened by means of expanding the social protection network, supporting workers for the loss of their livelihood activities and pandemic-induced insecurities. Some state governments instead scrambled to save the employer from the annoyance of the pandemic. These governmental (and legislative) actions failed labour law's justice mission by failing to treat workers fairly. While these pandemic-triggered governmental responses are exceptional in their ignorance of labour law's social justice mission, the 2020 parliamentary reforms of labour laws suffer from some of the same conceptual confusions seen in these governmental actions.

The 2020 reforms seem to perceive labour law as predominantly the regulation of market exchanges. In this formulation, the Indian Parliament's ideological position buttresses laissez-faire market relations. Because of this ideological commitment, Parliament has minimised the role of the government – that is, the role of political intervention – in labour market relations. This approach to the reforms fails to appreciate the market-consolidating role of labour law. In its move from status to contract – from master–servant relations to employment relationships – the aim of labour law has been to promote the freedom of contract of the worker. This regulatory attempt sought to remove the unfreedoms that emanated from the masters' legal right to control the servant and penalise disobedience of such control. This transition from master–servant relationship to employment relationship, then, facilitates workers' 'free' access to the market. However, mere facilitation of contractual freedom of workers is not enough in promoting contract-based resource distribution. Labour law simultaneously constrains the more expansive market freedom (resulting from property ownership) of the employer, which is what the governmental intervention in labour market relations has historically done in India. By substantially withdrawing the government's monitoring role from labour market relations, the 2020 reforms de facto expose workers to the unfreedoms of the market. Workers' unfreedoms, in turn, impede the market's capacity for resource distribution, thereby eventually unsettling Parliament's very attraction for, and commitment to, the market.

Additionally, the historical and continued prominence of informal workers in India somewhat blunts the Indian Parliament's freshly revived optimism for laissez-faire market relations. Labour law safeguards that existed to promote market freedom of formal workers and limit the freedom of employers have been generally absent for informal workers. In the absence of substantive safeguards securing the preconditions of their free market participation, in their divergent relationships to the market, informal workers have always been part of the laissez-faire market conditions. To be sure, this absence of legal safeguards does not mean that informal workers were completely unregulated and existed outside the purview of the state's administrative and bureaucratic structure. Although informal workers are often subject to municipal laws, criminal laws and social norms regulating work,[39] they have broadly remained outside the purview of the labour law framework, securing the preconditions for their market participation. In the absence of the latter, informal workers have been a part of the 'unregulated' (laissez-faire) market. At the same time, informal workers are some of the most exploited, vulnerable and marginalised workers in the country. What follows is that laissez-faire markets, in isolation, are no recipe for workers' well-being. Market exchanges must be complemented with a comprehensive social protection mechanism so as to enable workers to lead a more secure and better life.

As has been repeatedly emphasised by the judiciary, social protection is an indispensable requirement for a dignified life for workers.[40] By addressing health, nutrition, education, disability, sickness, unemployment, maternity support, employment injury, old-age security, and so on, legal entitlement to social protection strengthens workers' ability to lead a dignified life by expanding their choices in the ways of leading such a life.[41] Legal entitlement to an expansive range of social resources (or public goods) is also foundational in minimising inequalities in society. While, on the one hand, social security entitlements offer basic support to workers who are largely left out of the market-based distributive structure, on the other, they help develop workers' competence to gainfully participate in market transactions. In the latter sense, social protection is also the foundation of workers' market participation. Social protection entitlements to health, nutrition, education and training also have a market-constitutive role.[42] Because of the egalitarian underpinning of social protection, entitlement to social protection is becoming an increasingly important baseline for a diverse range of workers whose divergent relationships and experiences at work are difficult to capture through conventional legal categories and, accordingly, fit the traditional workplace standards.

Thus, understanding social protection as an inseparable component of labour law provides coherence and wholesomeness to the narrative of labour law in India. Such a narrative is coherent because it accounts for the socially contributory nature of worker-citizens' agency. In this manner of conceiving labour law, while the market (that is, employment contract) compensates workers for the tasks they perform, society secures a minimum living standard for workers for their contribution towards higher levels of endeavour and achievement of society.[43] These two commitments of labour law are, then, complementary and interdependent. While social contribution can occur without market involvement (for example, in unpaid care work), under most circumstances one does not exist without the other. These two aspects are held together by the third commitment of labour law, which is the entitlement to participatory law-making, thereby completing the social justice narrative of labour law. Thus, Indian labour law should be understood as an instrument for realising the worker-citizen's claim to social justice (not mere market participation).

The idea of social justice under the Constitution is not a fixed notion of institutional permanence. While the institutional spaces of social justice (such as the market and social protection) may have some permanent structure, the exact manner in which these spaces will be shaped is to be collectively decided through deliberative participation. It is on this front that the labour law reforms of 2020 have substantially faltered. The entirety of the unionised workforce in the country objected to the reforms and alleged that trade unions and workers' representatives were not adequately consulted during the reforms. Trade unions specifically objected to the increased exposure of the formal workforce to the neoliberal logic of the market. However, such objections were not heeded by the government and Parliament. In prioritising diminishing state monitoring of the market, Parliament mistakenly focused only on the tasks performed by workers ignoring their broader social contribution. Such withdrawal narrowly understands labour regulation as only a contractual exchange that is overburdened through regulation. This is a partisan understanding of the foundational rationale of labour law.

Arguably, exposure of workers to the neoliberal market logic and failure to consolidate social security for the increased insecurities of the market exposure could potentially fall within the permissible range of possibilities contemplated under the Constitution. The marginalisation of consultation, deliberation and participatory law-making process violates the very essence of the constitutional social justice framework. Because of the sidelining of participatory deliberation, Parliament's faulty understanding of labour law mainly as a contractual phenomenon was easily transmitted to some of the state governments, which attempted to suspend labour laws to ease the burden on the more powerful player in market relations (that is, employers). In view of this perception, perhaps trade unions and other representative organisations could derive some satisfaction from the fact that, after the 2020 reforms, the government is a lesser player in labour market relations. Contrary to what the trade unions have been protesting since the 2020 reforms, less governmental intervention in labour relations may not be such a bad thing if the governments – using their mandate of oversight of the market – end up bidding for the employers, as happened through the suspension of labour laws led by the government of Uttar Pradesh. In this sense, state withdrawal from labour market relations may be a blessing in disguise.

In any case, labour or work is a political idea under the Indian Constitution, an idea that helps elevate the nation through workers' agency. The organising principle of Indian labour law is the principle of social justice. The values underpinning such organisation are liberty, equality, solidarity and deliberative participation. Different components of labour law promote the social justice agenda by consolidating these values in their specific contexts. Because of the diversity of working relationships, including the prominence of informal work and newer modes of organising businesses, these contextual interventions may look different in divergent contexts. Trade unions and workers' representative organisations occupy centre stage in giving effect to these contextual interventions by mainstreaming actual experiences of workers in these varied contexts. In this sense, even though the labour law reforms emphasised the formal justificatory basis of employment contracts, the future of labour law de facto lies in the political space, to be led by participatory deliberative processes. Happily, because of contextual variability, statutory entitlements are incidental rather than foundational to this political deliberative space. This political space is where the opposition to the 2020 labour law reforms should take place in an unwavering manner. We should, then, look up to politics, rather than the judiciary, to challenge the narrow understanding of labour law in the recent reforms. The following section concludes the book by offering a commentary on the largely dependent juridical attitude to labour law in the country.

## A Concluding Note on Overcoming the Slave (Juridical) Mentality

As noted in Chapter 1, at independence, one of the foremost concerns of India's first prime minister was to establish constitutional conditions through which the 'slave mentality' of Indians could be overcome and Indians could become citizens from colonial subjects. As much as the notion of slave mentality was employed rhetorically, its significance for constitutional social justice and labour jurisprudence could not be overemphasised. Although formal self-determination is achieved at independence, the process of (mental) transformation from subjects to citizens is not an automatic one. If the slave mentality is understood to mean an orientation to abide by (worldviews and dogmas set by) a master, overcoming such mentality would require a fundamental conceptual reorientation to making sense of the world on the basis of one's own experiences, faculties and history, thereby becoming one's own master, having control over one's worldviews and life situations. Active mediation by means of education, cultural cultivation and practice must occur in order to bring about such reorientation. This mediation is, then, premised on the ability to create contextual knowledge on the basis of lived experiences of citizens without the compulsions – intellectual or political – of external forces.

Legal knowledge and conceptual categories, the purpose and architecture of conventional labour law in particular, are overwhelmingly products of the colonial narrative of industrial capitalism and its (potential) role in uplifting colonised people from backwardness to progress.[44] As part of the coloniser's burden to civilise and modernise the backward (and pre-capitalist) Indian society, they transported the legal structure that facilitated industrial capitalism in Europe while turning a blind eye to the sui generis conditions prevailing in India. This narrative and structure of industrial capitalism conceive of labour welfare in a specific manner, primarily in its relationship to market exchanges (in distinction to social relationships). This narrative, then, led to specific conceptual and institutional categories and functions (as discussed in this book), which, as has now been widely acknowledged, mostly remained distant from the lived experiences of the majority of the workers in the country.[45]

In the aforementioned sense, then, the creation of legal knowledge in India was part of the power structure and intellectual domination that largely evicted colonised peoples from participating in the knowledge production process. Power and domination shaped not only what is considered to be valid legal knowledge (ontology) but also the process through which such knowledge is created (epistemology). Except for parts of the social life (such as personal laws), the justificatory process to (what constitutes) legal knowledge has been largely European. Legal knowledge produced under such domination is inextricably linked to the coloniser's will to dominate.[46] Unsurprisingly, knowledge created within the overall normative purpose of domination has been – and (unfortunately) continues to be – exclusionary. Such exclusion pertains to the exclusion of agency of the dominated people as much as it relates to the ignorance of their realities. Exclusion along both of these trajectories is obnoxious for legal conceptualisation of a framework aiming to regulate livelihood activities of a remarkably diverse workforce. The gap between legal imagination and lived realities of Indian workers is a legacy of the political illegitimacy of the colonial legislative agenda.

It is by means of the colonisation-induced knowledge production process that an ethnocentric (that is, European) legal account presented and rooted itself as the universal account of law. Labour law emerged in India as an indispensable instrument of a well-managed capitalist modernisation process. By associating employment relationship-based industrial relations with the very understanding of capitalist modernisation, labour law failed to see the diverse realities of working arrangements and the varied ways by which such diverse productive arrangements relate to the capitalist modernisation process. The same hegemonic attitude currently prevails through the universal justificatory supremacy of neoliberal capitalism and globalisation. As the narrative goes, the division of labour between the Global North and the Global South is an opportunity for all workers to make best use of this global neoliberal capitalist modernisation agenda. Although the division of labour is conceived in global terms, labour laws remain stuck to their primitive (colonial) and local market exchange rationale.[47] This primitive understanding of labour law validates exploitative cost externalisation to the Global South as a legitimate neoliberal strategy.[48]

Accordingly, when the Indian judiciary interprets labour law in light of the rationales offered by global neoliberal capitalism,[49] it gets entrapped in intellectual subservience to an exploitative hegemonic logic, thereby showing signs of the slave mentality. It is true that this universalised neoliberal justification is also wholeheartedly accepted by a significant section of the political elites, including the incumbent executive of the country. However, such political inclination per se does not absolve the judiciary from the accusation of the slave mentality. The judiciary's principal allegiance lies with the Constitution, not the politics of the day. As much as the politics of the day seeks to diverge from foundational constitutional principles, it is the duty of the judiciary to remain faithful to the Constitution. In this sense, the judicial role in the interpretation of labour law is particularly delicate. In remaining true to the Constitution, on the one hand, the judiciary cannot unquestionably defer to a position agreed to by the global hegemons and local elites; on the other, its interpretation of labour law cannot merely defer to the conventional logic of the (English) common law.

The common law continues to imagine labour law in its exclusive relationship to the market exchange logic, as an instrument of negotiation between capital and labour. The constitutional foundation of labour law gets undermined in such an overtly market capitalism-focused understanding of the subject matter. There are two aspects of this problem: first, a strictly contractual understanding of labour law ties its principles to the market exchange logic; second, once such tie-up occurs, all market exchange rationales (that is, global neoliberalism) have a direct bearing on the understanding of labour law. Thus, the foundation exposes the jurisprudence to continued hegemonic domination. The primitive logic continues in a modern form. Accordingly, a primitive understanding of labour law does a disservice to concerns of (constitutional) justice by remaining true to the borrowed (colonial) logic of the subject. Primitive labour law has been merely market constitutive; modern (postcolonial) labour law is an instrument of justice.

Under the aforementioned circumstances, it is the responsibility of Indian jurists, including the judiciary, to overcome the (primitive) constrained and received rationale of labour regulation. The diversity of labour relations and the varied rationales of such relations in the country demand that juridical authorship of labour law for the sui generis conditions of the country be reclaimed. Reclaiming juridical authorship should not only be seen as a legitimate demand from workers, it should also be seen as a core responsibility of the practitioners of labour law. In particular, development of labour law jurisprudence should be mindful of the heterogeneous working relationships and labour law's traditional exclusions in the country. To be sure, this heterogeneity does not merely pertain to the existence of different kinds of working arrangements and relationships; it also relates to the diverse manner in which various working relationships interact with conventional labour law and its conceptual categories (such as collective bargaining, trade unionism, works council, conciliation, strike and a range of social security provisioning). Taking cognisance of heterogeneous experiences in developing a labour law jurisprudence would mean that such justificatory process should be contextual and based on lived experiences of workers instead of being faithful to the institutional formulation of conventional labour law. This juridical approach would naturally mean that labour jurisprudence in the country should unfold through deliberative and contextual law-making through workers' participation. Effective institutionalisation of such participation is a future juridical (and political) challenge. As argued in this book, the social security boards could become one of the prominent institutions for promoting such experience-based participatory law-making.

The constitutional social justice mandate offers the broader ideological and conceptual backdrop in furthering such a contextual idea of labour law. While any understanding of labour law must conform to constitutional ideals, its specific interpretations should heed to how such ideals relate to specific circumstances. In this respect, the impracticalities of completely discarding labour law's conventional (colonial) justifications must also be recognised. As forced as labour law's original justifications may have been, they are still partly valid in the country. Market exchange-based industrial relations and formal employment contracts continue to be realities of the Indian labour market. Formal industrial relations, therefore, continue to shape the overall context of the Indian workforce. Thus, although uncritical acceptance of the conventional jurisprudence of labour law is a recipe for disaster and an indication of the continued slave mentality of Indian legal practitioners, undeniably many of the foundations of Indian labour law are supplied by the industrial relations logic (even though such logic is more suitable to jurisdictions with homogeneous industrial workforce).[50] The challenge, then, for Indian labour jurisprudence is how to take cognisance of the conventional common law framework without losing sight of the unacceptable exclusions under such legal formulation. To be sure, reclaiming juridical authorship does not amount to the denial of intellectual exchanges and juridical conversations among different jurisdictions. While ongoing conversations with external juridical approaches should be strengthened, unquestioned deference to international jurisprudence, including conceptual categories, which are not contextualised in the realities of domestic situations, should be avoided.

As argued in this book, work is the primary means for individuals to participate in social cooperation. If fairness is to be a guiding principle in such social cooperation,[51] the ideal of social justice should inform the normative ordering of work-based relationships, including the relationship between workers and the state.[52] Labour law is the chief instrument for such normative ordering, consolidating (fair) entitlements for workers in their social cooperation. However, in furthering social justice for workers, labour law has traditionally adopted a universalised and homogeneous form, which is at odds with the heterogeneous configurations of work in India. The allegiance to the inherited – colonial-capitalist – universalised legal form has largely failed to further social justice for workers whose actual experiences at work fail to conform to the inherited conventional form. This failure of labour law, then, also implies its inability to offer an effective platform for inclusive deliberation by heterogeneous (that is, excluded) workers. This lack of institutional opportunities for expansive deliberation stands in stark contrast to modern ideals of social justice, which increasingly allocate a coveted space for broadly inclusive, multifaceted and continuing deliberations on questions of social justice, as noted in this book.[53] A sui generis Indian perspective on labour law has the potential to strengthen labour law by truly becoming an instrument of social justice by centralising heterogeneity and epistemological diversity in the reformulation of the subject matter.

Freedom from the slave (juridical) mentality would entail challenging the prominence of legal form over actual behaviour and relationships at work. Such an Indian approach to labour law, by challenging the domination of an inherited legal form over heterogeneous actual experiences of marginalised workers, may also pioneer reformulation of labour law in other jurisdictions, including jurisdictions in the Global North, which are increasingly struggling to remain faithful to the conventional model in view of the challenges posed by newer modes of organising work (such as gig work and platform-based work). Additionally, the prominence of subcontracting, supply chain networks, platform-based work on demand, machine-based cost reduction initiatives and large-scale labour migration has created an economic–cultural weld between societies in the Global South and the Global North. In view of these newly emergent circumstances, which limit the ability of the conventional model to account for varied labour relations, imaginations of labour law in postcolonial societies of the Global South including India – both its justificatory basis and its institutions – will also induce behavioural changes, and eventually institutional changes, in hegemonic societies of the Global North.

Overcoming the slave mentality would also mean imagining Indian labour law in the broadest possible sense articulated under the Constitution, in contrast to the narrower common law imagination of private labour market exchange. This imagination, in turn, would entail moving away from a strictly contractual to a more justice-centred understanding of labour law. Although modern capitalism emerged on the back of colonisation and the slave trade, in normatively ordering the capitalist political economy, including the idea of labour law, the agency of the impoverished workers in the Global South has been mostly denied. Therefore, the pertinence of reconceptualisation of labour law lies in its principled challenge to European ways of understanding and organising the globalised world mediated by market capitalism. By taking seriously the agency of workers in India, a reimagined labour law could offer a more inclusive alternative legal ontology. In this sense, the Indian labour law project is not only an undertaking in domestic jurisprudence; it is also part of a global project on reimagination of the subject matter.

## Notes

1. Hugh Collins, Gillian Lester and Virginia Mantouvalou, 'Introduction: Does Labour Law Need Philosophical Foundations?' in *Philosophical Foundations of Labour Law*, ed. Hugh Collins, Gillian Lester and Virginia Mantouvalou, 1–30 (New York: Oxford University Press, 2018), 7.
2. Brian Langille, 'Labour Law's Theory of Justice', in *The Idea of Labour Law*, ed. Guy Davidov and Brian Langille, 101–119 (Oxford and New York: Oxford University Press, 2011).
3. John Gardner, 'The Contractualisation of Labour Law', in *Philosophical Foundations of Labour Law*, ed. Hugh Collins, Gillian Lester and Virginia Mantouvalou, 33–47 (New York: Oxford University Press, 2018).
4. See Mark Freedland and Nicola Kountouris, *The Legal Construction of Personal Work Relations* (New York: Oxford University Press, 2012).
5. Elizabeth S. Anderson, 'What Is the Point of Equality?' *Ethics* 109, no. 2 (1999): 287–337.
6. Constitution of India, 1950, Article 51A(j) (hereinafter, 'Constitution').
7. Constitution, Article 51A(j).
8. See Constitution, Preamble.
9. See Katherine V. W. Stone, *From Widgets to Digits: Employment Regulation for the Changing Workplace* (New York: Cambridge University Press, 2004). See the different chapters in Brian Dolber, Michelle Rodino-Colocino, Chenjerai Kumanyika and Todd Wolfson, *The Gig Economy: Workers and Media in the Age of Convergence* (New York: Routledge, 2021). Also see the different chapters in Deepa Das Acevedo (ed.), *Beyond the Algorithm: Qualitative Insights for Gig Work Regulation* (Cambridge [UK] and New York: Cambridge University Press, 2021); Cynthia Estlund, *Automation Anxiety: Why and How to Save Work* (New York: Oxford University Press, 2021).
10. While newer forms of work do pose this challenge, the challenge itself is not new. Particularly in the Indian context, one is familiar with this challenge because of the prominence of informal economic activities that do not fit the conventional contractual structure.

11. For example, judicial decisions on legal entitlements (and legal exclusion) of online platform-based 'on-demand' drivers in common law countries offer conflicting rationales in seeking to find the fit of Uber drivers with the conventional employer–employee account of labour law. There is, however, an increasing convergence (albeit with internal variations) in different jurisdictions categorising such drivers as 'employees'. For a discussion, see Ronald C. Brown, 'Ride-Hailing Drivers as Autonomous Independent Contractors: Let Them Bargain!' *Washington International Law Journal* 29, no. 3 (2020): 533–574. Also see Jeremias Adams-Prassl, Sylvaine Laulom and Yolanda Maneiro Vazquez, 'The Role of National Courts in Protecting Platform Workers: A Comparative Analysis', in *Collective Bargaining and the Gig Economy: A Traditional Tool for New Business Models*, ed. José Maria Miranda Boto and Elizabeth Brameshuber, 75–98 (Oxford: Hart Publishing, 2022).
12. Alain Supiot, *Governance by Numbers* (Oxford: Hart Publishing, 2015); Supriya Routh, 'Embedding Work in Nature: The Anthropocene and Legal Imagination of Work as Human Activity', *Comparative Labor Law and Policy Journal* 40 (2018): 29–60; Simon Deakin, 'The Law of the Anthropocene', in *Concerter Les Civilisations: Mélanges en L'honneur d'Alain Supiot*, ed. Samantha Besson and Samuel Jubé, 113–122 (Paris: Éditions du Seuil, 2020); Alain Supiot, 'Labour Is Not a Commodity: The Content and Meaning of Work in the Twenty-First Century', *International Labour Review* 160 (2021): 1–20; Paolo Tomassetti, 'Energy Transition: A Labour Law Retrospective', *Industrial Law Journal* 52, no. 1 (2023): 34–67.
13. Simon Deakin, 'Law and (Un)Sustainability in the Age of the Anthropocene', in *Prospects and Policies for Global Sustainable Recovery: Promoting Environmental and Economic Sustainability*, ed. Philip Arestis and Malcolm Sawyer, 91–131 (London: Palgrave Macmillan, 2023).
14. Karl Polanyi, *The Great Transformation: The Political and Economic Origins of Our Time* (Boston, MA: Beacon Press, 2001 [1944]), 74–77.
15. See Deakin, 'Law and (Un)Sustainability in the Age of the Anthropocene'; David J. Doorey, 'Just Transitions Law: Putting Labour Law to Work on Climate Change', *Journal of Environmental Law and Practice* 30, no. 2 (2017): 201–239, 230–238.
16. Deakin, 'Law and (Un)Sustainability in the Age of the Anthropocene'.
17. Ania Zbyszewska, 'Regulating Work with People and "Nature" in Mind: Feminist Reflections', *Comparative Labor Law and Policy Journal* 40, no. 1 (2018): 9–28.

18. Manfred Weiss, 'The Future of Labour Law in Europe: Rise or Fall of the European Social Model', *European Labour Law Journal* 8, no. 4 (2017): 344–356, 344.
19. See the discussion in Gautam Bhatia and Emilios Christodoulidis, 'Social Rights' in *Democratic Constitutionalism in India and the European Union: Comparing the Law of Democracy in Continental Polities*, ed. Philipp Dann and Arun K Thiruvengadam, 223–251 (Cheltenham, UK: Edward Elgar, 2021). Also see Niraja Gopal Jayal, *Citizenship and Its Discontents: An Indian History* (Cambridge [MA] and London: Harvard University Press, 2013), 15.
20. Collins, Lester and Mantouvalou, 'Introduction', 8–9.
21. Collins, Lester and Mantouvalou, 'Introduction', 9; Alain Supiot, María Emilia Casas, Jean de Munck, Peter Hanau, Anders L. Johansson, Pamela Meadows, Enzo Mingione, Robert Salais and Paul van der Heijden, *Beyond Employment Changes in Work and the Future of Labour Law in Europe* (Oxford and New York: Oxford University Press, 2001).
22. Ewan McGaughey, 'Otto von Gierke: The Social Role of Private Law', *German Law Journal* 19, no. 4 (2018): 1017–1116, 1036, 1040, 1044, 1048, 1050.
23. Collins, Lester and Mantouvalou, 'Introduction'. Also see Ruth Dukes, *The Labour Constitution: The Enduring Idea of Labour Law* (New York: Oxford University Press, 2014).
24. Bhatia and Christodoulidis, 'Social Rights'.
25. For example, see Stone, *From Widgets to Digits*, where Katherine Stone calls for such a comprehensive conceptualisation of labour law.
26. John Rawls, *A Theory of Justice* (Cambridge, MA: Harvard University Press, 1999 [1971]); John Rawls, *The Law of Peoples* (Cambridge [MA] and London: Harvard University Press, 1999).
27. Anderson, 'What Is the Point of Equality'.
28. Supiot, Casas, de Munck, Hanau, Johansson, Meadows, Mingione, Salais and van der Heijden, *Beyond Employment Changes in Work*; Langille, 'Labour Law's Theory of Justice'.
29. Langille, 'Labour Law's Theory of Justice'.
30. Alain Supiot, *The Spirit of Philadelphia: Social Justice vs. the Total Market*, trans. Saskia Brown (New York: Verso Books, 2012).
31. Langille, 'Labour Law's Theory of Justice'; Supiot, *The Spirit of Philadelphia*.
32. For example, see Riccardo Del Punta, 'Is the Capability Theory an Adequate Normative Theory for Labour Law?' in *The Capability Approach to Labour Law*, ed. Brian Langille, 82–102 (New York: Oxford University Press,

2019); Alan Bogg, 'The Constitution of Capabilities: The Case of Freedom of Association', in *The Capability Approach to Labour Law*, ed. Brian Langille, 241–267 (New York: Oxford University Press, 2019); Guy Davidov, 'Distributive Justice and Labour Law', in *Philosophical Foundations of Labour Law*, ed. Hugh Collins, Gillian Lester and Virginia Mantouvalou, 141–155 (New York: Oxford University Press, 2028).

33. John Gardner, 'The Contractualisation of Labour Law'.
34. See the different chapters in Douglas Hay and Paul Craven (eds.), *Masters, Servants, and Magistrates in Britain and the Empire, 1562–1955* (Chapel Hill [NC] and London: University of North Carolina Press, 2004). Also see Simon Deakin and Frank Wilkinson, *The Law of the Labour Market: Industrialization, Employment, and Legal Evolution* (New York: Oxford University Press, 2005).
35. Mark Freedland and Nicola Kountouris, *The Legal Construction of Personal Work Relations* (New York: Oxford University Press, 2012); Mark Freedland, 'The Legal Structure of the Contract of Employment', in *The Contract of Employment*, ed. Mark Freedland (general editor), Alan Bogg, David Cabrelli, Hugh Collins, Nicola Countouris, A. C. L. Davies, Simon Deakin and Jeremias Prass, 28–51 (New York: Oxford University Press, 2016).
36. Dukes, *The Labour Constitution*.
37. See Thomas Pogge, *World Poverty and Human Rights* (Cambridge, UK: Polity Press, 2008); Iris Marion Young, 'Responsibility and Global Labor Justice', *Journal of Political Philosophy* 12, no. 4 (2004): 365–388.
38. See Constitution, Article 300A. Also see Namita Wahi, 'Property', in *The Oxford Handbook of the Indian Constitution*, ed. Sujit Choudhry, Madhav Khosla and Pratap Bhanu Mehta, 943–964 (Oxford: Oxford University Press, 2016). It is arguable that by suspending labour laws, the governments were trying to promote the 'right to trade or business' of the employer, a fundamental right (Article, 19[1][g]). However, this proposition will be found to be problematic on deeper scrutiny. First, since both the employer and the employee possess the right to trade, prioritising one group's right over the other (who are more vulnerable) is violative of the principle of substantive equality. Second, restricting the substantive market freedom of employees without a simultaneous mandate on the employers to carry on their business does not meet the public interest threshold. The governmental actions should, therefore, be seen as a trade-off between workers' freedom of contract and employers' right to property rather than a trade-off between two co-equal fundamental rights.

39. See Supriya Routh, 'Examining the Legal Legitimacy of Informal Economic Activities', *Social and Legal Studies* 31, no. 2 (2022): 282–308; Hila Shamir, 'What's the Border Got to Do with It? How Immigration Regimes Affect Familial Care Provision: A Comparative Analysis', *American University Journal of Gender, Social Policy and the Law* 19, no. 2 (2011): 601–669, 619.
40. For example, see *Francis Coralie v. Union Territory of Delhi*, (1981) 2 SCR 516, 529. Also see *Bandhua Mukti Morcha v. Union of India*, (1984) 2 SCR 67; *Consumer Education and Research Centre v. Union of India*, (1995) MANU 0175 SC; *Kirloskar Brothers Limited v. Employees' State Insurance Corporation*, (1996) MANU 0873 SC.
41. Amartya Sen, *The Idea of Justice* (Cambridge, MA: Harvard University Press, 2009); Langille, 'Labour Law's Theory of Justice'.
42. See Deakin and Wilkinson, *The Law of the Labour Market*.
43. Constitution, Article 51A(j).
44. Jayal, *Citizenship and Its Discontents*, 18, 230, 233–237; Homi K. Bhabha, *The Location of Culture* (Abingdon and New York: Routledge, 1994), 100–120; Leela Gandhi, *Postcolonial Theory: A Critical Introduction* (Abingdon and New York: Routledge, 2020 [1998]), 64–80. In particular, for an outline of the colonial imprint on Indian labour law, see K. R. Shyam Sundar, 'Dynamics of Reforms of Labour Market and the Industrial Relations System in India', in *Globalization, Labour Market Institutions, Processes and Policies in India: Essays in Honour of Lalit K. Deshpande*, ed. K. R. Shyam Sundar, 521–544 (Singapore: Palgrave Macmillan, 2019). Also see Richard Mitchell, Petra Mahy and Peter Gahan, 'The Evolution of Labour Law in India: An Overview and Commentary on Regulatory Objectives and Development', *Asian Journal of Law and Society* 1 (2014): 413–453, 415–421. Also see Bushan Tilak Kaul, '"Industry", "Industrial Dispute", and "Workman": Conceptual Framework and Judicial Activism', *Journal of the Indian Law Institute* 50, no. 1 (2008): 3–50, for a discussion of some of the prominent conceptual categories in labour law (that is, industry, industrial dispute and workman) and how they were originally transplanted from, and interpreted with reference to, the labour jurisprudence in the United Kingdom (and other common law jurisdictions); Jaivir Singh, 'Who Is a Worker? Searching the Theory of the Firm for Answers', in *Labour, Employment and Economic Growth in India*, ed. K. V. Ramaswamy, 265–291 (Delhi: Cambridge University Press, 2015), for colonial and imperial juridical conceptualisation of the idea of worker (the author also evaluates the idea from an economic perspective as a potential guidance for labour law reforms).

45. For example, see, generally, Mitchell, Mahy and Gahan, 'The Evolution of Labour Law in India'. Also see the different chapters in Hay and Craven (eds.), *Masters, Servants, and Magistrates*. Also see, generally, Simon Deakin, Priya Lele and Mathias Siems, 'The Evolution of Labour Law: Calibrating and Comparing Regulatory Regimes', *International Labour Review* 146, nos. 3-4 (2007): 133-162 (Although authors of this study, employing their specific methodology, do not find the imprints of the British common law on post-war Indian labour law framework, they do recognise the complexities of labour regulation triggered by the very large informal workforce in the country. However, it is in these complexities of labour law, operating in a sui generis heterogeneous labour relations scenario, that colonial common law concepts linger on.)

46. Edward W. Said, *Orientalism* (New York: Vintage Books, 1979). For a note on how the British government's interests dictated colonial India's labour policy, see Pankaj Kumar and Jaivir Singh, *Issues in Law and Public Policy on Contract Labour in India: Comparative Insights from China* (Singapore: Springer, 2018), 35-36. For an analysis of the role of the colonial labour law to promote interests of colonial tea plantation owners, see Rebekah McCallum, 'The Business of Tea: British Tea Companies and Plantation Labour Law in India, 1901-1951 (With Special emphasis on James Finlay & Co.)', PhD dissertation, Department of History and Classical Studies, Faculty of Arts, McGill University, Montreal, December 2021. The general preoccupation to dominate the colonies, India in particular, insofar as labour regulation is concerned, has also unfolded in the manner in which colonial India interacted with the International Labour Organization (ILO) and ratified its instruments. See Amritha V. Shenoy, 'Colonial India in the ILO and International Law', *Christ University Law Journal* 11, no. 2 (2022): 63-78.

47. Gayatri Chakravorty Spivak, *In Other Worlds: Essays in Cultural Politics* (Abingdon and New York: Routledge, 1998 [1987]), 230-231.

48. Chakravorty Spivak, *In Other Worlds*.

49. See Supriya Routh, 'The Judiciary and (Labour) Law in the Development Discourse in India', *Verfassung und Recht in Ubersee* 44, no. 2 (2011): 237-257; Supriya Routh, 'Developing Human Capabilities through Law: Is Indian Law Failing?' *Asian Journal of Law and Economics* 3, no. 1 (2012): Article 4 (1-20). Also see Bhatia and Christodoulidis, 'Social Rights'; Ramapriya Gopalakrishnan, 'Labour Jurisprudence of the Supreme Court: Recent Trends', in *Labour, Employment and Economic Growth in India*, ed. K. V. Ramaswamy, 292-318 (Delhi: Cambridge University Press, 2015),

for an analysis of judicial reasonings explicitly based on the neoliberal economic logic and the urgency to globalise Indian industry. However, Gopalakrishnan also notes that although the general trend of the Indian Supreme Court judgments has been to facilitate neoliberal economic globalisation, decisions protesting against such general trend could also be sporadically identified. Also see Girish Balasubramanian, Surendra Babu Talluri and Santanu Sarkar, 'The Curious Case of Judicial Interpretation and Labour Flexibility in India', *Industrial Law Journal* 52, no. 3 (2023): 696–720, wherein the authors analyse 196 judgments of appellate courts in India on the Contract Labour (Regulation and Abolition) Act, 1970 (Act no. 37 of 1970) and conclude that in the majority of judgments the judiciary has favoured a narrative of labour flexibilisation, contributing to the political cause of labour flexibility in keeping with the neoliberal rationale. For a similar conclusion on the basis of a study of the Calcutta High Court judgments on the Industrial Disputes Act, 1947 (Act no. 14 of 1947), see Supurna Banerjee and Zaad Mahmood, 'Judicial Intervention and Industrial Relations: Exploring Industrial Disputes Cases in West Bengal', *Industrial Law Journal* 46, no. 3 (2017): 366–396. Also see Santanu Sarkar, 'How Independent Is India's Labour Law Framework from the State's Changing Economic Policies?' *Economic and Labour Relations Review* 30, no. 3 (2019): 422–440.

50. Simon Deakin and Antara Haldar, 'How Should India Reform Its Labour Laws?' *Economic and Political Weekly* 50, no. 12 (2015): 48–55, 48–50.
51. See John Rawls, *A Theory of Justice*, 10–11.
52. Langille, 'Labour Law's Theory of Justice'.
53. See, for example, Sen, *The Idea of Justice*; Martha C. Nussbaum, *Creating Capabilities: The Human Development Approach* (Cambridge [MA] and London: Belknap Press of Harvard University Press, 2011); Jürgen Habermas, *Between Facts and Norms: Contributions to a Discourse Theory of Law and Democracy*, trans. William Rehg (Cambridge, MA: MIT Press, 1996 [1992 in German]); Seyla Benhabib, 'Toward a Deliberative Model of Democratic Legitimacy', in *Democracy and Difference: Contesting the Boundaries of the Political*, ed. Seyla Benhabib, 67–94 (Princeton, NJ: Princeton University Press, 1996).

# Bibliography

## Published and Unpublished Works

Adams-Prassl, Jeremias, Sylvaine Laulom and Yolanda Maneiro Vazquez. 'The Role of National Courts in Protecting Platform Workers: A Comparative Analysis'. In *Collective Bargaining and the Gig Economy: A Traditional Tool for New Business Models*, edited by José Maria Miranda Boto and Elizabeth Brameshuber, 75–98 (Oxford: Hart Publishing, 2022).

Agarwala, Ramgopal, Nagesh Kumar and Michelle Riboud. 'Reforms, Labour Markets and Social Security Policy in India: An Introduction'. In *Reforms, Labour Markets and Social Security in India*, edited by Ramgopal Agarwala, Nagesh Kumar and Michelle Riboud, 1–19 (New Delhi: Oxford University Press, 2004).

Agarwala, Rina. *Informal Labor, Formal Politics, and Dignified Discontent in India* (New York: Cambridge University Press, 2013).

———. 'Reshaping the Social Contract: Emerging Relations Between the State and Informal Labor in India'. *Theory and Society* 37, no. 4 (2008): 375–408.

Agarwala, Rina, and Shiny Saha. 'The Employment Relationship and Movement Strategies among Domestic Workers in India'. *Critical Sociology* 44, nos. 7–8 (2018): 1207–1223.

Anderson, Elizabeth. 'Equality and Freedom in the Workplace: Recovering Republican Insights'. *Social Philosophy and Policy* 31, no. 2 (2015): 48–69.

———. 'Justifying the Capabilities Approach to Justice'. In *Measuring Justice: Primary Goods and Capabilities*, edited by Harry Brighouse and Ingrid Robeyns, 81–100 (New York: Cambridge University Press, 2010).

———. 'What Is the Point of Equality?' *Ethics* 109, no. 2 (1999): 287–337.

Anuja, S. 'Lifting the Veil through Judicial Activism: Access to Justice Model during COVID-19'. In *Labour Law Reforms 2021*, edited by Jeet Singh Mann, 185–200 (Delhi: Centre for Transparency and Accountability in Governance, 2021).

Arendt, Hannah. *The Human Condition* (Chicago, IL: University of Chicago Press, 1969).

Arunachalam, Jaya, and Brunhild Landwehr (eds.). *'Structuring a Movement and Spreading it On': History and Growth of the Working Women's Forum (India) 1978–2003* (Frankfurt and London: IKO – Verlag für Interkulturelle Kommunikation, 2003).

Austin, Granville. *The Indian Constitution: Cornerstone of a Nation* (Bombay: Oxford University Press, 1966).

Babu, Sharath, and Rashmi Shetty. *Social Justice and Labour Jurisprudence: Justice V.R. Krishna Iyer's Contributions* (New Delhi: SAGE Publications, 2007).

Badigannavar, Vidu, and John Kelly. 'Do Labour Laws Protect Labour in India? Union Experiences of Workplace Employment Regulations in Maharashtra, India'. *Industrial Law Journal* 41, no. 4 (2012): 439–470.

Balasubramanian, Girish, Surendra Babu Talluri and Santanu Sarkar. 'The Curious Case of Judicial Interpretation and Labour Flexibility in India'. *Industrial Law Journal* 52, no. 3 (2023): 696–720.

Banerjee, Supurna, and Zaad Mahmood. 'Judicial Intervention and Industrial Relations: Exploring Industrial Disputes Cases in West Bengal'. *Industrial Law Journal* 46, no. 3 (2017): 366–396.

Bast, Jürgen, and Arun K. Thiruvengadam. 'Origins and Pathways of Constitutionalism'. In *Democratic Constitutionalism in India and the European Union: Comparing the Law of Democracy in Continental Polities*, edited by Philipp Dann and Arun K Thiruvengadam, 75–103 (Cheltenham, UK: Edward Elgar, 2021).

Baxi, Upendra. 'The Place of Dignity in the Indian Constitution'. In *The Cambridge Handbook of Human Dignity: Interdisciplinary Perspectives*, edited by Marcus Düwell, Jens Braarvig, Roger Brownsword and Dietmar Mieth, 429–436 (Cambridge, UK: Cambridge University Press, 2014).

Bayly, C. A. *Recovering Liberties: Indian Thought in the Age of Liberalism and Empire* (New York: Cambridge University Press, 2012).

Benassi, Chiara, and Milena Tekeste. 'Employment Relations and Precarious Work'. In *The Routledge Companion to Employment Relations*, edited by Adrian Wilkinson, Tony Dundon, Jimmy Donaghey and Alexander Colvin, 307–320 (London: Routledge, 2018).

Benhabib, Seyla. 'Toward a Deliberative Model of Democratic Legitimacy'. In *Democracy and Difference: Contesting the Boundaries of the Political*, edited by Seyla Benhabib, 67–94 (Princeton, NJ: Princeton University Press, 1996).

Beyleveld, Deryck, and Roger Brownsword. *Human Dignity in Bioethics and Biolaw* (Oxford: Oxford University Press, 2001).

Bhabha, Homi K. *The Location of Culture* (Abingdon and New York: Routledge, 1994).

Bhargava, Rajeev. 'Liberal, Secular Democracy and Explanations of Hindu Nationalism'. *Commonwealth and Comparative Politics* 40, no. 3 (2002): 72–96.

Bhatia, Gautam, and Emilios Christodoulidis. 'Social Rights'. In *Democratic Constitutionalism in India and the European Union: Comparing the Law of Democracy in Continental Polities*, edited by Philipp Dann and Arun K. Thiruvengadam, 223–251(Cheltenham, UK: Edward Elgar, 2021).

Bhatt, Ela R. *We Are Poor but So Many: The Story of Self-Employed Women in India* (New Delhi: Oxford University Press, 2006).

Bhattacharjea, Aditya. 'Labour Market Flexibility in Indian Manufacturing: A Critical Survey of the Literature'. *International Labour Review* 160, no. 2 (2021): 197–218.

Bhattacharjee, Saurabh. 'Adapting Social Security to 21st Century Indian Economy: A Case for Universalisation'. *NUJS Journal of Regulatory Studies* 1, no. 1 (2016): 1–15.

———. 'COVID-19 and Labour Law: India'. *Italian Labour Law e-Journal* 13, no. 1 (2020): 1–7.

Bhowmik, Sharit K., and Kanchan Sarker. 'Worker Cooperatives as Alternative Production Systems'. *Work and Occupations* 29, no. 4 (2002): 460–482.

Bhuta, Aishwarya. 'Imbalancing Act: India's Industrial Relations Code, 2020'. *Indian Journal of Labour Economics* 65, no. 3 (2022): 821–830.

Bogg, Alan. 'Common Law and Statute in the Law of Employment'. *Current Legal Problems* 69, no. 1 (2016): 67–113.

———. 'The Constitution of Capabilities: The Case of Freedom of Association'. In *The Capability Approach to Labour Law*, edited by Brian Langille, 241–267 (New York: Oxford University Press, 2019).

Bogg, Alan, and Ruth Dukes. 'The Contract of Employment and Collective Labour Law'. In *The Contract of Employment*, edited by Mark Freedland (general editor), Alan Bogg, David Cabrelli, Hugh Collins, Nicola Countouris, A. C. L. Davies, Simon Deakin and Jeremias Prassl, 96–123 (New York: Oxford University Press, 2016).

Bordoloi, Mridusmita. Mohammad Hamza Farooqui and Sharad Pandey. *Social Security for Informal Workers in India: Exploring India's Labour Market Policies on Provisioning of Social Security to Informal Workers in the Unorganised Sector* (New Delhi: Centre for Policy Research), November 2020 (Research Brief).

Borghi, Vando. 'Transforming Knowledge into Cognitive Basis of Policies: A Cosmopolitan from Below Approach'. In *Science and Scientification in South Asia and Europe*, edited by Axel Michaels and Christoph Wulf, 242–254 (Abingdon and New York: Routledge, 2020).

Brown, Ronald C. 'Ride-Hailing Drivers as Autonomous Independent Contractors: Let Them Bargain!' *Washington International Law Journal* 29 (2020): 533–574.

Cammett, Melani, and Lauren M. MacLean. 'Introduction'. In *The Politics of Non-State Social Welfare*, edited by Melani Cammett and Lauren M. MacLean, 1–16 (Ithaca, NY: Cornell University Press, 2014).

Chakravorty Spivak, Gayatri. *In Other Worlds: Essays in Cultural Politics* (Abingdon and New York: Routledge, 1998 [1987]).

Chatterjee, Partha. *Lineages of Political Society: Studies in Postcolonial Democracy* (New York: Columbia University Press, 2011).

———. *The Politics of the Governed: Reflections on Popular Politics in Most of the World* (New York: Columbia University Press, 2004).

Chen, Martha. 'COVID-19, Cities and Urban Informal Workers: India in Comparative Perspective'. *Indian Journal of Labour Economics* 63 (2020): S41–S46.

Chigateri, Shraddha. *Labour Law Reforms and Women's Work in India: Assessing the New Labour Codes from a Gender Lens* (New Delhi: Institute of Social Studies Trust, 2021).

Choudhry, Sujit, Madhav Khosla and Pratap Bhanu Mehta. 'Locating Indian Constitutionalism'. In *The Oxford Handbook of the Indian Constitution*, edited by Sujit Choudhry, Madhav Khosla and Pratap Bhanu Mehta, 1–14 (Oxford: Oxford University Press, 2016).

Clark, Barry, and Herbert Gintis. 'Rawlsian Justice and Economic Systems'. *Philosophy & Public Affairs* 7, no. 4 (1978): 302–325.

Cohen, Joshua. 'The Economic Basis of Deliberative Democracy'. *Social Philosophy and Policy* 6, no. 2 (1989): 25–50.

Collins, Hugh. 'Is the Contract of Employment Illiberal?' In *Philosophical Foundations of Labour Law*, edited by Hugh Collins, Gillian Lester and Virginia Mantouvalou, 48–67 (New York: Oxford University Press, 2018).

Collins, Hugh, Gillian Lester, and Virginia Mantouvalou. 'Introduction: Does Labour Law Need Philosophical Foundations?' In *Philosophical Foundations of Labour Law*, edited by Hugh Collins, Gillian Lester and Virginia Mantouvalou, 1–30 (New York: Oxford University Press, 2018).

'Constituent Assembly of India Debates (Proceedings)', vol. 1. Friday, 13 December 1946. https://eparlib.nic.in/bitstream/123456789/760449/3/CA_Debate_Eng_Vol_01_edited_page_217-218.pdf. Accessed on 14 December 2023.

'Constituent Assembly of India Debates (Proceedings)', vol. 7. 19 November 1948 (Opinion of Dr. B R Ambedkar). https://www.constitutionofindia.net/constitution_assembly_debates/volume/7/1948-11-19. Accessed on 16 August 2023.

Dann, Philipp, and Arun K. Thiruvengadam. 'Comparing Constitutional Democracy in the European Union and India: An Introduction'. In *Democratic Constitutionalism in India and the European Union: Comparing the Law of Democracy in Continental Polities*, edited by Philipp Dann and Arun K Thiruvengadam, 1–41 (Cheltenham, UK: Edward Elgar, 2021).

Das Acevedo, Deepa (ed.). *Beyond the Algorithm: Qualitative Insights for Gig Work Regulation* (Cambridge [UK] and New York: Cambridge University Press, 2021).

Das Gupta, Ranajit. 'A Labour History of Social Security and Mutual Assistance in India'. *Economic and Political Weekly* 29, no. 11 (1994): 612–620.

Davidov, Guy. 'Distributive Justice and Labour Law'. In *Philosophical Foundations of Labour Law*, edited by Hugh Collins, Gillian Lester and Virginia Mantouvalou, 141–155 (New York: Oxford University Press, 2018).

———. 'Setting Labour Law's Coverage: Between Universalism and Selectivity'. *Oxford Journal of Legal Studies* 34, no. 3 (2014): 543–566.

D'Cruz, Premilla, and Ernesto Noronha. 'Indian Freelancers in the Platform Economy: Prospects and Problems'. In *Globalization, Labour Market Institutions, Processes and Policies in India: Essays in Honour of Lalit K. Deshpande*, edited by K. R. Shyam Sundar, 257–276 (Singapore: Palgrave Macmillan, 2019).

Deakin, Simon. 'Law and (Un)Sustainability in the Age of the Anthropocene', in *Prospects and Policies for Global Sustainable Recovery: Promoting*

*Environmental and Economic Sustainability*, ed. Philip Arestis and Malcolm Sawyer, 91–131 (London: Palgrave Macmillan, 2023).

———. 'The Law of the Anthropocene'. In *Concerter Les Civilisations: Mélanges en L'honneur d'Alain Supiot*, edited by Samantha Besson and Samuel Jubé, 113–122 (Paris: Éditions du Seuil, 2020).

Deakin, Simon, and Antara Haldar. 'How Should India Reform Its Labour Laws?' *Economic and Political Weekly* 50, no. 12 (2015): 48–55.

Deakin, Simon, and Frank Wilkinson. *The Law of the Labour Market: Industrialization, Employment, and Legal Evolution* (New York: Oxford University Press, 2005).

Deakin, Simon, and Gillian S. Morris. *Labour Law* (London: Butterworths, 2001 [1995]).

Deakin, Simon, Priya Lele and Mathias Siems. 'The Evolution of Labour Law: Calibrating and Comparing Regulatory Regimes'. *International Labour Review* 146, nos. 3–4 (2007): 133–162.

Del Punta, Riccardo. 'Is the Capability Theory an Adequate Normative Theory for Labour Law?' In *The Capability Approach to Labour Law*, edited by Brian Langille, 82–102 (New York: Oxford University Press, 2019).

DeVault, Marjorie. 'Introduction'. In *People at Work: Life, Power, and Social Inclusion in the New Economy*, edited by Marjorie L. DeVault, 1–22 (New York and London: New York University Press, 2008).

———. 'Mapping Invisible Work: Conceptual Tools for Social Justice Projects'. *Sociological Forum* 29, no. 4 (2014): 775–790.

Dewan, Ritu, Indira Rani, Ravi S. K., Radha Sehgal, Aruna Kanchi and Swati Raju. 'Contextualising and Visibilising Gender and Work in Rural India: Economic Contribution of Women in Agriculture'. *Indian Journal of Agricultural Economics* 71, no. 1 (2016): 49–58.

Dewan, Ritu, Indira Rani, Ravi S. K., Radha Sehgal, Aruna Kanchi and Swati Raju. *Invisible Work, Invisible Workers: The Sub-Economies of Unpaid Work and Paid Work—Action Research on Women's Unpaid Labour* (New Delhi: ActionAid, 2017).

Dolber, Brian. Michelle Rodino-Colocino, Chenjerai Kumanyika and Todd Wolfson. *The Gig Economy: Workers and Media in the Age of Convergence* (New York: Routledge, 2021).

Donaghey, Jimmy, and Juliane Reinecke. 'Global Supply Chains and Employment Relations'. In *The Routledge Companion to Employment Relations*, edited by Adrian Wilkinson, Tony Dundon, Jimmy Donaghey and Alexander Colvin, 342–356 (London: Routledge, 2018).

Doorey, David J. 'Just Transitions Law: Putting Labour Law to Work on Climate Change'. *Journal of Environmental Law and Practice* 30, no. 2 (2017): 201–239.

Drèze, Jean, and Amartya Sen. *India Development and Participation* (New Delhi: Oxford University Press, 2002).

Dukes, Ruth. *The Labour Constitution: The Enduring Idea of Labour Law* (New York: Oxford University Press, 2014).

Dworkin, Ronald. *Justice for Hedgehogs* (Cambridge [MA] and London: Belknap Press of Harvard University Press, 2011).

Employees' State Insurance Corporation. Circular No. N-11/12/2003-Bft.II/Vol. II, Sub. 'Rajiv Gandhi Shramik Kalyan Yojana'. 9 February 2009.

Estlund, Cynthia. *Automation Anxiety: Why and How to Save Work* (New York: Oxford University Press, 2021).

Evans, Peter. 'Collective Capabilities, Culture, and Amartya Sen's Development as Freedom'. *Studies in Comparative International Development* 37, no. 2 (2002): 54–60.

Freedland, Mark. 'The Legal Structure of the Contract of Employment'. In *The Contract of Employment*, edited by Mark Freedland (general editor), Alan Bogg, David Cabrelli, Hugh Collins, Nicola Countouris, A. C. L. Davies, Simon Deakin and Jeremias Prassl, 28–51 (New York: Oxford University Press, 2016).

Freedland, Mark, and Nicola Kountouris. *The Legal Construction of Personal Work Relations* (New York: Oxford University Press, 2012).

Gandhi, Leela. *Postcolonial Theory: A Critical Introduction* (Abingdon and New York: Routledge, 2020 [1998]).

Gardner, John. 'The Contractualisation of Labour Law'. In *Philosophical Foundations of Labour Law*, edited by Hugh Collins, Gillian Lester and Virginia Mantouvalou, 33–47 (New York: Oxford University Press, 2018).

Ghosh, Arun Kumar. 'Cooperative Movement and Rural Development in India'. *Social Change* 37, no. 3 (2007): 14–32.

Ghosh, Jayati. 'A Critique of the Indian Government's Response to the COVID-19 Pandemic'. *Journal of Industrial and Business Economics* 47 (2020): 519–530.

———. 'Gendered Labour Markets and Capitalist Accumulation'. *Japanese Political Economy* 44, nos. 1–4 (2018): 25–41.

———. 'The Uses and Abuses of Inequality'. *Journal of Human Development and Capabilities* 20, no. 2 (2019): 181–196.

Gopalakrishnan, Ramapriya. 'Labour Jurisprudence of the Supreme Court: Recent Trends'. In *Labour, Employment and Economic Growth in India*, edited by K. V. Ramaswamy, 292–318 (Delhi: Cambridge University Press, 2015).

Government of India. *All India Report of Sixth Economic Census, 2016*. http://mospi.nic.in/all-india-report-sixth-economic-census. Accessed on 10 November 2021.

———. *Economic Survey 2018–19*, vol. 2 (New Delhi: Government of India, 2019).

Government of India, Ministry of Labour and Employment. 'Atal Bimit Vyakti Kalyan Yojana'. https://www.india.gov.in/spotlight/atal-beemit-vyakti-kalyan-yojana. Accessed on 16 August 2023.

———. *Report of the National Commission on Labour*, vols. 1–2 (New Delhi: Ministry of Labour, Government of India, 2002).

———. 'Welfare Schemes for Unorganised Workers'. 22 March 2021. https://pib.gov.in/PressReleaseIframePage.aspx?PRID=1706609. Accessed on 16 August 2023.

Gulati, Ashok, and Kavery Ganguly. 'The Changing Landscape of Indian Agriculture'. *Agricultural Economics* 41, no. 1 (2010): 37–45.

Gunawardana, Samanthi J. 'Emerging Economies, Freedom of Association and Collective Bargaining for Women Workers in Export-Oriented Manufacturing'. In *The Routledge Companion to Employment Relations*, edited by Adrian Wilkinson, Tony Dundon, Jimmy Donaghey and Alexander Colvin, 372–386 (London: Routledge, 2018).

Habermas, Jürgen. *Between Facts and Norms: Contributions to a Discourse Theory of Law and Democracy*. Translated by William Rehg (Cambridge, MA: MIT Press, 1996 [1992 in German]).

Harriss-White, Barbara. 'Work and Wellbeing in Informal Economies: The Regulative Roles of Institutions of Identity and the State'. *World Development* 38, no. 2 (2010): 170–183.

Hay, Douglas, and Paul Craven. 'Introduction'. In *Masters, Servants, and Magistrates in Britain & the Empire, 1562–1955*, edited by Douglas Hay and Paul Craven, 1–58 (Chapel Hill [NC] and London: University of North Carolina Press, 2004).

——— (eds.), *Masters, Servants, and Magistrates in Britain and the Empire, 1562–1955* (Chapel Hill [NC] London: University of North Carolina Press, 2004).

*Hindu Business Line*. 'Trade Unions Go on Nationwide Strike against Centre's "Anti-People" Policies'. 8 January 2020. https://www.thehindubusinessline.com/news/10-central-trade-unions-go-on-nationwide-strike/article3051 1129.ece. Accessed on 16 August 2023.

*Hindustan Times*. 'Ola and Uber Taxis May Go On Strike in Mumbai Tomorrow'. 27 February 2017.

———. 'Ola, Uber Strike: Who Gained and Who Lost'. 27 February 2017.

Hirway, Indira. 'Unpaid Work and the Economy: Linkages and their Implications'. *Indian Journal of Labour Economics* 58, no. 1 (2015): 1–21.

Holston, James. *Insurgent Citizenship: Disjunctions of Democracy and Modernity in Brazil* (Princeton, NJ: Princeton University Press, 2008).

Hsieh, Nien-he. 'Rawlsian Justice and Workplace Republicanism'. *Social Theory and Practice* 31, no. 1 (2005): 115–142.

International Labour Organization. 'ILO Monitor: COVID-19 and the World of Work: Updated Estimates and Analysis' (2nd edition). 7 April 2020. https://www.ilo.org/wcmsp5/groups/public/---dgreports/---dcomm/documents/briefingnote/wcms_740877.pdf. Accessed on 16 August 2023.

———. 'ILO Monitor on the World of Work' (9th edition). 23 May 2022. https://www.ilo.org/wcmsp5/groups/public/---dgreports/---dcomm/---publ/documents/briefingnote/wcms_845642.pdf. Accessed on 16 August 2023.

———. *India: A Provident Fund for Unorganized Workers (West Bengal)*, ILO Subregional Office for South Asia. https://www.ilo.org/wcmsp5/groups/public/---ed_protect/---soc_sec/documents/publication/wcms_secsoc_6581.pdf. Accessed on 16 August 2023.

———. *India Labour Market Update*. ILO Country Office for India, July 2017 (New Delhi: International Labour Organization).

———. *Situation Analysis on the COVID-19 Pandemic's Impact on Enterprises and Workers in the Formal and Informal Economy in India* (New Delhi: International Labour Organization, 2021).

———. 'Statistical Update on Employment in the Informal Economy'. June 2012. http://www.ilo.org/wcmsp5/groups/public/---dgreports/---stat/documents/presentation/wcms_182504.pdf. Accessed on 16 August 2023.

International Alliance of Waste Pickers. 'List: Waste Pickers around the World'. https://globalrec.org/waw/list. Accessed on 16 August 2023.

Jayal, Niraja Gopal. *Citizenship and Its Discontents: An Indian History* (Cambridge [MA] and London: Harvard University Press, 2013).

Jenkins, Jean, and Paul Blyton. 'In Debt to the Time-Bank: The Manipulation of Working Time in Indian Garment Factories and "Working Dead Horse"'. *Work, Employment and Society* 31, no. 1 (2017): 90–105.

John, Mathew. 'Social Institutions in the Shadow of Liberal Constitutionalism: An Indian Perspective'. In *Constitutionalism beyond Liberalism*, edited by

Michael W. Dowdle and Michael A. Wilkinson, 129–148 (Cambridge, UK: Cambridge University Press, 2017).

Kahn-Freund, Otto. 'A Note on Status and Contract in British Labour Law'. *Modern Law Review* 30, no. 6 (1967): 635–644.

Kapur, Ratna. 'Gender Equality'. In *The Oxford Handbook of the Indian Constitution*, edited by Sujit Choudhry, Madhav Khosla and Pratap Bhanu Mehta, 742–755 (Oxford: Oxford University Press, 2016).

Kannan, K. P., and Jan Breman (eds.). *The Long Road to Social Security: Assessing the Implementation of National Social Security Initiatives for the Working Poor in India* (New Delhi: Oxford University Press, 2013).

Kaul, Bushan Tilak. '"Industry", "Industrial Dispute", and "Workman": Conceptual Framework and Judicial Activism'. *Journal of the Indian Law Institute* 50, no. 1 (2008): 3–50.

Kaushik, Archana. 'From Hunger Deaths to Healthy Living: A Case Study of Dalits in Varanasi District, Utter Pradesh, India'. *Contemporary Voice of Dalit* 10, no. 2 (2018): 173–181.

Kelly, Erin. 'Equal Opportunity, Unequal Capability'. In *Measuring Justice: Primary Goods and Capabilities*, edited by Harry Brighouse and Ingrid Robeyns, 61–80 (New York: Cambridge University Press, 2010).

Khaitan, Tarunabh. *A Theory of Discrimination Law* (New York: Oxford University Press, 2015).

———. 'Directive Principles and the Expressive Accommodation of Ideological Dissenters'. *International Journal of Constitutional Law* 16, no. 2 (2018): 389–420.

———. 'Equality: Legislative Review under Article 14'. In *The Oxford Handbook of the Indian Constitution*, edited by Sujit Choudhry, Madhav Khosla and Pratap Bhanu Mehta, 699–719 (Oxford: Oxford University Press, 2016).

———. 'Killing a Constitution with a Thousand Cuts: Executive Aggrandizement and Party–State Fusion in India'. *Law and Ethics of Human Rights* 14, no.1 (2020): 49–95.

Khosla, Madhav. 'Constitutional Amendment'. In *The Oxford Handbook of the Indian Constitution*, edited by Sujit Choudhry, Madhav Khosla and Pratap Bhanu Mehta, 232–250 (Oxford: Oxford University Press, 2016).

———. *India's Founding Moment: The Constitution of a Most Surprising Democracy* (Cambridge [MA] and London: Harvard University Press, 2020).

Krishna, Anirudh. 'The Naya Netas: Informal Mediators of Government Services in Rural North India'. In *The Politics of Non-State Social Welfare*, edited by

Melani Cammett and Lauren M. MacLean, 175–192 (Ithaca, NY: Cornell University Press, 2014).

Krishnaswamy, Sudhir. *Democracy and Constitutionalism in India: A Study of the Basic Structure Doctrine* (New Delhi: Oxford University Press, 2009).

Kumar, Anjani, Ashok K. Mishra, Sunil Saroj and P. K. Joshi. 'Institutional versus Non-Institutional Credit to Agricultural Households in India: Evidence on Impact from a National Farmers' Survey'. *Economic Systems* 41, no. 3 (2017): 420–432.

Kumar, Pankaj, and Jaivir Singh. *Issues in Law and Public Policy on Contract Labour in India: Comparative Insights from China* (Singapore: Springer, 2018).

Kwok, Chi. 'Work Autonomy and Workplace Democracy: The Polarization of the Goods of Work Autonomy in the Two Worlds of Work'. *Review of Social Economy* 78, no. 3 (2020): 351–372.

Langille, Brian. 'Labour Law's Theory of Justice'. In *The Idea of Labour Law*, edited by Guy Davidov and Brian Langille, 101–119 (Oxford and New York: Oxford University Press, 2011).

———. 'The Narrative of Global Justice and the Grammar of Law'. In *Global Justice and International Labour Rights*, edited by Yossi Dahan, Hanna Lerner and Faina Milman-Sivan, 186–208 (Cambridge, UK: Cambridge University Press, 2016).

Lerche, Jens. 'A Global Alliance against Forced Labour? Unfree Labour, Neo-Liberal Globalization and the International Labour Organization'. *Journal of Agrarian Change* 7, no. 4 (2007): 425–452.

Mangubhai, Jayshree P. *Human Rights as Practice: Dalit Women Securing Livelihood Entitlements in South India* (New Delhi: Oxford University Press, 2014).

Marshall, T. H., and Tom Bottomore. *Citizenship and Social Class* (London: Pluto Press, 1992).

Mayer, Robert. 'Robert Dahl and the Right to Workplace Democracy'. *Review of Politics* 63, no. 2 (2001): 221–247.

McCallum, Rebekah. 'The Business of Tea: British Tea Companies and Plantation Labour Law in India, 1901–1951 (With Special emphasis on James Finlay & Co.)'. PhD dissertation, Department of History and Classical Studies, Faculty of Arts, McGill University, Montreal, December 2021.

McCrudden, Christopher. 'Human Dignity and Judicial Interpretation of Human Rights'. *European Journal of International Law* 19, no. 4 (2008): 655–724.

McGaughey, Ewan. 'Otto von Gierke: The Social Role of Private Law'. *German Law Journal* 19, no. 4 (2018): 1017–1166.

Menkel-Meadow, Carrie. 'Uses and Abuses of Socio-Legal Studies'. In *Routledge Handbook of Socio-Legal Theory and Methods*, edited by Naomi Creutzfeldt, Marc Mason and Kirsten McConnachie, 35–57 (Abingdon and New York: Routledge, 2020).

Mitchell, Richard, Petra Mahy and Peter Gahan. 'The Evolution of Labour Law in India: An Overview and Commentary on Regulatory Objectives and Development'. *Asian Journal of Law and Society* 1, no. 2 (2014): 413–453.

Mundlak, Guy. 'Industrial Citizenship, Social Citizenship, Corporate Citizenship: I Just Want My Wages'. *Theoretical Inquiries in Law* 8, no. 2 (2007): 719–748.

Nath, Damini. 'Can't Keep Deferring Labour Reforms in the Name of Consultation, Says Labour Minister Gangwar'. *The Hindu*, 2 October 2020.

National Commission for Enterprises in the Unorganised Sector. *Report on Definitional and Statistical Issues Relating to Informal Economy* (New Delhi: National Commission for Enterprises in the Unorganised Sector, 2008).

Nehru, Jawaharlal. 'The Psychology of Indian Nationalism'. In *Selected Works of Jawaharlal Nehru*, vol. 2, edited by Sarvepalli Gopal, 259–270 (New Delhi: Orient Longman, 1972–1982).

Nussbaum, Martha C. *Creating Capabilities: The Human Development Approach* (Cambridge [MA] and London: Belknap Press of Harvard University Press, 2011).

———. *Women and Human Development: The Capabilities Approach* (Cambridge, UK: Cambridge University Press, 2000).

Paskalia, Vicki. *Free Movement, Social Security and Gender in the EU* (London: Hart Publishing, 2007).

Patra, Rabi N., and Mahendra P. Agasty. 'Cooperatives, Agriculture and Rural Development: Role, Issues and Policy Implications'. *IOSR Journal of Humanities and Social Sciences* 13, no. 2 (2013): 14–25.

Pence, Ellen. 'Safety for Battered Women in a Textually Mediated Legal System'. *Studies in Cultures, Organizations and Societies* 7, no. 2 (2001): 199–229.

Poddar, Mihika, and Alex Koshy. 'Legislating for Domestic "Care" Workers in India: An Alternative Understanding'. *NUJS Law Review* 12 (2019): 67–117.

Pogge, Thomas. 'A Critique of the Capability Approach'. In *Measuring Justice: Primary Goods and Capabilities*, edited by Harry Brighouse and Ingrid Robeyns, 17–60 (New York: Cambridge University Press, 2010).

———. *World Poverty and Human Rights* (Cambridge, UK: Polity Press, 2008).

Polanyi, Karl. *The Great Transformation: The Political and Economic Origins of Our Time* (Boston, MA: Beacon Press, 2001 [1944]).

Prabhat, Shantanu, Sneha Nanavati and Nimmi Rangaswamy. 'India's "Uberwallah" Profiling Uber Drivers in the Gig Economy'. Paper presented at the Tenth International Conference on Information and Communication Technologies and Development (ICTD '19), 4–7 January 2019, Ahmedabad.

Rajalakshmi, T. K. 'The New Labour Codes: Labour's Loss'. *Frontline*, 23 October 2020.

Ram-Prasad, Chakravarthi. 'Pluralism and Liberalism: Reading the Indian Constitution as a Philosophical Document for Constitutional Patriotism'. *Critical Review of International Social and Political Philosophy* 16, no: 5 (2013): 676–697.

Rawls, John. *A Theory of Justice* (Cambridge, MA: Harvard University Press, 1999 [1971]).

———. *The Law of Peoples* (Cambridge [MA] and London: Harvard University Press, 1999).

Ray, Aditya. 'Unrest in India's Gig Economy: Ola–Uber Drivers' Strikes and Worker Organization'. *Futures of Work*, 9 December 2019.

Raz, Joseph. *The Authority of Law: Essays on Law and Morality* (New York: Oxford University Press, 1979).

Robeyns, Ingrid, and Harry Brighouse. 'Introduction: Social Primary Goods and Capabilities as Metrics of Justice'. In *Measuring Justice: Primary Goods and Capabilities*, edited by Harry Brighouse and Ingrid Robeyns, 1–14 (New York: Cambridge University Press, 2010).

Routh, Supriya. 'Constituting a Right to Association: A Postcolonial Exploration'. *International Journal of Comparative Labour Law and Industrial Relations* 36, no. 4 (2020): 523–552.

———. 'Developing Human Capabilities through Law: Is Indian Law Failing?' *Asian Journal of Law and Economics* 3, no.1 (2012): Article 4 (1–20).

———. 'Do Human Rights Work for Informal Workers?' In *Re-Imagining Labour Law for Development: Informal Work in the Global North and Global South*, edited by Diamond Ashiagbor, 101–122 (London: Hart Publishing, 2019).

———. 'Embedding Work in Nature: The Anthropocene and Legal Imagination of Work as Human Activity'. *Comparative Labor Law and Policy Journal* 40, no. 1 (2018): 29–60.

———. *Enhancing Capabilities through Labour Law: Informal Workers in India* (Abingdon and New York: Routledge, 2014).

———. 'Examining the Legal Legitimacy of Informal Economic Activities'. *Social and Legal Studies* 31, no. 2 (2022): 282–308.

———. 'Informal Workers' Aggregation and Law'. *Theoretical Inquiries in Law* 17, no. 1 (2016): 283–320.

———. 'The Judiciary and (Labour) Law in the Development Discourse in India'. *Verfassung und Recht in Ubersee* 44, no. 2 (2011): 237–257.

———. 'Workers and Competition Law in India: Workers' Associations Are Mostly Not Cartels'. In *The Cambridge Handbook of Labor in Competition Law*, edited by Sanjukta Paul, Shae McCrystal and Ewan McGaughey, 193–207 (Cambridge, UK: Cambridge University Press, 2022).

Routray, Sanjeev. *The Right to Be Counted: The Urban Poor and the Politics of Resettlement in Delhi* (Redwood City, CA: Stanford University Press, 2022).

Roy, Gopal Krishna, Amaresh Dubey and Suresh Ramaiah. 'Labour Market Flexibility and Changes in Employment: Spatial and Temporal Evidence from Indian Manufacturing'. *Indian Journal of Labour Economics* 63, no. 1 (2020): 81–98.

Roy, Indrajit. *Politics of the Poor: Negotiating Democracy in Contemporary India* (New Delhi: Cambridge University Press, 2018).

Roychowdhury, Anamitra. 'Application of Job Security Laws, Workers' Bargaining Power and Employment Outcomes in India'. *Economic and Labour Relations Review* 30, no. 1 (2019): 120–141.

———. *Labour Law Reforms in India: All in the Name of Jobs* (Abingdon and New York: Routledge, 2018).

Roychowdhury, Anamitra, and Kingshuk Sarkar. 'Labour Law Reforms in a Neo-Liberal Setting: Lessons from India'. *Global Labour Journal* 12, no. 1 (2021): 58–64.

Said, Edward W. *Orientalism* (New York: Vintage Books, 1979).

Saini, Debi S. 'Labour Legislation and Social Justice: Rhetoric and Reality'. *Economic and Political Weekly* 34, no. 39 (1999): L-32–L-40.

Samantroy, Ellina and Subhalakshmi Nandi. 'Introduction'. In *Gender, Unpaid Work and Care in India*, edited by Ellina Samantroy and Subhalakshmi Nandi, 1–9 (Abingdon and New York: Routledge, 2022).

Sankaran, Kamala. 'Emerging Perspectives in Labour Regulation in the Wake of COVID-19'. *Indian Journal of Labour Economics* 63 (2020): S91–S95.

Sapkal, Rahul Suresh, and K. R. Shyam Sundar. 'Determinants of Precarious Employment in India: An Empirical Analysis'. In *Precarious Work*, edited by Arne L. Kalleberg and Steven P. Vallas, 335–361 (Bingley: Emerald Publishing Limited, 2018).

Sarkar, Santanu. 'How Independent Is India's Labour Law Framework from the State's Changing Economic Policies?' *Economic and Labour Relations Review* 30, no. 3 (2019): 422–440.

———. 'The 2019 Code on Wages: Truth versus Hype'. *Indian Journal of Industrial Relations* 57, no. 1 (2021): 1–12.

Sen, Amartya. *Development as Freedom* (New York: Alfred A. Knoph, 1999).

———. '"Equality of What?" The Tanner Lecture on Human Values, delivered at Stanford University, May 22, 1979'. In *The Tanner Lectures on Human Values*, vol. 1, 195–220 (Salt Lake City, UT: University of Utah Press; Cambridge [UK], London, Melbourne and Sydney: Cambridge University Press, 1980).

———. 'Human Rights and Capabilities'. *Journal of Human Development* 6, no. 2 (2005): 151–166.

———. *The Idea of Justice* (Cambridge, MA: Harvard University Press, 2009).

———. 'The Place of Capability in a Theory of Justice'. In *Measuring Justice: Primary Goods and Capabilities*, edited by Harry Brighouse and Ingrid Robeyns, 239–253 (New York: Cambridge University Press, 2010).

Sengupta, Mitu. 'Economic Liberalization, Democratic Expansion and Organized Labour in India: Towards a New Politics of Revival'. *Just Labour: A Canadian Journal of Work and Society* 14 (2009): 13–32.

Shamir, Hila. 'What's the Border Got to Do with It? How Immigration Regimes Affect Familial Care Provision: A Comparative Analysis'. *American University Journal of Gender, Social Policy and the Law* 19, no. 2 (2011): 601–669.

Sharma, Yogima Seth. 'Central Trade Unions Want Ministry to Put on Hold Four Labour Codes & Re-Start Discussions'. *Economic Times*, 20 January 2021.

Shenoy, Amritha V. 'Colonial India in the ILO and International Law'. *Christ University Law Journal* 11, no. 2 (2022): 63–78.

Shenoy, Deepti. 'Courting Substantive Equality: Employment Discrimination Law in India'. *University of Pennsylvania Journal of International Law* 34, no. 3 (2013): 611–640.

Shukla, Somanshu, and Aryan Bhat. 'Migrant Workers in Unorganised Sector: Socio-Legal and Policy Analysis'. In *Labour Law Reforms 2021*, edited by Jeet Singh Mann, 387–416 (Delhi: Centre for Transparency and Accountability in Governance, 2021).

Singh, Jaivir. 'Who Is a Worker? Searching the Theory of the Firm for Answers'. In *Labour, Employment and Economic Growth in India*, edited by K. V. Ramaswamy, 265–291 (Delhi: Cambridge University Press, 2015).

Singh, Mahendra Pal (ed.). *VN Shukla's Constitution of India* (12th edition) (New Delhi: Eastern Book Company, 2013).

Smith, Dorothy E. *The Everyday World as Problematic: A Feminist Sociology* (Toronto: University of Toronto Press, 1987).

Sood, Atul, and Paaritosh Nath. 'Labour Law Changes: Innocuous Mistakes or Sleight of Hand?' *Economic and Political Weekly* 55, no. 22 (2020): 33–37.

Srivastava, S. C. 'Labour Law Reforms on Unorganised, Gig and Platform Workers under the Code on Social Security: Issues and Challenges'. In *Labour Law Reforms 2021*, edited by Jeet Singh Mann, 1–40 (Delhi: Centre for Transparency and Accountability in Governance, 2021).

Stone, Katherine V. W. *From Widgets to Digits: Employment Regulation for the Changing Workplace* (New York: Cambridge University Press, 2004).

Stranded Workers Action Network. '32 Days and Counting: COVID-19 Lockdown, Migrant Workers, and the Inadequacy of Welfare Measures in India'. 1 May 2020.

Sudesh, V. 'Domestic Worker Rights Violation During COVID-19 Lockdown: Need for Labour Law Protection'. In *Labour Law Reforms 2021*, edited by Jeet Singh Mann, 86–94 (Delhi: Centre for Transparency and Accountability in Governance, 2021).

Sundar, K. R. Shyam. 'Dynamics of Reforms of Labour Market and the Industrial Relations System in India'. In *Globalization, Labour Market Institutions, Processes and Policies in India: Essays in Honour of Lalit K. Deshpande*, edited by K. R. Shyam Sundar, 521–544 (Singapore: Palgrave Macmillan, 2019).

———. 'Labour Flexibility Debate in India: A Comprehensive Review and Some Suggestions'. *Economic and Political Weekly* 40, nos. 22–23 (2005): 2274–2285.

———. 'No Dialogue with Trade Unions, India's Labour Laws Are Now a Product of Unilateralism'. *The Wire*, 7 July 2020.

———. 'Second National Commission on Labour (SNCL) and Reform of Industrial Relations System: Some Comments'. *Indian Journal of Industrial Relations* 42, no. 2 (2006): 252–270.

Sundar, K. R. Shyam, and Rahul Suresh Sapkal. 'Changes to Labour Laws by State Governments Will Lead to Anarchy in the Labour Market'. *Economic and Political Weekly* 55, no. 23 (2020). https://www.epw.in/engage/article/changes-labour-laws-state-market-anarchy-labour-market. Accessed on 30 November 2023.

Supiot, Alain. *The Spirit of Philadelphia: Social Justice vs. the Total Market*. Translated by Saskia Brown (New York: Verso Books, 2012).

Supiot, Alain. 'Grandeur and Misery of the Social State'. *New Left Review* 82 (2013): 99–113.

———. *Governance by Numbers* (Oxford: Hart Publishing, 2015).

———. 'Labour Is Not a Commodity: The Content and Meaning of Work in the Twenty-First Century'. *International Labour Review* 160, no. 1 (2021): 1–20.

Supiot, Alain, María Emilia Casas, Jean de Munck, Peter Hanau, Anders L. Johansson, Pamela Meadows, Enzo Mingione, Robert Salais and Paul van der Heijden. *Beyond Employment Changes in Work and the Future of Labour Law in Europe* (Oxford and New York: Oxford University Press, 2001).

Surendranath, Anup. 'Life and Personal Liberty'. In *The Oxford Handbook of the Indian Constitution*, edited by Sujit Choudhry, Madhav Khosla and Pratap Bhanu Mehta, 756–776 (Oxford: Oxford University Press, 2016).

Surie, Aditi. 'Tech in Work: Organising Informal Work in India'. *Economic and Political Weekly* 52, no. 20 (2017): 12–15.

*The Hindu*. 'Trade Unions to Strike on November 26 against Labour Laws'. 2 October 2020.

Thiruvengadam, Arun. *The Constitution of India: A Contextual Analysis* (Oxford and Portland [OR]: Hart Publishing, 2017).

Tilly, Charles. 'Citizenship, Identity and Social History'. *International Review of Social History* 40, supp. 3 (1995): 1–17.

———. 'Where Do Rights Come From?' In *Collective Violence, Contentious Politics, and Social Change: A Charles Tilly Reader*, edited by Ernesto Castaneda and Cathy Lisa Schneider, 168–182 (New York and Abingdon: Routledge, 2017).

Tomassetti, Paolo. 'Energy Transition: A Labour Law Retrospective'. *Industrial Law Journal* 52, no. 1 (2023): 34–67.

Tushnet, Mark. 'State Action, Social Welfare Rights, and the Judicial Role: Some Comparative Observations'. *Chicago Journal of International Law* 3, no. 2 (2002): 435–453.

———. 'The Indian Constitution Seen from Outside'. In *The Oxford Handbook of the Indian Constitution*, edited by Sujit Choudhry, Madhav Khosla and Pratap Bhanu Mehta, 1019–1032 (Oxford: Oxford University Press, 2016).

Verma, Anil, and Ana Virginia Moreira Gomes. 'Labor Market Flexibility and Trajectories of Development: Lessons from Brazil, India and China'. *Indian Journal of Industrial Relations* 50, no. 1 (2014): 51–74.

Wahi, Namita. 'Property'. In *The Oxford Handbook of the Indian Constitution*, edited by Sujit Choudhry, Madhav Khosla and Pratap Bhanu Mehta, 943–964 (Oxford: Oxford University Press, 2016).

Waldron, Jeremy. *Law and Disagreement* (New York: Oxford University Press, 1999).

———. *The Dignity of Legislation* (New York: Cambridge University Press, 1999).

Webber, Grégoire, Paul Yowell, Richard Ekins, Maris Köpcke, Bradley W. Miller and Francisco J. Urbina. *Legislated Rights: Securing Human Rights through Legislation* (New York: Cambridge University Press, 2018).

Weber, Max. 'Freedom and Coercion'. In *Max Weber on Law in Economy and Society*, edited by Max Rheinstein, 188–191 (Cambridge, MA: Harvard University Press, 1954).

Weiss, Manfred. 'The Future of Labour Law in Europe: Rise or Fall of the European Social Model'. *European Labour Law Journal* 8, no. 4 (2017): 344–356.

Werden, Gregory J. 'Antitrust's Rule of Reason: Only Competition Matters'. *Antitrust Law Journal* 79, no. 2 (2014): 713–759.

Young, Iris Marion. 'Between Liberalism and Social Democracy: A Comment on Tushnet'. *Chicago Journal of International Law* 3, no. 2 (2002): 471–476.

———. 'Responsibility and Global Labor Justice'. *Journal of Political Philosophy* 12, no. 4 (2004): 365–388.

———. 'Self-Determination and Global Democracy: A Critique of Liberal Nationalism'. *NOMOS* 42 (2000): 147–183.

Zaidi, Mubashira. 'Work and Women's Economic Empowerment in Tribal Rajasthan, India'. In *Gender, Unpaid Work and Care in India*, edited by Ellina Samantroy and Subhalakshmi Nandi, 147–164 (Abingdon and New York: Routledge, 2022).

Zbyszewska, Ania. 'Regulating Work with People and "Nature" in Mind: Feminist Reflections'. *Comparative Labor Law and Policy Journal* 40, no. 1 (2018): 9–28.

## Legislation

Beedi and Cigar Workers (Conditions of Employment) Act, 1966 (Act no. 32 of 1966)

Beedi Workers Welfare Fund Act, 1976 (Act no. 62 of 1976)

Bonded Labour System (Abolition) Act, 1976 (Act no. 19 of 1976)

Building and Other Construction Workers (Regulation of Employment and Conditions of Service) Act, 1996 (Act no. 27 of 1996)

Cine-Workers and Cinema Theatre Workers (Regulation of Employment) Act, 1981 (Act no. 50 of 1981)

Code on Social Security, 2020 (Act no. 36 of 2020)

Code on Wages, 2019 (Act no. 29 of 2019)

Competition Act, 2002 (Act no. 12 of 2003)
Constitution (Ninety-Seventh Amendment) Act, 2011
Constitution of India, 1950
Contract Labour (Regulation and Abolition) Act, 1970 (Act no. 37 of 1970)
Dock Workers (Safety, Health and Welfare) Act, 1986 (Act no. 54 of 1986)
Employees' Compensation Act, 1923 (Act no. 8 of 1923)
Employees' Provident Funds and Miscellaneous Provisions Act, 1952 (Act no. 19 of 1952)
Employees' State Insurance Act, 1948 (Act no. 34 of 1948)
Equal Remuneration Act, 1976 (Act no. 25 of 1976 as amended by Act no. 49 of 1987)
Factories Act, 1948 (Act no. 63 of 1948)
Industrial Disputes (Amendment) Act, 1982 (Act no. 46 of 1982)
Industrial Disputes Act, 1947 (Act no. 14 of 1947)
Industrial Employment (Standing Orders) Act, 1946 (Act no. 20 of 1946)
Industrial Relations Code, 2020 (Act no. 35 of 2020)
Inter-State Migrant Workmen (Regulation of Employment and Conditions of Service) Act, 1979 (Act no. 30 of 1979)
Kerala Recognition of Trade Unions Act, 2010 (Act no. 16 of 2010)
Maharashtra Recognition of Trade Unions and Prevention of Unfair Labour Practices Act, 1971 (Act no. 1 of 1972)
Maternity Benefit Act, 1961 (Act no. 53 of 1961)
Mines Act, 1952 (Act no. 35 of 1952)
Minimum Wages Act, 1948 (Act no. 11 of 1948)
Motor Transport Workers Act, 1961 (Act no. 27 of 1961)
Occupational Safety, Health and Working Conditions Code, 2020 (Act no. 37 of 2020)
Payment of Bonus Act, 1965 (Act no. 21 of 1965)
Payment of Gratuity Act, 1972 (Act no. 39 of 1972)
Personal Injuries (Compensation Insurance) Act, 1963 (Act no. 37 of 1963)
Plantations Labour Act, 1951 (Act no. 69 of 1951)
Scheduled Tribes and Other Traditional Forest Dwellers (Recognition of Forest Rights) Act, 2006 (Act no. 2 of 2007)
Unorganised Workers' Social Security Act, 2008 (Act no. 33 of 2008)
West Bengal Trade Unions Rules, 1998 (issued under the Trade Unions Act, 1926 [Act no. 16 of 1926], as amended by the Trade Unions [West Bengal Amendment] Act, 1983 [West Bengal Act no. 48 of 1983])
Working Journalists (Fixation of Rates of Wages) Act, 1958 (Act no. 29 of 1958)

Working Journalists and Other Newspaper Employees (Conditions of Service) and Miscellaneous Provisions Act, 1955 (Act no. 45 of 1955)

## Cases

*All India Bank Employees' Association v. National Industrial Tribunal and Others*, (1962) 3 SCR 269 (SC)
*Bandhua Mukti Morcha v. Union of India*, (1984) 2 SCR 67
*Bangalore Water Supply and Sewerage Board v. A. Rajappa and Others*, AIR 1978 SC 548
*Calcutta Electricity Supply Corporation (India) Limited v. Subhash Chandra Bose*, AIR 1992 SC 573
*Competition of India v. Steel Authority of India Limited and Another*, (2010) Civil Appeal No. 7779 of 2010 (SC)
*Consumer Education and Research Centre v. Union of India*, (1995) 3 SCC 42
*Dharangadhara Chemical Works Limited v. State of Saurashtra*, (1957) 1 LLJ 477 (SC)
*Excel Crop Care Limited v. Competition Commission of India and Another*, (2014) Civil Appeal No. 2480 of 2014 (SC)
*Excel Crop Care Limited v. Competition Commission of India and Another*, (2014) Civil Appeal No. 6691 of 2014 (SC)
*Ficus Pax Private Limited and Others v. Union of India and Ors*, W.P. (C) Diary No. 10983 of 2020
*Francis Coralie v. Union Territory of Delhi*, (1981) 2 SCR 516
*Gujarat Mazdoor Sabha and Another v. State of Gujarat*, (2020) 13 S.C.R. 886
*His Holiness Kesavananda Bharati Sripadagalvaru v. State of Kerala*, (1973) MANU 0445 (SC)
*Hussainbhai v. The Alath Factory Tezhilali Union and Others*, AIR 1978 SC 1410
*International Airport Authority of India v. International Air Cargo Workers' Union*, AIR 2009 SC 3063
*Justice K S Puttaswami (Retired) v. Union of India*, Writ Petition (Civil) No. 494 of 2012 (SCC, 2018)
*Kirloskar Brothers Limited v. Employees' State Insurance Corporation*, (1996) 2 SCALE 1
*M. C. Mehta v. State of Tamil Nadu*, AIR 1997 SC 699
*Managing Director, Hassan Co-Operative Milk Producer's Society Union Limited v. Assistant Regional Director, Employees' State Insurance Corporation*, (2010) 11 SCC 537

*Maneka Gandhi v. Union of India*, 1978 (1) SCC 248

*People's Union for Democratic Rights v. Union of India*, (1982) 3 SCC 235

*Rajasthan Cylinders and Containers Limited v. Union of India and Another*, (2014) Civil Appeal No. 3546 of 2014 (SC)

*Regional Director, Employees' State Insurance Corporation v. Francis D'Costa*, AIR 1995 SC 1811

*Secretary, State of Karnataka and Others v. Umadevi and Others*, 2006 (4) SCC 1

*Silver Jubilee Tailoring House and Others v. Chief Inspector of Shops and Establishments and Another*, AIR 1974 SC 37

*State of Uttar Pradesh v. Jai Vir Singh*, 2005 MANU 0360 SC

*T. K. Rangarajan v. Government of Tamil Nadu and Others*, (2003) Appeal (Civil) 5556 of 2003 (SC)

*Workmen of Nilgiri Cooperative Marketing Society Limited v. State of Tamil Nadu*, (2004) 3 SCC 514

# Index

access to information, 45
accident insurance, 13, 110
active citizenry, 29
actual realisation, 171
actual social context, 9–10
adjudicative exercise, 175
agency
   capacity for agency, 33
   collective agency, 30
   human agency, 100
   individual agency, 4, 33, 101, 181
   worker agency, 18, 31, 159, 181, 185, 187
agents of change, 30
amalgamations, 154
amending power, 52
annual leave, 88
anthropological narratives, 8
anti-competitive, 139, 153–156, 158, 160, 167n74, 167n77
arbitration, 147
associations, 3, 6, 46, 119, 144, 148–149, 154–155, 158–160

authentic
   authenticity, 33, 182
authority of law, 5
autonomy
   autonomous action, 31, 57n10, 102
   autonomously decided, 34
   contractual, 78, 173
   individual, 18, 68–92, 136

bargaining equality, 137
basic essentials, 32
basic structure
   doctrine, 35, 58n34
*beedi* and cigar, 88
bill of rights, 5–7, 17–18
Bonded Labour System (Abolition) Act (1976), 60n66, 83
bonded worker, 38, 111
bonus, 80, 89–90
Building and Other Construction Workers (Regulation of Employment and Conditions of Service) Act (1996), 83

Building and Other Construction
    Workers' Welfare Boards, 128n49,
    151–152

capacity of choice, 69
capacity to contract, 73
care work, 30, 48, 118–119, 121–122, 180,
    186
caste, 2, 118–120, 122, 133n101, 141–142, 152
Central Board of Trustees of Employees'
    Provident Fund, 151
central government, 13–14, 26n66, 88,
    110–111, 115–116, 128n49, 129n52,
    151–152, 156
certifying officer, 78, 87, 145
Chatterjee, Partha, 53
child labour, 37–38, 83
Child Labour (Prohibition and
    Regulation) Act (1986), 38, 83
choice, 2, 11, 33–34, 40–41, 43–45, 48,
    62n100, 68–69, 71, 73, 76, 84, 102,
    138, 154–155, 158, 164n38, 185
citizenship
    idea of, 31
civil disobedience, 149
civil society, 32, 34, 44–47, 51–54, 56,
    63n123, 64n130, 117, 124, 152–153
classical liberalism, 2
classification test, 103
closed networks, 120, 122
closure
    closure of the business, 78, 87, 90
Code on Social Security (2020), 10, 12–13,
    26n65–66, 106, 108, 110, 115, 117–118,
    121, 124, 128n47–49, 151–153, 165n46
Code on Wages (2019), 10, 85
collective action, 3–4, 7, 14, 19, 32, 53–54,
    56, 73, 75, 83, 85, 115, 119, 123–124,
    135–160, 171–173, 175
collective bargaining
    bargaining agenda, 3

collective governance, 136
collectivisation, 73
colonial-capitalist, 191
colonial legislative agenda, 189
combined methods, 10
common political framework, 5
community perspective, 142
compensation for injury at employment,
    13, 104
compensatory, 89, 99n95, 138
competition, 19, 139, 153–160, 167n77, 172
Competition Act (2002), 153–154,
    156–159, 166n71, 167n74
Competition Commission of India
    (CCI), 155–156, 158
conceptual categories, 148–149, 188,
    190–191, 197n44
conciliation, 16, 37, 143–144, 147, 190
Concurrent List, 9
consequentialist idea, 41
constitutional adjudication, 5, 37, 39
constitutional amendments, 35, 52
constitutional authority, 5
constitutional concern, 101
constitutional duties, 48, 100
constitutionalism, 53
constitutional jurisprudence, 31
constitutional mandate, 1, 3, 6, 18, 55, 75,
    81, 100, 110, 113, 121, 128n47, 135
constitutional metric, 7
constitutional principles, 7, 29, 43, 69,
    138, 172, 189
Constitution of India (1950)
    basic structure, 4, 17–18, 35–36, 51, 101
    constitutional framework, 1, 4, 6, 30,
        33, 52, 177
    constitutional ideal, 3–4, 18, 30,
        54–55, 81, 191
    justiciable constitutional rights, 2, 6,
        19
    labour mandate, 1

INDEX 223

Part III, 6–7, 17, 36, 135, 144
Part IV, 6–7 17, 19, 36, 50, 135, 144
Preamble, 1, 17
redistributive agenda, 19, 51
construction, 13, 37, 88, 104, 127n33, 128n49, 152
construction workers' welfare fund, 13, 104
context-sensitivity, 7, 46, 136
contextual deliberation, 118, 121, 141
contextual investigation, 151
contextual knowledge, 188
contextual realities, 170
Contract Labour (Regulation and Abolition) Act (1970), 23–24n51, 83, 198–199n49
contractual employment, 7, 79
control, 3, 10, 28n90, 33, 71–74, 76, 79–80, 82, 87, 94n30, 95n37, 105, 115, 117, 136–138, 146–147, 152, 154, 161n11, 184, 188
cooperative societies
   workers' cooperatives, 3
corporate profits, 176
cost externalisation, 189
COVID-19 pandemic, 15, 89, 108–109, 111, 118, 183
childcare, 13, 110, 119
customary norms, 120

decentralised
   law-making, 88, 139
deliberative law-making, 117–118, 151
democratic deliberation, 11, 14, 136
democratic evaluation, 52
dependent juridical mentality, 170
dependent worker, 111, 141, 157
deposit-linked life insurance, 13
deregulation
   deregulating, 72
   deregulatory, 72, 89, 92

dignity
   dignified existence, 31
   dignified life, 3, 17, 32, 38, 50, 91, 101–103, 185
   human dignity, 31–33, 39, 49, 57n10, 58n24, 102, 124
   individual dignity, 31
dignity-affirming rights, 31
Directive Principles of State Policy, 19, 36, 144
disadvantaged workers, 103
discriminatory effect, 103
distributive justice
   distributional fairness, 17
   theories, 40
divergence, 16, 45, 139, 141, 160
diversity
   diversity of labour relations, 17, 190
   empirical diversity, 179
docks, 79, 88
domestic work, 12, 82, 141
dominant market position, 154

ease of doing business, 10, 15
economic democracy, 3, 161n5
economic development, 29, 32, 91, 154–155
educational provisioning, 13
efficacy of legislation, 6
egalitarian, 7, 121–122, 185
electoral representative, 45, 56
embodied experiences, 115, 117, 124
Employees' State Insurance
   Corporation, 14, 32, 107, 151
employment contract
   formal, 7, 10, 105, 107, 111, 114, 191
   freedom, 6, 89
employment injury benefit, 13, 102, 105–106, 110
employment relationship, 10–11, 69–76, 79–80, 85–87, 89–91, 100, 102,

104–106, 111, 116, 136, 143, 145, 149–151, 160, 161n7, 165n47, 172, 174, 184, 189
empowerment, 31, 34, 36, 57n10, 125n11
enslavement, 33
entitlement framework, 46
epistemological diversity, 192
equality
  formal, 2, 15, 73, 112, 115
  negotiating, 78
  of opportunity, 42, 44
  of status, 100
  substantive equality, 48–49, 104, 110, 112–113, 116, 126n22, 196n38
equal protection, 75, 103, 112–113, 128n47
Equal Remuneration Act (1976), 83
equitable outcomes, 100
essential services, 112
ethnicity, 118, 141–142
Europe, 26n65, 155, 167n77, 177, 188–189, 192
exchange of labour, 34, 48, 69, 71–74, 173
executive, 13–14, 26n69, 32, 35–38, 48, 51, 58n34, 78, 102, 116, 124, 144, 189
executive actions, 32, 35, 48
executive schemes, 13, 26n69, 32, 116
exploitative relations, 111

factories, 14, 79, 87–89, 126n28, 134n105
fairness, 17, 34, 40, 48, 54–55, 78, 81, 87, 109, 111, 114, 174–179, 191
fixed-term workers, 12
floor of rights, 85, 87, 173
forced labour, 31, 39, 60n66, 71
foundational rationale, 186
fraternity, 3–4, 31, 34, 42, 101, 174
freedom
  of business, 2, 68
  constrained, 77, 92
  of contract, 10–11, 18, 40–42, 49, 68–92, 107, 136, 172–173, 183–184, 196n38
  contractual, 11–12, 18, 49, 68–70, 72, 75–77, 79–87, 90–92, 107, 173, 184
  of dissent, 45
  expansive, 77
  from exploitation, 36, 38, 39
  individual freedom, 2–4, 7, 36, 43, 45, 48–50, 69, 75, 135, 161n7
  market freedom, 2, 18, 56, 73, 81–86, 90–92, 104, 109, 143, 171, 182–184, 196n38
  of occupation, 68
  of profession, 18, 68, 70
  real, 43, 68–70, 75, 80–81, 83–85, 96n44
  of speech, 45
  of trade, 2, 48–49, 68–71, 74, 76, 78, 80–81, 84–86, 90–92
fundamental duties, 3, 30
fundamental rights, 18, 35–39, 49–50, 57n9, 65n146–147, 68, 75, 81, 92, 101, 103, 128n47, 144, 146, 159, 171, 174–175, 182, 196n38
funeral assistance, 13, 110
future-guiding, 170

gender, 37, 44, 79, 88, 118–120, 141
gig work, 12, 20, 26n65, 103, 192
Global South, 170, 180, 189, 192
governance, 6–7, 19, 50, 121, 135–136, 138, 143, 159, 161n8
governmental monitoring, 109, 114
governmental oversight, 111, 114
gratuity, 13–14, 104–107, 116, 165n16
gratuity at termination, 13
guild-based system, 73

harmonious coexistence, 159
hazardous industries, 37–38

INDEX

health, 2, 10, 13, 18, 26n69, 32–33, 37–39, 44, 50, 61n83, 70, 77, 79, 85, 88–90, 95n36, 102, 105, 108, 110, 116, 119, 129n52, 151, 166n55, 173–174, 185
health and maternity benefits, 13, 110, 129n52
heterogeneity
  of work, 139
heterogeneous workers
  heterogeneous informal workers, 16, 114–115, 119, 151
hire-and-fire regime, 15
historical wrong, 111
housing provisioning, 13

ideal-type citizen, 30
ideological commitment, 34, 173, 184
impoverished workers, 192
independence movement, 29, 35
independent commercial entities, 153
Indian independence, 29
Indian jurisprudence, 126n22, 177
Indian workforce, 7, 12, 14, 26n64, 81, 90, 92, 105–106, 109, 113, 138, 141, 174, 191
individual freedom, 2–4, 7, 36, 43, 45, 48–50, 69, 75, 135, 161n7
individual liberty, 17–19, 36–37, 40–44, 46–50, 65n145, 68, 75, 80–81, 113
industrial democracy, 9, 14–17, 19, 118, 135–160
Industrial Disputes Act (1947), 11, 78, 162n23, 164n43, 165n46, 198–199n49
industrial relations, 6, 10–13, 15–20, 24–25n52, 26n65, 70, 78, 85, 97n68, 117–118, 121–123, 137, 142–146, 153, 162–163n24, 189, 191
Industrial Relations Code (2020), 6, 25n53, 70, 97n68, 145
industry, 6, 8–20, 23–24n51, 24n52, 28n90, 37–38, 55, 70, 72–73, 77–82, 84–86, 97n68, 101, 106, 108–109, 117–118, 121–123, 135–160, 162–163n24, 164n41, 164n43, 165n46, 188–189, 191, 197n44, 198–199n49
inequalities, 9, 10–12, 16, 25n56, 42, 50, 61n88, 69–70, 74, 77, 94n30, 100, 103–104, 110, 112–113, 128n47, 135, 158–159, 161n6, 173, 176–177, 185
inequitable, 81, 85, 101, 173
informal associations, 46
informal economic activities, 19, 82, 90, 105, 153, 193n10
informal support systems, 118, 120
informal workers, 7–9, 13, 16, 19, 26n64, 26n69, 38, 71, 81–84, 90–92, 102–105, 109–123, 128n46, 128n48, 128n51–53, 130n63–64, 132n87, 138–139, 148–153, 156–158, 160, 165n47, 172, 184–185
inspector-cum-facilitator(s), 88
institutionalised dialogue, 118
institutional permanence, 186
institutions
  fundamental institutions, 43
instrumental
  instrumental reasoning, 37
instrument of exchange, 69
insurance, 9, 13–14, 26n69, 32, 38, 40, 104–116, 119, 129n52, 130n64, 151, 165n46, 174, 183
intellectual domination, 188
interdisciplinary analysis, 8
intermediary, 82, 111, 121
International Labour Organization, 111, 114, 198n46
Inter-State Migrant Workmen (Regulation of Employment and Condition of Service) Act (1979), 83
intrinsically important, 30, 43, 49, 65n145, 101

judicial interpretation, 9, 37, 104
judicial review, 5
juridical authorship, 190, 191
justiciable rights, 7, 19, 49–50, 101–102, 144–145, 150
justificatory basis, 89, 112, 178–179, 187, 192

kinship, 112, 118, 121–122, 138, 141

labour
   contributions of, 34
   personal labour, 102, 172, 179–180
labour law
   alternative approach, 170
   conceptual and doctrinal account, 8
   contextual assessment, 8
   doctrinal scrutiny, 8
   evaluation of labour law, 7–17
   holistic approach, 8
   labour law discourse, 7–8
   labour law scheme, 9
   post-reform, 8, 31, 48, 113, 123
   suspension of, 20, 182, 187
   theorising, 20, 41, 170, 178–181
labour law reforms
   hard reforms, 10, 23n49
labour market
   uncertainties, 18, 70
labour movement, 16
labour process, 34, 48
labour relations
   withdrawal of the state, 24n52, 84, 91, 105–106
laissez faire, 76–77, 80–81, 89–92, 146, 161n7, 171, 179, 182, 184–185
language, 115, 118, 140, 162n18
law-making power, 9, 35
lay-off, 10–12, 78–79, 82, 86–87, 90, 106, 112, 144
least advantaged groups/people, 42, 161n6

legal enumeration, 124
legal fiction, 146–147
legal knowledge, 188
legal ontology, 192–193
legislation
   enacted legislation, 4–6
   legislative action, 3, 184
   legislative amendments, 9
   legislative entitlements, 3, 48, 103, 139
   legislative evaluation, 47
   legislative intervention, 6, 72–74, 80
   role of legislation, 5–8
legislative exclusions, 13, 106–107
legislative power
   division of legislative power, 9
legislature, 5–6, 9, 12, 22n42, 32, 36–37, 73, 79, 83, 107, 141, 163n28
legitimacy
   legitimacy deficit, 7
life and disability coverage, 13
life cycle, 118, 177
lived experiences, 67n170, 123–124, 139–143, 146, 151–152, 159, 188, 190
livelihood
   activity, 138, 178, 181, 183, 189
   right to, 38
locality, 118, 141
lockdown, 111–112

Mahatma Gandhi National Rural Employment Guarantee Scheme (2005), 109, 119
market
   competitive markets, 41, 44
   market-based distribution, 3, 45, 48–49, 51, 53, 55–56, 70, 92, 137, 139, 143–150, 175
   market-distorting, 18, 159
   market exchange, 2–3, 12, 18, 20, 42, 48–49, 55, 68–69, 75–77, 90–92, 96n44, 101, 109, 111, 119, 136–138, 150,

159–160, 172–177, 180, 182, 184–185, 188–192
  market forces, 79–80, 166n71
  market liberalisation, 171
  market turmoil, 183
  neoliberal logic, 186
  reasonable limits, 11, 49–50, 77
market access, 77, 101
market efficiency, 15, 89, 154, 179
mass unemployment, 108
master–servant
  model, 72, 85
  relationship, 12, 76, 184
material resources, 34, 42, 45, 49–50, 135, 137–139, 141, 143, 150–153
maternity benefit, 2, 9, 13–14, 34, 83, 102, 105–108, 110, 116, 119, 129n52, 165n46
Maternity Benefit Act (1961), 83
medical insurance, 13–14, 107, 165n46
mergers, 154
mines, 14, 79, 87–88, 107
minimise inequalities, 3, 100, 103–104, 110, 128n47, 173
minimum standards, 33, 74, 83, 87, 89–92, 111, 173
minimum wage, 18, 37, 70, 72, 75, 79–80, 82–83, 85, 87–89
Minimum Wages Act (1948), 79, 83
Motor Transport Workers Act (1961), 83

National Social Security Board for Unorganised Workers, 151
nation building, 29, 34, 101, 124, 174
negotiating union, 146
non-alienable commodity, 173
non-discrimination, 2, 79, 98n71, 113, 173–174
non-human nature, 177–178
non-traditional bargaining, 172
Nussbaum, Martha, 41, 43

Occupational Safety, Health and Working Conditions Code (2020), 10, 85
Ola, 157, 168n92
old-age benefits, 13, 110, 113–114
on-demand work, 12, 20, 26n65, 100, 110–111, 175, 192
on-demand worker, 110–111, 117, 152
organised sector, 24–25n52
overtime, 79, 88–89
own-account worker, 84, 111, 141, 149, 160

pandemic, 15, 89, 108–109, 111–112, 114, 118, 123, 129n53, 182–184
Parliament
  Indian Parliament, 9–10, 152, 162–163n24, 184
participatory citizenship, 3
participatory deliberation
  democratic participation, 4, 10, 19, 44, 137–138
  legitimacy to legal entitlements, 7
  participatory deficit, 56
participatory law-making, 4, 138–140, 142, 150–151, 154–160, 186, 190–191
pay equity, 79, 83, 88
Payment of Bonus Act (1965), 79–80
penal sanctions, 71
pension, 9, 13–14, 105–106, 111, 113–116, 119, 129n52, 151, 177
permissible inequality, 10
permissible range, 51–52, 55, 186
plantations, 14, 79, 87–88, 107, 198n46
platform-based work, 12–13, 19, 26n65, 26n69, 103, 110, 116–117, 152, 160, 166n55, 175, 181, 192
political citizen, 30
political commitment, 34
political deficiency, 171
political freedoms, 29
political narrative, 180

political party, 10, 144
political philosophy, 30, 40
political process, 32–34, 52, 152, 160
political theory, 8
power structure, 188
precarious conditions, 31, 38
primary goods, 40–43, 46, 61n83, 64n131
primitive logic, 190
private freedom, 51
private markets, 4, 48, 136
private property, 41, 72
pro-market, 15
provident fund, 9, 13–14, 34, 83, 104, 106–107, 110, 115–116, 126n23, 151, 165n46
public deliberation, 44
public entitlement, 142–143, 160
public interest, 2, 38, 49, 76, 78–80, 89, 155–157, 182, 196n38
public intervention, 51
public provisioning, 77, 96n44, 102
public utility, 16, 78, 147–148, 164n43
punitive, 71, 89, 99n95

Rawls, John, 40–46, 54, 61n88, 62–63n104, 64n130–131, 161n6
reciprocal recognition, 178
redistribution
 of common good, 6, 34
redistributive framework, 55–56, 135–136
redistributive policies, 36
religion, 2, 6, 118, 120, 122, 133n101, 141
representative organisations, 15–16, 141, 145, 159, 186–187
reskilling, 108, 114, 118, 120
resource distribution, 3, 42, 50, 75, 102, 175, 184
retrenchment, 144
right to life, 32, 38, 101
right to work, 19, 37

safety, 10, 18, 31, 38, 70, 79, 85, 88–90, 106–107, 149
Sales Promotion Employees (Conditions of Service) Act (1976), 83
Scheduled Caste, 152
Scheduled Tribe, 152
secular Indian identity, 29–30
self-determination, 29, 139–140, 187–188
Self-Employed Women's Association, 119–120, 148, 150, 165n48, 168n90
self-employed workers, 13, 82, 84, 106, 111, 128n49, 141, 150–151, 157–158
self-respect, 33, 41
Sen, Amartya, 41, 44–46, 62n100
SEWA (Self-Employed Women's Association) Bank, 119
skilling, 118
skill upgradation, 13, 110
slave mentality
 juridical, 187, 189, 191–192
social citizenship, 178–179
social cohesiveness, 140
social connectedness, 101
social contribution, 34, 174–175, 177–181, 186
social cooperation, 30, 42, 48, 119, 171, 191
social democracy, 2
social development, 55, 174, 178–179, 181
social embeddedness, 37
social identities, 118, 120, 122
social institutions, 7, 43, 118, 120–121
socialist republic, 86
social justice
 agenda, 1–4, 8, 17, 40, 47, 53, 55–56, 135–136, 145, 147, 159, 171–172, 175, 177, 187
 approach to labour law, 170, 192
 capability-sensitive idea, 41, 43, 62n103
 constitutional balance, 18, 50, 113
 constitutional programme, 3, 106

ideal of social justice, 3–5, 30, 48, 54–55, 175, 191–192
just social order, 3
just social outcomes, 3
liberal idea, 36, 40
narrative, 4, 30, 48, 51–53, 78, 179–181, 186
normative goal, 7, 154, 177, 179
rules of social justice, 42
social justice in actual contexts, 5, 7, 54
social justice mission, 7–8, 19, 54, 171, 184
worker-centric, 35, 140–141
social law, 177
social network, 112, 122
social protection, 6, 9, 37–38, 40, 50, 91–92, 105, 119, 122–123, 130n62, 183, 185–186
social provisioning
of public goods, 45
social reform, 29
social relational, 55, 101, 174
social rights, 50, 177
social security
programme, 104–105, 118–121, 128n48–49, 130n63
social security regime, 12–13, 106, 109, 114
universal social security coverage, 13
Social Security Board, 13, 16, 26n66, 110–111, 113, 115, 117–124, 151–152, 172, 190–191
social space
contraction of, 15
social state, 3, 104–105, 118
social support, 31, 34, 101–102, 118, 122, 183
social welfare
public social welfare, 4
socio-ecological work, 48

socio-economic exchanges, 36
socio-economic rights, 37, 39, 49
solidarity
principle of, 34, 48, 92, 155, 183
social solidarity, 2–4, 7, 17–18, 31, 37, 42, 47, 104, 112, 118, 171
standing order, 77, 86–87, 145
state
constitutional duty of, 48, 100
state-based redistribution, 3, 47, 50–51, 56, 139
state inaction, 103
state–citizen relationship, 121
State List, 9, 22n42
state paternalism, 75–85, 90–92
state responsibility, 33–34, 50
State Unorganised Workers' Social Security Board, 151
statutory entitlements, 75, 116, 145, 149, 187
statutory limits, 79
street vending, 12
strike
cessation of work, 16, 156, 164n41
industrial strike, 16, 146
right to strike, 16, 146–149, 157, 160, 171–172
sub-contracted workers, 12
subject matter of distribution, 135
Supreme Court, 3, 22n36, 31–33, 35, 37–39, 57n10, 76, 84–86, 95n37, 98n71, 101–104, 108–109, 113, 125n15, 128n47, 134n105, 144–147, 154–155, 159, 160, 165n46, 198–199n49
sustainability of nature, 176
sustainable development, 181

techno-managerial innovations, 181
termination
terminating, 10–11, 79, 87
theory of justice, 30, 40–41

trade unions
    mandatory recognition, 15
    right to unionise, 3
    unions, 3, 9–10, 14–16, 19, 23n49, 27n82, 46, 53, 75, 81, 83, 94n30, 119, 137, 139, 141, 143–150, 153–160, 162–163n24, 163n29, 163n35, 165n48, 167n74, 168n90, 171, 186–187
Trade Unions Act (1926), 83
transportation, 12, 19, 79, 138, 153, 164n43, 179
tripartite relationship, 10–11

Uber, 157, 168n92, 179, 194n11
ultra vires, 5, 17, 92, 106, 182–183
unemployment insurance, 107–109, 111–116, 183
unfair dismissal, 83
unfair labour practice, 145
unfreedom, 74–75, 77, 81, 91, 95–96n43, 96n44, 172–173, 184
unorganised sector/workers, 12, 26n65, 81, 110, 116, 137, 145, 148, 152, 166n55
Unorganised Workers Social Security Act (2008), 110, 130n63
unpaid work
    unpaid care work, 118–119, 121, 180, 186
unwaged worker, 111
utilitarianism, 41, 43

Waldron, Jeremy, 5, 54
waste recycling, 12, 148, 150, 178
weaker sections, 135

welfare rights, 2
welfare state, 4, 50–51, 72
withdrawal of the state, 24–25n52, 84–91, 105–106
women workers, 88–89, 119–120, 129n53
work
    conditions of, 9, 11, 32, 38–39, 97n60
    as a human activity, 178
    humane conditions of, 32, 38–39
    newer forms of, 175, 193n10
    political idea, 187
    regulation of, 178, 180
    socio-ecological contribution, 177
    work and environment, 20
work cessation, 3
worker as a contractor, 173
worker autonomy, 2, 18, 106, 139, 173–175
worker-citizens, 29–31, 34, 36, 55, 101–102, 136, 138, 149, 157, 171, 174, 177–178, 181, 183, 185–186
worker identity, 30
worker organisations, 10, 16, 54, 141, 143, 153
workers' participation in management, 3
worker voice, 16, 143
working arrangements, 7–8, 12–13, 34, 71, 91, 105, 110, 116, 141, 148–149, 151–152, 181, 189–190
workplace democracy, 136–137, 161n5
workplace republicanism, 136–137
workplace safety, 18, 70, 149
World Bank's Ease of Doing Business (EoDB), 15

Milton Keynes UK
Ingram Content Group UK Ltd.
UKHW042043111124
451073UK00006B/130